Foundations for
Biblical Christian Counseling

The Counsel
of Heaven on Earth

IAN F. JONES

PUBLISHING GROUP

Nashville, Tennessee

Listen to counsel and receive wise instruction;
Many plans are in the heart of people,
but the counsel of the Lord, that will stand.

Proverbs 19:20–21

CONTENTS

PREFACE

Books on counseling have a variety of emphases. Some books address the theories of counseling; others deal with the techniques and tools. In my own library I have books that focus on the history of counseling and the cure of souls, counseling topics and issues, listings of Bible verses organized according to specific problems, assessment and criticism of other counselors and counseling texts, exegesis and analysis of the Scriptures dealing with psychology and human nature, brain-scan technology and counseling; spiritual healing, emotional wholeness, counseling skills, treatment plans, and counselor training and supervision. Some books argue for specific theological approaches to counseling, others present detailed descriptions of interventions and strategies in such areas as trauma and crises, marriage and family, forgiveness, adultery, conflict resolution, and healing prayers. A number of counseling books cover individual and group counseling practices across a spectrum from secular and even antireligious viewpoints to positions that embrace a basic spiritual and biblical perspective. All the authors of these books hold certain assumptions about our personality and human nature, our ability to change, and the role of the social, biological, psychological, and spiritual dimensions in the counseling process. A few writers specifically acknowledge these areas; however, in many cases, the underlying suppositions and beliefs are not clearly articulated.

My experience over the past twenty-five years, both in my counseling practice and in teaching and training counselors in graduate school, has taught me the importance of knowing the basic components of competent counseling, understanding the direction and purpose of counseling, and, most importantly, having a solid biblical foundation for counseling practice. Proverbs 19:20-21 instructs us to listen attentively to wise counsel and instruction; however, we are reminded that ultimately it is the counsel of God and his plans that will prevail. In this book I have tried to identify and explain the essential features of biblical Christian counseling. No attempt has been made to engage in formal theory building or to develop systematically any counseling strategies or techniques. My intention is to show how the Bible, from Genesis to Revelation, provides counselors with the blueprint for developing an effective counseling ministry.

A number of people need to be acknowledged for their assistance in this effort. Thanks must go to the president and trustees of Southwestern Baptist Theological Seminary for granting me a sabbatical leave in 2002 and 2003, which allowed me the time for research and writing. During this period I was a visiting lecturer at Queensland Baptist College of Ministries in Australia and a visiting professor at Malaysia Baptist Theological Seminary in Penang, Malaysia. The faculty and staff at both these institutions offered assistance and support.

The late Jim Headrick, professor at New Orleans Baptist Theological Seminary, provided a number of suggestions and ideas that have been incorporated into the book. He was a colleague, good friend, and spiritual advisor. I will miss our long discussions on biblical counseling and his words of encouragement.

Helpful suggestions and corrections were made by David Allen, Scott Floyd, Paige Patterson, Lori Moore, Paul Carlin, Marsha Lawson, Dana Wicker, Malinda Fasol, Donnie Holden, and David Penley. The work of Kevin Forrester was particularly helpful in the chapter on biblical traits and spiritual gifts. While I bear responsibility for the final product, the insights and support of these people and other colleagues have contributed immeasurably to the value of this work. Finally, I am indebted to my wife Linda for her assistance and support and to our children Andrew and Kathryn, who represent the future generation of wise Christians who seek the counsel of the Lord.

1

WHERE DO WE START?

Varied Options in Counseling
Discovering a Standard of Truth
Counseling from the Whole Bible

Varied Options in Counseling

Christian counseling has come a long way in the last quarter of the twentieth century and early into the twenty-first century. More and more people are appending the prefix *Christian, biblical,* or *pastoral* to their title of counselor. In addition to the increased professionalization of the psychotherapy field, signified by the introduction of licensing requirements in many U.S. states, Christian counselors also face an array of options to choose from in counseling organizations and associations, with a variety of memberships designed to address their needs. The American Association of Pastoral Counselors (AAPC), Christian Association for Psychological Studies (CAPS), American Association of Christian Counselors (AACC), and the National Association of Nouthetic Counselors (NANC) provide alternatives to such secular associations as the American Psychological Association (APA), the American Counseling Association (ACA), National Council on Family Relations (NCFR), National Board for Certified Counselors (NBCC), and the American Association for Marriage and Family Therapy (AAMFT).

This alphabet soup of options can be confusing for individuals who believe that God is calling them into a counseling ministry. Students regularly ask me for advice on the courses, degrees, and programs needed for work in counseling and psychotherapy. Invariably, they are overwhelmed by the options. Past professional choices were limited to psychiatry, psychology, the pastorate, and chaplaincy or the clinical pastoral education (CPE) programs. Now students are faced with the additional alternatives of social work, which offers the Licensed Clinical Social Worker (LCSW); the Licensed Professional Counselor (LPC), which is a minimum requirement in many states; the Licensed Marriage and Family Therapist (LMFT), which is being offered in an increasing number of states; the National Certified Counselor (NCC), which is administered by the NBCC, and even the burgeoning field of applied and clinical sociology with its attempts to introduce certification as a sociological practitioner.

All these alternatives represent underlying assumptions about counseling. They rest on foundations or philosophies concerning the nature of counseling and the components required to produce an effective counselor. Aspiring Christian counselors may find themselves living in states where licensing requirements dictate the number and type of courses they must take, particularly if they plan to practice outside the local church setting. More than ever before, Christians entering the counseling field need a clear and strong foundation, a firm understanding of the elements and origin of biblical caregiving. For the Christian counselor, the beginning does not lie in selecting a particular program or licensure; the origin and knowledge of Christian counseling must be far more fundamental.

Discovering a Standard of Truth

Whether or not we care to admit it, we all have a basic source of authority upon which we base our beliefs and evaluate the world around us. What is yours? For millennia the basic sources of truth centered on what we were told. Tradition dictated our view of life and interpreted the world around us. Elders passed on truths to younger generations. In the Western world around the seventeenth century, emphasis began shifting away from tradition. Scientific inquiry involving observation and the measurement of phenomena led to a belief that reason and formal procedures of investigation could reveal basic truths in the natural world around us. Early scientific pioneers like Francis Bacon (1561–1626) were careful to point out that their methods and results revealed orderliness in our world and affirmed the work and the existence of a Creator. The rational and inductive approach to science was a tool that complemented biblical truth and was subject to the grace of God. One outcome of this new inquiry, however, was that reason and grace became separated as science became more secularized.[1]

Modern scientific inquiry has developed meticulous methods that generally rest on a belief in a universe of natural cause and effect that views the realm of grace and faith as supercilious fantasy at best or unnecessarily meddlesome at worst. Science systematically studies humans and their environment and identifies the facts, truths, and laws governing the material or physical world. Hence, the argument goes, faith, theology, and religion should either recognize scientific knowledge as the supreme arbiter of reality or stay on their own nonscientific turf of rituals and church dogma while maintaining a policy of noninterference. Evidence for this position may appear in the form of horror stories about religious bodies that have interfered with scientific progress and caused pain and suffering as a result. The story of Galileo is often cited as a case in point.[2] The problem with this position is that science does not occur in a vacuum. Scientific inquiry rests on decisions, attitudes, philosophies, belief systems, and even interpretations that have moral and religious foundations. In fact, debates about the separation of science and religion and the tension and antagonism between the two fields cloud the important role that religion has played in the development of modern science.

In his 1905 book *The Protestant Ethic and the Spirit of Capitalism*, Max Weber suggested that certain branches of Protestantism (Pietists, Methodists, and Anabaptists) following the Reformation reframed the biblical concept of calling to apply not only to the work of the clergy but also to the laity and to trades and occupations in general. In other words, any honorable work or activity could become a means of glorifying God. The Protestant doctrine of the priesthood of every believer, not just the professional priesthood or clergy, meant that all Christians had a calling to honor and glorify God in whatever trade or profession they were engaged. Weber claimed that this belief resulted in higher levels and a better quality of work as people sought to express their obedience to God. Weber demonstrated that Protestant areas in Europe showed higher levels of economic production than other areas. The goal of these Christians was not to increase their rates of production in order to earn more money; rather, increased wealth was a by-product of their efforts.

Sociologist Robert Merton studied the effects of this Protestant ethic on scientific development in the seventeenth century. In 1957, Merton argued that the cultural attitudes embraced by the Protestant ethic promoted rational and empirical scientific inquiry. If this is true, we should see a higher proportion of successful seventeenth-century scientists affiliated with the branches of Protestantism that embraced the Protestant ethic. These scientists would be driven by a desire to discover the truths and laws of God in his creation. They would accept their enterprise as a divine calling and evaluate their work by the way it glorifies God. One effect of their endeavor would be an increase in the likelihood of these believers rising to the top of their profession. In England the Protestant group most representative of the beliefs that Weber and Merton described was the Puritans.

Merton examined the religious affiliation of the founders of the Royal Society in England, a prestigious organization that accepted only scientists who had made significant contributions to their field. Puritans in England at the time represented a small minority of Christians, so it would be highly unlikely for any of them to be members of such an elite group. Merton's findings were surprising. Of the ten founders of the society in 1645, seven were clearly Puritan; one, Scarbrough, definitely was not; and of the two remaining there was some uncertainty, although one, Merret, had some Puritan training. Among the sixty-eight members in 1663 about whom we have information on their religious orientation, forty-two were clearly Puritan.[3]

A small religious group was responsible for producing some of the most highly regarded scientists of the century. Puritan values promoted scientific knowledge and education. In fact, these scientists would often formally dedicate their work to the glory of God, and they regarded the true goal of science as revealing the works of the Creator. This relationship between Protestantism and science was also evident in New England, where scientists affiliated with the Royal Society were all trained in Calvinism and where this Calvinistic culture was instrumental in the founding of Harvard University

Although changes have occurred in both the economic and scientific fields, Protestants are still disproportionately represented among Western scientists in comparison to the general population.[4] Yet a separation has arisen between the Protestant work ethic and the spirit of capitalism. The early work ethic based on a desire to honor God has faded, and a secularized version has replaced it. Money and materialism are no longer the side effects of holy activity; they have become independent goals—the new idols in our culture. Hard work has become a means of accumulating wealth and honoring self, and selfish greed has replaced service to God as the motivating factor in life (cf. 1 Tim. 6:10).

The same separation that has occurred in the economic field has also transpired in the scientific field. In science the standard of truth has shifted as faith has become secondary to nature. Scientific ideologies have fostered opposition and intellectual challenges to religion. The irony is that the scientific field is constantly changing. New discoveries demolish old "truths," and textbooks require constant updating. Science is, in effect, a moving target where information and investigation are always in motion, producing new insights and more ideas for further study. Yet science is no longer motivated by a desire to glorify God but rather by a desire to serve the self and others. This shift in focus is no less evident in the field of counseling and humanistic psychotherapy where an idolatrous form of selfism has emerged.[5]

A Christian worldview provides a stark contrast to secular perceptions of knowledge and truth about human nature. We acknowledge the revealed truth of God in the Bible and accept Scripture as the infallible standard by which all values, ideas, and concepts are evaluated. The Bible, through the illumination of the Holy Spirit, gives us the true and undistorted picture of human nature, our purpose, and how we are related to our Creator (Rom. 15:4; 16:23–26; 2 Tim. 3:15–17; Heb. 4:12; 1 Pet. 1:25; 2 Pet. 1:21; 1 John 5:6–8). It is the standard by which we are able to interpret and make sense of the general revelation of God in creation (2 Tim. 3:16).

The Bible tells us that there are an order and a purpose in our world and that all of creation, both the living and the inanimate, depends on God's will for their design, development, and survival or continued existence (Pss. 104; 135:6–7,9–10). A common grace from God allows both believers and nonbelievers the wisdom to identify some of the laws, patterns, and truths found in creation and the natural world (Esther 1:13; Ps. 19; Prov. 31:1; Dan. 2:12–18; Matt. 7:9–11; Rom. 1:18–23) and to develop an orderly and moral society. Theologians throughout church history, including Justin Martyr (AD 110–165),[6] Augustine (AD 354–430),[7] and John Calvin (1509–1564),[8] among others,[9] have recognized the value of discovering and appropriating truth wherever it is found, even among profane and ungodly sources.

A full and complete explanation of human nature and our world necessary for an effective counseling ministry cannot be understood outside the revelation of God (Acts 17:22–31). In comparison to the wisdom of God, our knowledge appears as foolishness (1 Cor. 3:18–21; James 4:6; Prov. 16:5,18). Attempts to develop systems of counseling and caregiving will always be inadequate without an awareness and acceptance of the biblical revelation. The ideas, research, theories, and techniques in counseling warrant our attention; but unless they are built on the foundational truths of Scripture, they will inevitably be distorted, lacking a complete and true context; and they will be at times misleading and harmful.[10]

Christian counselors must guard against spiritual arrogance that unilaterally dismisses truth claims and ideas based solely on a superficial and judgmental evaluation of a particular theory or theorist. They must avoid *ad hominem* arguments and narrow-mindedness that take the place of wisdom and discernment or become confused with them. Further, although all of Scripture reveals truth, not every known truth is found in the Bible. In addition, we must be humble and realize that some things lie beyond all human wisdom and understanding and can be revealed only through the Spirit of God (1 Cor. 2:8–11).

Counseling from the Whole Bible

This book will not tell you which counseling certification to pursue or which organization to join. It will not present a formal training model in counseling or give a detailed description of techniques and procedures. The focus will be on building a foundation and developing the components necessary for a biblical approach to counseling and on the attitude and disposition of a biblical Christian counselor. In order to do this, we must go back to the beginning. But where, exactly, should we begin?

Books on Christian counseling usually stress the importance of building models and approaches to counseling on a biblical foundation. They suggest various ways to accomplish this task. Some books stress biblical themes on the nature of God and humankind as they apply to pastoral care; others focus on techniques, skills, and theories in counseling, often borrowed, with varying degrees of caution, from secular models; still others address a particular word or theological concept as an organizing principle for counseling.

Most Christian counseling texts will reveal that most of them draw heavily from the New Testament with examples from the ministry of Jesus and the disciples and biblical quotations drawn regularly from the writings of Paul. This tendency to cite Paul is natural in light of the rational organization and structure of his epistles. Writers of these counseling books usually have advanced degrees in theology or psychology. They have been trained in an academic arena that emphasizes rational thinking and systematic development of thought and argument. They are comfortable with Paul's didactic style; it has an air of familiarity to them, a reminder of sermons, graduate lectures, and studies. Paul's style also fits well with a Western or European mode of logical thinking.

I do not wish to challenge these approaches in any way, least of all to question the value of the Pauline epistles. There can be no doubt as to their inspiration and authority, and we will refer regularly to them, particularly in discussing spiritual gifts. The epistles are at the end of God's biblical revelation chronologically and in the canon. As such, they interpret for us the themes of the Old Testament and the narratives of the Gospels and Acts, and they develop basic theological principles that are foundational for biblical Christian counseling. Yet nearly 70 percent of Scripture is written in a narrative form. The didactic approach, as a style of communication, represents around 30 percent of Scripture. What does this mean? I do not pretend to have all the answers to this question, but I would suggest that a closer examination of the other writing styles, particularly the narratives, is warranted. God is conveying the message of his Word in more than one form or style of communication. One obvious area of study for finding directions and insights into models of caregiving would be the Old Testament.

Our study should emulate the Bereans, whose noble character was expressed in their eager desire to search and examine the Scriptures to ascertain the truth of Paul's words to them (Acts 17:11).[11] Rather than going over old ground and limiting our focus to the New Testament alone, I believe that we can find edification and some valuable lessons about counseling by examining the Word of God, starting "In the beginning."

Questions and Exercises for Reflection

1. What is your view of biblical authority in counseling? Give your definition of the term as it applies to Christian caregiving.
2. Where do you believe counseling should begin? In other words, what should be the first principles or starting place for Christian counseling from a biblical perspective?
3. Examine and compare the mission and beliefs of some of the counseling organizations mentioned in the chapter (e.g., AAPC, CAPS, AACC, NANC, APA, ACA, NCFR, NBCC, and AAMFT). You can find most of this information on the official Web sites of each of these organizations.
4. How should scientific inquiry relate to biblical truth in counseling?

5. Review some books on biblical and Christian counseling and describe the different ways they approach the subject.

References

Augustine. *On Christian Doctrine* in Nicene and Post-Nicene Fathers, First Series, vol. 2, *Augustine: City of God, Christian Doctrine*. Ed. Philip Schaff. Christian Literature Publishing Company, 1887; reprint, Peabody, Mass.: Hendrickson Publishers, 1994.

Calvin, John. *Institutes of the Christian Religion.* Translation of *Institutio Christianae Religionis.* Trans. Henry Beveridge. Reprint, with new introduction. Edinburgh: Calvin Translation Society, 1845–1846. Oak Harbor, Wash.: Logos Research Systems, Inc., 1997.

Erickson, Millard J. *Christian Theology,* 2nd ed. Grand Rapids, Mich.: Baker Book House, 1998.

Holmes, Arthur F. *All Truth Is God's Truth.* Grand Rapids, Mich.: William B. Eerdmans, 1977.

Martyr, Justin. *The Second Apology of Justin,* in Ante-Nicene Fathers, vol. 1, *The Apostolic Fathers, Justin Martyr, Irenaeus.* Eds. Alexander Roberts and James Donaldson. Christian Literature Publishing Company, 1885; reprint, Peabody, Mass.: Hendrickson Publishers, 2004.

Merton, Robert King. *Social Theory and Social Structure,* Revised and enlarged ed. Glencoe, Ill.: The Free Press, 1957.

Schaeffer, Francis A. *Escape from Reason.* Downers Grove, Ill.: InterVarsity Press, 1968.

Shaeffer, Francis A. *How Should We Then Live? The Rise and Decline of Western Thought and Culture.* Old Tappan, N.J.: Fleming H. Revell Company, 1976.

Vitz, Paul. *Psychology as Religion: The Cult of Self Worship,* 2nd ed. Grand Rapids, Mich.: William B. Eerdmans, 1994.

Endnotes

1 See Francis A. Schaeffer, *Escape from Reason* (Downers Grove, Ill.: InterVarsity Press, 1968); and Francis A Shaeffer, *How Should We Then Live? The Rise and Decline of Western Thought and Culture* (Old Tappan, N.J.: Fleming H. Revell, 1976), 130–66.

2 Galileo (1564–1642) argued from scientific observation that the sun, not the earth, is the center of the universe. Although he attempted to defend his views as consistent with Scripture, he was tried for heresy in 1633 and forced by the religious authorities to recant his views.

3 See Robert King Merton, *Social Theory and Social Structure,* rev. and enlarged ed. (Glencoe, Ill.: Free Press, 1957), 574–85.

4 Ibid., 588, 602. The views and values leading to the advancement of science and the positions averse and hostile to scientific inquiry are both present in the Calvinistic tradition and among the Dissenters, including Baptists. The debate continues into the twenty-first century, but the point is that both positions have a common theological ancestry and both approaches originated in a desire to glorify God and honor his Word. See Merton, 600.

5 See Paul Vitz, *Psychology as Religion: The Cult of Self Worship,* 2nd ed. (Grand Rapids, Mich.: William B. Eerdmans, 1994). Vitz does not engage in a blanket generalization and condemnation of psychology. He states that his focus is on humanistic self-psychology and that his discussion does not include an evaluation of experimental psychology, behaviorism, psychoanalysis, and psychologists who hold a genuine respect for the religious dimension in people. See Vitz, xvii–xviii.

6 "Whatever things were rightly said among all men, are the property of us Christians." Justin Martyr, *The Second Apology of Justin,* in Ante-Nicene Fathers, vol. 1, *The Apostolic Fathers, Justin Martyr, Irenaeus,* eds. Alexander Roberts and James Donaldson (Christian Literature Publishing Company, 1885; reprint, Peabody, Mass.: Hendrickson Publishers, 1994), 193.

7 For example, "For no one ought to consider anything his own, except perhaps what is false. All truth is of Him who says, 'I am the truth,'" and, "Nay, but let every good and true Christian understand that wherever truth may be found it belongs to his Master." Augustine, *On Christian Doctrine,* Preface, 8; 2.18.28, in Nicene and Post-Nicene Fathers, First Series, vol. 2, *Augustine: City of God, Christian Doctrine,* ed. Philip Schaff (Christian Literature Publishing Company, 1887; reprint, Peabody, Mass.: Hendrickson Publishers, 1994), 521, 545. Augustine elaborates on this principle in Book 2 (40.60) of *On Christian Doctrine,* 554:

> Moreover, if those who are called philosophers, and especially the Platonists, have said aught that is true and in harmony with our faith, we are not only not to shrink from it, but to claim it for our own use from those who have unlawful possession of it. For the Egyptians had not only the idols and heavy burdens which the people of Israel hated and fled from, but also vessels and ornaments of gold and silver, and garments, which the same people when going out of Egypt appropriated to themselves, designing them for a better use, not doing this on their own authority, but by the command of God, the Egyptians themselves, in their ignorance, providing them with things which they themselves were not making a good use of (Ex. 3:21,22; 12:35,36); in the same way all branches of heathen learning have not only false and superstitious fancies and heavy burdens of unnecessary toil, which every one of us, when going out under the leadership of Christ from the fellowship of the heathen, ought to abhor and avoid; but they contain also liberal instruction which is better adapted to the use of the truth, and some most excellent precepts of morality; and some truths in regard even to the worship of the One God are found among them. Now these are, so to speak, their gold and silver, which they did not create themselves, but dug out of the mines of God's providence which are everywhere scattered abroad, and are perversely and unlawfully prostituting to the worship of devils. These, therefore, the Christian, when he separates himself in spirit from the miserable fellowship of these men, ought to take away from them, and to devote to their proper use in preaching the gospel. Their garments, also,—that is, human institutions such as are adapted to that intercourse with men which is indispensable in this life,—we must take and turn to a Christian use.

8 "Therefore, in reading profane authors, the admirable light of truth displayed in them should remind us, that the human mind, however much fallen and perverted from its original integrity, is still adorned and invested with admirable gifts from its Creator. If we reflect that the Spirit of God is the only fountain of truth, we will be careful, as we would avoid offering insult to him, not to reject or condemn truth wherever it appears. In despising the gifts, we insult the Giver. . . . But if the Lord has been pleased to assist us by the work and ministry of the ungodly in physics, dialectics, mathematics, and other similar sciences, let us avail ourselves of it, lest, by neglecting the gifts of God spontaneously offered to us, we be justly punished for our sloth." John Calvin, *Institutes of the Christian Religion,* translation of: *Institutio Christianae religionis,* trans Henry Beveridge, reprinted with new introduction (Edinburgh: Calvin Translation Society, 1845–1846; Oak Harbor, Wash.: Logos Research Systems, 1997), II, ii, 15–16.

9 For example: "Truth arrived at apart from special revelation is still God's truth." Millard J. Erickson, *Christian Theology,* 2nd ed. (Grand Rapids, Mich.: Baker Book House, 1998), 199; and, "Whatever men know they know by the grace of God, for all truth is God's truth wherever it be found." Arthur F. Holmes, *All Truth Is God's Truth* (Grand Rapids, Mich.: William B. Eerdmans, 1977), 23.

10 Similar problems can arise in theology, where, for example, Jesus exposed the inadequate biblical anthropology of the Sadducees in Matthew 22:23–33.

11 Scripture warns us about difficulties that can arise in reading Paul's epistles. In 2 Peter 3:16, we are told that in Paul's letters there are "some things that are hard to understand" and that some people distort his message, as they do the rest of Scripture. The Greek word Peter uses is *dysnoetos*, and it is found only in this passage in the New Testament. The word describes people who lack spiritual insight into the acts and will of God. They misread and misunderstand what Paul is trying to say and so distort or twist the meaning of Scripture to suit their particular interest or purpose. Underlying this problem, Peter implies, is the fact that, although Paul wrote with a godly wisdom (2 Pet. 3:15), his meaning is not always clear to his readers. This word of caution should not discourage us; rather, it should encourage us to be careful in our scholarship.

2

CREATION: THE STARTING PLACE FOR BIBLICAL CHRISTIAN COUNSELING

Our Family of Origin
Born to Relationship
The Distorted Image
Deceit and Our Family History
God's Work of Redemption
A Fundamental Flaw in All Secular Counseling Theories

E ach counselor brings prior beliefs, training, and a repertoire of gifts and techniques to the counseling encounter. The person in need also brings an array of attitudes, experiences, and competencies to the situation. At the heart of the counseling relationship lies a set of assumptions about healing and human nature. How would you describe the essential nature of human beings? Who are we? Are we simply biological machines designed to respond to behavioral stimuli, perhaps with some unconscious forces or some external social pressures driving our feelings, attitudes, and actions? Variations on these views of human nature are the foundation of most secular counseling theories. The Bible presents a different picture of who we are, and the book of Genesis gives us the foundation for a complete model of counseling.

Our Family of Origin

In the beginning the Creator designed and built a garden in a place that had been barren, containing no trees, grass, or plants—a place he

15

had created out of nothing. He filled this empty environment with beautiful trees, including fruit trees and a river to water the land. In the midst of this idyllic setting, he placed two tenants with the instructions that they were to nurture and cultivate the garden. They were his representatives in the garden, providing order and control. They were blessed with a comprehensive understanding of the will of the Owner; in fact, in their nature they bore a clear resemblance to him.

The Owner told the two tenants that they had access to all the fruit in the garden. Like him they were free to choose where they went and what they did, with one exception. The Owner made clear that one tree in the garden was to remain his personal property. They were not to trespass and eat any fruit from this tree.

This was a necessary order. The Owner had provided the two tenants with the freedom to choose. They could listen to his instructions and obey him, or they could reject his Word. This freedom would be a sham unless a clear choice existed between his way and a way contrary to his will. True freedom requires at least two alternatives in a situation. Without the tree, the tenants would be the equivalent of slaves or robots programmed to be caretakers of a garden, but they would lack any resemblance to their Creator's ability to exercise free will.

The Owner of the garden was good enough to reveal his reason for asking them not to eat from the tree. (He was under no obligation to give them an explanation.) Basically, the rule was for their own protection. He alone was strong enough to handle all things, including the power found in the fruit of this tree. The tree was there to teach obedience. By not eating the fruit, they would grow in understanding the true knowledge of God, the Builder, Owner, and Manager. They would learn to distinguish right from wrong without having to experience evil in their lives. On the other hand, eating this fruit would result in death. To assist them further, the Owner placed another tree in the garden. This one offered the transforming power of eternal life. It was a visual indicator of the consequences and reward of obedience: life without end, in the presence of and in full communication with the Creator. The choices were clear and observable.

The freedom to choose was emphasized further when the Owner allowed the presence in the garden of a voice of opposition to his way. The caretakers were free to communicate with their Creator, or they could listen to the misguided words of an opponent, the serpent *(Nachash)*. As you know, they chose to listen to the latter.

"I can't believe this god has told you not to eat from any tree in the garden," mused the snake. "You won't die."

Of course, the Owner in his goodness had forbidden access to only one tree; everything else he had created was available to them, but our tenants were drawn into the lies of Satan.

The new message sowed seeds of doubt in place of assurance. The Creator was not to be trusted; in fact he was a liar who was intent on stunting the growth and development of his tenants. They would gain far more knowledge if they just ignored God. The irony is that the appointed rulers of the garden had been given all that they needed for intellectual and moral development, physical needs, and fulfillment of their designed purpose; but they chose to listen to the words of the evil one. They accepted a false and distorted image of their Creator and chose to live their lives according to this new vision.

When the Creator confronted his tenants, the destructive effects of the fruit were revealed. The man blamed God and the woman; the woman blamed the snake; and the Owner banished the couple from the garden. As a consequence, we have been blaming others for our own misbehavior, acting like gods, and searching for the garden of Eden ever since.

Banishment from the garden meant that the couple no longer had access to the tree of life. This was actually the first step in a redemptive plan on the part of the Creator. The tenants no longer faced the horror of an eternity of sin and evil. In time there would be another tree that would herald the possibility of a new path to eternal life. A new Adam, filled with the unbroken image of God, would face temptation from the same devil; but this time the outcome would be different.

The tree of life found in Genesis would reappear in the last chapter of the book of Revelation (Rev. 22:2) and in the end times. "To him who overcomes," says the Spirit of God, "I will give the right to eat from the tree of life" (Rev. 2:7 NIV). But how does a person overcome? Access to this eternal life would be found at the intersection of history in the cross of Christ, which spans the breadth of the Word of God, from the tree of the knowledge of good and evil to the tree of life—the narrow way that reestablished full communication with the Creator (John 14:6).

The authority and power of all the world's kingdoms were given over to Satan, who offered them to Christ, the new Adam, if he would worship him. This time the temptation was rejected (Luke 4:5–8), and the way was made for the redemption of mankind through pain and suffering on a new tree. The penalty of the curse of the law was paid on the cross. Cursed is everyone who hangs on a tree, says the Scripture (Deut. 21:23), and Christ became the curse of the law for us (Gal. 3:13). The new tree designed by the destructive forces of evil to bring pain, suffering, and death to the new Adam, God would transform redemptively into a path and symbol of salvation. He would destroy the Devil's work (1 John 3:8b).

Born to Relationship

The importance of relationship is seen in the opening verses of the Bible. The first letter of the first word in Genesis, *Beit,* is the second letter in the Hebrew alphabet. As a prefix, the letter is translated as "in"; but Jewish scholars, particularly those in the mystical tradition, tell us that the letter also represents the number "two," duality, sharing or plurality.[1] While it is translated, quite correctly, as "in" in Genesis 1:1, it is interesting and perhaps significant that the first letter of the first verse of the first chapter of the first book of the Bible should be one that points to the importance of relationships. We do not exist as individuals in isolation. We are connected to our Creator and to other people.

Further evidence of the importance of relationships is found in other verses in the first chapter of Genesis. The word translated "God" in the opening phrase of Genesis 1:1, *Bereshith . . . Elohim* ("In the beginning, God") is *Elohim*, the plural form of *El*. The term *El* conveys the idea of "first" in terms of his lordship and his strength or power. God is all-powerful, our supreme Lord. The word is often used in the Old Testament in a compound form with other descriptive names for God; for example *El Shaddai*—God Almighty, and *El Elyon*—God Most High. The plural form *Elohim* is a way of intensifying the nature and attributes of God, telling us that our Creator's power, majesty, and authority are matchless and that he alone is eternal. The plural term should in no way imply a form of polytheism. God is one. Yet, for Christians, the term also indicates the triune nature of God.

Francis Schaeffer considered the Trinity a fundamental doctrine because without it God would require something or someone outside himself for relationship.[2] Creation with a rational humanity is not an absolute necessity in order for God to commune and have fellowship. He has relationship separate from mankind. God does not need us, but we do need him for our existence and continued survival. The presence of God is essential for any individual or community to achieve wholeness.

Community and Individuality

The theme of relationship is also seen in the creation of mankind (Gen. 1:26–28,31). God has created us as individuals, each with our own unique identity, and as people who need one another. We are both spiritual and material, and we are both personal and social. We were born to commune with God and with others.

As you read the first chapter of Genesis, pay attention to the weaving together of the singular and plural terms that reflect our nature.

> Then God said, "Let Us make man [humankind] in Our image, according to Our likeness. . . ." And God created the [man] (singular) in His own image, in the image of God he created him (singular); male and female he created them (plural) God blessed them (plural); and God said to them (plural), "Be fruitful and multiply, and fill the earth, and subdue it; and rule over the fish of the sea and over birds of the sky, and over every living thing

that moves on the earth." . . . God saw all that He had made; and behold, it was very good!

We bear the image (*tselem*) of God, and this likeness sets us apart from all other forms of creation. This is our Genesis identity. It tells us that we were created for a special purpose and that we have a special relationship with our Creator, but sin has broken this relationship.

Uniqueness and Unity

We are different from all other creations. God "formed (*yyat-sar*— ייצר) man of dust from the ground" (Gen. 2:7), and he separately "formed (*yatsar*— יצר) every beast of the field" (Gen. 2:19). Our identity is unique. We are not a result of chance and genetic happenstance; we have been designed and crafted like a work of art as part of the Creator's plan. We were created in his image to be his administrators on earth, and the special relationship that Adam and Eve had with God was distinct from any other in all creation.[3]

We have both separateness and unity in our relationships. Each person has an individual identity. God created a single man, and he gave him a name. Adam was a unique individual with a personality that separated him from Eve. Yet God also created "them" (Gen. 1:27), male and female, with the command to "be fruitful and multiply" (Gen. 1:28). The couple was to be united, both physically and in community. God was to be the central focus for the individual and for the community at both the family and society levels.

The Distorted Image

Human identity is unique among all creation. We are made in the image of God, but we are no longer perfect and free of sin. Sin has brought condemnation and separation from God. Sin has led to physical and spiritual death. Part of Adam's soulishness (Hebrew: *nephesh*) was his physical existence. The fall created a separation between us and God, but our bodies are not intrinsically evil. The incarnation affirms this view (John 1:14; Heb. 2:14,17). Jesus was God, but he was also fully human with a physical body. Our bodies are members of Christ himself

(1 Cor. 6:15–20), the temple of the Holy Spirit, so we are to honor God with our bodies, and present them as a gift to him (Rom. 12:1–2). The coming resurrection will provide us with new bodies (1 Cor. 15:35–44, 53–54; Phil. 3:20–21).[4]

The relationship Adam and Eve had with God before the fall was gone. The image they bore of their Creator had become distorted, and they were no longer able to realize their full potential in creation. They would need a new spirit and a new body. The effects of their decision have continued through the generations. All people now have an inherent predisposition to sin as soon as they are aware of moral actions and personal responsibility. The only hope for people who are dead in their trespasses and sins is in a new Adam who brings new life (Eph. 2:1–6) and a new birth in the Spirit (John 3:7–8; Rom. 8:10).

Deceit and Our Family History

The fall brought separation into our lives. The deception exhibited by Satan in the garden (Gen. 3:3) has become a trait that permeates our relationships. Our personalities are predisposed to sin, and we wear masks in our relationships that cover our true thoughts and feelings. In fact, the word *personality* is derived from the Latin word *persona,* which means "mask," and it refers to the stage masks that actors wore in Greek plays to depict various emotions. Sociologists use the term "impression management" to describe how we stage our actions and responses in situations in order to present ourselves in ways we wish to be seen.

Deceit can be conscious and deliberate, or it can be unintentional. We pass on deceptive traits from generation to generation. The family of Abraham provides a good illustration of the generational transference of deceptive behavior. When Abram (Abraham) entered Egypt, he grew afraid that Pharoah would desire his beautiful wife Sarai (Sarah). He was afraid that the Egyptians would have him put to death. To avoid this possibility, Abram passed his wife off as his sister (Gen. 12:11–13). Abram's fear and subsequent deception resulted in God's inflicting disease upon the Egyptian royal household until the subterfuge was revealed.

What did Abraham learn from this incident? In Genesis 20, we find him repeating the same deception. This time he is in Gerar, and once again fear leads him to present Sarah as his sister. Abimelech, the king of Gerar, takes Sarah, but God warns him in a dream of the deception, and tragedy is avoided.

What model does Abraham present to his son Isaac? Abraham is clearly a man of faith (Heb. 11:11–12), and yet he is not perfect. His son Isaac would have heard the stories about Egypt and Gerar. He would have observed how his father reacted in times of great pressure and fear.

Isaac married Rebekah, and the day arrived when he and his family were faced with a famine. Isaac sought aid in Gerar; but like his father before him, he passed his wife off as his sister (Gen. 26:7). God had reminded Isaac of his promise to Abraham of protection through the provision of land and descendants too numerous to count, but once again fear drove Abraham's family to deceive. Fortunately, the king discovered the deceit, and Isaac's tenure in Gerar became a time of blessing from God.

We now enter the third generation. Surely the stories of Abraham and Isaac have been taught to the children, and the dangers of deception have been learned. Yet in Genesis 27, we find Rebekah teaching her son Jacob to deceive his father, manipulating Isaac into giving him and not his brother, Esau, the patriarchal blessing.

Nations and peoples suffer for the poor decisions of their leaders, and children suffer for the unwise behavior of their parents. The Bible describes cases such as Abraham where children pick up deceptive and sinful practices from their parents. We learn from the people around us how to think, speak, and behave, and the most influential people in our early stages of development are usually our parents and relatives. The principle behind this learning process led to the ancient adage, "The fathers have eaten sour grapes, and the children's teeth are set on edge" (Ezek. 18:2 KJV). In other words, the actions of one generation, for better or worse, affect the following generation. A corollary belief was that offspring could be held accountable for the behavior of their parents and subsequently punished. As we shall see, this saying misrepresented God's teaching.

A study of your family history can reveal significant information on the people and events that have influenced your life and affect how you respond in a given situation. A helpful counseling exercise is to ask people to list and describe their current generation (siblings and cousins) and two to three previous generations (parents, grandparents, great grandparents) in their family history. Other significant people in addition to blood relatives can also be identified.

A detailed description of the most memorable and important influences can include any history of marriage and divorce, alcohol or drug abuse, honors and social recognitions, education, occupations and social status, ethnic and national origins, and any other noteworthy events. A religious history, in particular, can be collected that details the spiritual journey of the family. Information can also be gathered on the methods and styles of communication in the family, how problems were discussed, how strong emotions were handled, and how conflicts were resolved (or covered up and ignored).

Other areas include the role of love, faith, hope, and trust and examples of betrayal, deception, violence, and distrust in the various relationships. One effect of this exercise is that people become aware of just how much they are like their parents and previous generations, or, alternatively, how much they have reacted to or rebelled from these influences.

The Bible provides us with a family history of the nation of Israel, written in particular from the perspective of faith. We discover the strengths and human frailties of people in each generation as they relate to God and to others. The Bible makes clear, however, that even though parents influence their children (Prov. 22:6), each person is responsible for his or her own behavior. Children cannot blame parents for the way they turned out, and parents must not be punished for the crimes of their offspring. We all must be accountable for our own behavior (Deut.

24:16–18; 2 Kings 14:6; 2 Chron. 25:4). In fact, the Bible makes clear that God repudiates the teaching behind the adage "The fathers have eaten sour grapes, and the children's teeth are set on edge." Instead, "everyone will die for his own iniquity, each man who eats the sour grapes, his [own] teeth will be set on edge" (Jer. 31:29–30).

Ezekiel gives an extended discussion on this issue (Ezek. 18:1–32). God forbade Israel from ever using the proverb again (Ezek. 18:2–3), and he stressed that blame must not be placed on a parent for a child's sin or vice versa. "Behold, all souls are Mine; the soul of the father as well as the soul of the son is Mine. The soul who sins will die" (v. 4).

> Yet you say, "Why should the son not bear the punishment for the father's iniquity?" When the son has practiced justice and righteousness and has observed all My statutes and done them, he shall surely live. The person who sins will die. The son will not bear the punishment for the father's iniquity, nor will the father bear the punishment for the son's iniquity; the righteousness of the righteous will be upon himself, and the wickedness of the wicked will be upon himself (vv. 19–20).

God also made clear that repentance and following the path of righteousness would bring forgiveness from him and break these generational patterns. "But if the wicked man turns from all his sins which he has committed and observes all My statutes and practices justice and righteousness, he shall surely live; he shall not die" (Ezek. 18:21). The Bible also tells us that ultimately no person is righteous in the sight of the Lord (Pss. 14:2–3; 52:2–3; Rom. 3:10) but that God has provided the path to righteousness through his Son (Rom. 5:6–11). At the most basic level in our spirit and soul, we are unable to change ourselves.

God's Work of Redemption

The beginning of history, the centrality of the cross, and access to the tree of life are all part of a divine plan for humanity. An understanding of the creation story and, of course, the cross and salvation is fundamental to a theology of Christian counseling. The book of Genesis reveals important basic points about human nature and our relationship to God:

- We are created for relationship with God and with others.
- We are unique among all of creation.
- We have been given the freedom to choose, but our choices have led to sin and separation from God.
- God has not abandoned us; he is present, and he has a plan since we are incapable of saving ourselves.

This biblical picture stands in stark contrast to the secular models of counseling, which focus on the self and social systems, ignoring our fundamental spiritual nature and dependence on God.

A Fundamental Flaw in All Secular Counseling Theories

All secular counseling theories have one principle in common: the individual and the society are at the center of all change; they are the source of both the problems and the potential solutions in life. These theories focus on the horizontal dimension of relationships, but they ignore the divine or vertical dimension. They are built on a philosophy of naturalism, which acknowledges the existence only of material, measurable, observable, natural elements or forces in our world, to the exclusion, by definition, of the supernatural or spiritual.[5] The motivation for change and the behavioral drives originate somewhere on a continuum between individual freedom to choose and social or biological pressure to conform, depending on which theory you read. The implication of such theories is that counseling must address the self by increasing personal awareness or by reprogramming the cognitive or behavioral dimensions, or it must assist in reconfiguring the social or biological forces that shape a person's world.

When these theories consider the spiritual dimension, they often view God in functional cause-and-effect terms. God is a figment of your imagination that enables you to cope with life, or he is a supreme power of reciprocity that you believe must reward your good works. These views are not new. Satan offers a variation of the behaviorist cause-and-effect argument in his explanation for Job's exemplary behavior. The only reason that Job is righteous and doesn't curse you, he tells God, is that he has been blessed or rewarded with a family, wealth, and physical health (Job 1–2); Job's righteousness could be explained by a simple behavioral response. God's reply and the subsequent testing of Job reveal that human nature and human behavior are more than a two-dimensional product of a cause-and-effect universe. "Though He slay me, I will hope in Him," said Job (Job 13:15). Although Job had questions about his predicament, his faith and belief in God were not governed by his physical conditions and the satanic manipulation of his life.

A fundamental problem with all the secular theories of personality is that they cannot comprehend Genesis. They are unable to account for both the image of God in humanity and the fall—our pull toward altruism and the divine and our rebellious predisposition toward sin and evil. Either theories emphasize an underlying goodness in all human nature, or they stress a basic evil. We see examples of these two positions in the works of Sigmund Freud and the psychologist Carl Rogers.

In a letter to his friend Oskar Pfister, Freud said that he was not interested in studying the nature of good and evil, but his experience told him that most people were "trash" and that there was "little that is 'good' about human beings on the whole." [6] His psychoanalytic theory reflects this position. Human nature is driven by unconscious biological forces (in particular a sex drive), and the conflicting elements within the personality lead to neuroses and moral anxiety. Conflict is a hallmark of his theory. Up to a point, Freud has a blind man's grasp of the fall, but his insights lack the comprehensive context of Genesis. They lack any understanding of our creation in the image of God.

Carl Rogers believed that all people have an innate goodness. His person-centered theory of counseling stresses the importance of allowing this goodness to be expressed. The client, guided by experience and self-direction, will inherently be drawn toward mental health and responsible behavior. The function of the counselor in his approach is to nurture this self-awareness by showing an unconditional positive regard, without interfering or imposing his or her own values on the client. As a result of his focus on a natural potential for growth and goodness, Rogers overlooked or ignored any orientation toward dissimulation, evil, and sin in human nature. Neither Rogers nor Freud is able to account for both our creation in the image of God and the consequences of the fall on our human nature.

In the next chapter we will examine Freud and Rogers further to determine what value we might draw from their counseling theories and others like them.

Summary

1. We are designed for fellowship with God and with other people. We were created in the image of God, but our fall into sin has led to a separation from God and dissonance in our relationships with others.
2. God alone has the power to restore our relationship with him, and he has made the way possible for reconciliation.
3. A study of our biblical family history and our personal family history can teach us about our human condition and the influence of personal, social, and spiritual forces on our lives.
4. The failure of secular counseling theories lies in their inability to understand the biblical nature of human beings, and their reliance, by default, on the individual or social forces for the definition and causes of problems and the interventions for solutions.
5. An understanding of Genesis is fundamental to a biblical model of Christian counseling. Without the comprehensive biblical description of human nature and the connection with our Creator, we are left with an incomplete picture that will lead to an inadequate and insufficient model of caregiving and a deficient healing process.

Where Do We Go from Here?

With this foundation we now turn to the operational starting place for biblical counseling. I believe that biblical Christian counseling must use the example that God gives us. Our point of departure is God's response when he engaged in the first crisis counseling intervention in human history.

Adam and Eve were in crisis. Sin had entered their lives. They were separated from God, and their relationship with each other was already unraveling. Only God had the power to intervene, and he began his counsel not with a statement or a demand but with a question.

Did you know that the first question asked by God in recorded human history was a crisis-counseling intervention question? "Where are you?" (Gen. 3:9). And so began the counsel of heaven on earth.

Questions and Exercises for Reflection

1. How would you define "the image of God"? What are the implications of this image for Christian counseling?
2. Study and compare some secular theories of personality with Genesis 1–3. What are some significant differences in the descriptions?
3. Study the role of Jesus as the new Adam, and identify the differences between Christ and the old Adam. In what ways are we like the old Adam? How are we like the new Adam?
4. Complete a detailed genogram or history of your family over the past two to three generations. Whom in your family of origin are you most like? What areas in your family history have been most influential in your personal life?
5. How does the Bible deal with family influence and individual responsibility?

References

Gaede, S. D. *Where Gods May Dwell: On Understanding the Human Condition.* Grand Rapids, Mich.: Academie Books/Zondervan Publishing House, 1985.

Hoffman, Edward. *The Hebrew Alphabet: A Mystical Tradition.* San Francisco: Chronicle Books, 1998.

Meng, Heinrich, and Ernst L. Freud, eds. *Psychoanalysis and Faith: The Letters of Sigmund Freud and Oskar Pfister.* Trans. by Eric Mosbacher. New York: Basic Books, 1963.

Schaeffer, Francis A. *He Is There and He Is Not Silent.* Wheaton, Ill.: Tyndale House, 1972.

Endnotes

1 See, for example, Edward Hoffman, *The Hebrew Alphabet: A Mystical Tradition* (San Francisco: Chronicle Books, 1998), 25.

2 Francis A. Schaeffer, *He Is There and He Is Not Silent* (Wheaton, Ill., Tyndale House, 1972), 14–17.

3 A further example of the uniqueness of human creation is found in the original language in Genesis. The Bible tells us that God formed both humans and animals, but, although the same Hebrew word is used in both passages, there is a slight difference in the spelling used in Genesis 2:7 and 2:19.

• "God formed (*yyatsar*— רצייַ) man of dust from the ground" (Gen. 2:7).

• "God formed (*yatsar*— רצייַ) every beast of the field" (Gen. 2:19).

Perceptive readers will notice that the word for "formed" is spelled differently in the verses. In the original Hebrew, an additional letter called a *yod* has been added when referring to the forming of humans. Both verbs are in the imperfect tense in Hebrew, and in the imperfect the second *yod* is usually deleted. There is no grammatical or literary reason for this addition. The word has the same meaning without the extra letter, so the question arises about why the letter is there. A grammarian may explain it as simply a variance in the written language that occurs from time to time, whereas some branches of Judaism might have a more mystical interpretation. While there can be no definitive explanation, I believe the Bible makes clear in the context and possibly in the spelling of the actual words that something was different about the creation of humans in comparison to the creation of animals. Under the inspiration of the Holy Spirit, the writer of Genesis is demonstrating to us that an additional element went into the creation of mankind. Our creation in the image of God allowed us to have a special relationship with our Creator.

4 One implication of this principle is that pastoral care and counseling should address the whole person: body, psyche (cognitive and emotional), and spirit. See, e.g., Matthew 25:31–36.

5 Gaede notes that our assumptions or beliefs about the ultimate nature of our world can be reduced to three views of reality: naturalism, which argues that the material universe is the true reality and that it has always existed; pantheism, which sees the physical world as an illusion, with all material and nonmaterial elements and forces in the universe simply being manifestations of the divine; and theism, which views God as eternal or preexistent and the Creator and sustainer of our universe. The naturalistic philosophy has permeated Western science since the Enlightenment. See S. D. Gaede, *Where Gods May Dwell: On Understanding the Human Condition* (Grand Rapids, Mich.: Academie Books/Zondervan Publishing House, 1985), 33–39.

6 Heinrich Meng and Ernst L. Freud, eds., *Psychoanalysis and Faith: The Letters of Sigmund Freud and Oskar Pfister,* trans. by Eric Mosbacher (New York: Basic Books, 1963), 61–62.

3

LOSTNESS: THE HUMAN LOCATION

R eal estate agents tell us that the three most important things to remember when purchasing a house are location, location, and location. They want buyers to understand that the value of a house is determined not just by the quality and size of its construction but primarily by its desirable position in relationship to other things of value in a community, including quality schools, good utilities and public services, transportation, access to shops and churches, and attractive recreational facilities.

Adam and Eve moved, but they failed to pay attention to their location. Their new real estate agent had deceived them, and now they faced a crisis.

The first crisis counseling intervention in human history began with the question, "Where are you?" (Gen. 3:9). God's question provides us with a fundamental principle in witnessing and also in counseling. Effective Christian counseling requires us to start with the same question. We need to identify the precise location of the person in need.

31

> Then the LORD called to the man, and said to him,
> "Where are you?" He said, "I heard the sound of you
> in the garden, and I was afraid, for I was naked, so I
> hid myself." And He said, "Who told you that you were
> naked? Have you eaten from the tree of which I com-
> manded you not to eat?" The man said, "The woman
> whom You gave to be with me, she gave me from the
> tree, and I ate." Then the LORD said to the woman,
> "What is this you have done?" And the woman said,
> "The serpent deceived me, and I ate" (Gen. 3:9–13).

"Where are you?" Why would God ask such a question? After all, his knowledge is unlimited, and it would seem more reasonable that he simply dictate to Adam and Eve exactly what they had done wrong and spell out their punishment. He was obviously not asking for their physical location in a celestial game of hide-and-seek. God knew where they were physically hiding. I believe the question was asked not to assist God and discover the couple's whereabouts, but rather it was asked for Adam and Eve's benefit and for ours.

God asked Adam and Eve the same question he asks of all sinners. The question indicates that there has been a breakdown in communication. We are no longer in right relationship with our Creator. The fault lies in us not in anything God has done (Rom. 3:23). The question acknowledges that we are not slaves; instead we have limited freedom of choice. We can listen to God or we can reject him. The question also tells us that we are lost without God. We cannot find our own way. Our sin prevents us from finding God. Whereas religions of the world are human attempts to find God, the biblical picture reveals that God first seeks us.

Finally, the question reveals how God begins his counsel of heaven on earth. He comes to us and starts his healing where we are. He allows us first to define our situation, to recognize our current condition, to accept personal responsibility, and, most importantly, to acknowledge our need for him.[1] This approach gives us a key to effective biblical

Christian counseling, and it also has implications for evangelism and discipleship.

The Three Dimensions of Location

Adam's and Eve's responses to God's inquiries reveal three dimensions that must be addressed in Christian counseling: the discovery of location from the perspectives of self, of others, and of God.

1. *Location in Relationship to Self.* Adam's first response to God was to show fear. His attempts to cover himself physically and to hide were signs that he had been disobedient. Sin had led to separation from his Creator and had led to a distorted view of self. His self-understanding had become egocentric; his motivation was no longer to serve God but to protect himself and his own self-interest. The Bible makes clear that the cover-up was unsuccessful.

2. *Location in Relationship to Others.* The fall caused a breakdown in relationship with others. When God gave Adam the opportunity to confess, Adam instead responded by blaming both God and Eve ("The woman whom You gave *to be* with me, she gave me from the tree" [Gen. 3:12]). A dissonance now existed in the relationship between Adam and Eve, symbolized by the covering of their naked bodies and expressed in laying the responsibility and the culpability on someone else. In the Western world their actions would appear to have a sexual connotation and imply modesty along with the loss of innocence, but their behavior may have had additional implications. Creative power is a manifestation of the image of God; by covering their bodies at the place of procreation, Adam and Eve were indicating that they no longer fully reflected the image of their Creator. The fact that the act of childbirth would now be associated with pain is a further indication of this disruption.

The act of covering their bodies also signified that Adam and Eve were no longer completely open with each other; distrust and blame had entered their relationship. The unity of spirit they had shared together was now broken, and the action of covering themselves at the point of anatomical difference symbolized the relational differences and disagreements that they were now experiencing.

3. *Location in Relationship to God.* The most significant loss at the fall (and all others pale in comparison to it) is the breakdown in the relationship with God. "The serpent deceived me," said Eve. A shift in allegiance had occurred, and now humanity was listening to an authority other than God. Deception was now part of human relationships and our dealings with God. Their sin led to a separation from God. Idolatry had entered the relationship. The new gods on the throne were the self and social and demonic forces. Adam and Eve were lost, and they were incapable of rescuing themselves.

The Counseling Process: Finding the Best Path

Biblical Christian counseling addresses the problem of location and lostness. The counseling process is like trying to help a person who has wandered off track and has become lost in a forest. When I ask students what they would like to have if they were lost under such circumstances, the most common responses I get include a desire to have a compass and a map. (For the sake of my illustration, I am excluding the possibility of having a global positioning transmitter, an operational mobile phone, a homing pigeon, a very long string, and other such creative and imaginative solutions.) I point out to the students that neither a compass nor a map alone will help a lost person unless that individual has some additional information.

The first thing lost people need to know is where they are located on the map. The map is absolutely useless to them unless they can find their precise position on it. They need to identify enough familiar landmarks surrounding them to successfully determine their current location. But this knowledge, while necessary, is still insufficient for rescue from their problem. Even if they are able to pinpoint their location on a map, they are faced with a second dilemma: Which direction do they go? Where does the place of safety and rescue lie? What is their goal? The second thing then that our lost people need to identify is a place on the map that represents shelter and protection. They need to know where they are going.

I often ask my counselees to describe what their situation would look like if their problems were solved. How do you know when you have arrived at your destination or a place of safety? What does it look like? What key indicators tell you that you have met your goal? But even an awareness of current position and a clearly defined objective or goal will not be enough to get people out of the woods. There is still a third requirement.

After determining their current position and their destination, they still must decide the track they will take to reach their goal. The third requirement, then, is to develop a plan that effectively and safely directs them to their destination. The best track may not be in a straight line. Dangerous and unknown territory may need to be avoided by taking an indirect route. An assessment of equipment and physical, mental, emotional, and spiritual capabilities also needs to be made.

Problems and disagreements can occur at any one of these three steps. A map may not be accurate or contain enough details. People may not be able to interpret the map clearly, or they may fail to study it closely.

We were on the third day of a five-day walk along the southernmost point of mainland Australia. Our plan for the day was to hike three miles through mountainous terrain down to a lighthouse and then walk another four miles to a beach campsite. The rough map used by our leader showed two approaches to the lighthouse, a dirt road and a narrow walking track. We chose to follow the road, which was wider and smoother than the track. We labored up and down the steep inclines on the road until we arrived exhausted at the lighthouse. Later we looked at an accurate topographical map of the region.

A close examination revealed significant additional information about the route we had taken. The narrow hiking track that we had rejected followed a straight line and maintained about the same elevation all the way to the lighthouse. The path was not only less mountainous than the way we had taken; it was also about one-third shorter. We had exerted unnecessary energy, traveling at times in the wrong direction, to arrive at our destination. Under certain circumstances, such as a blizzard, our decision and direction could have had disastrous and even deadly consequences.

We learned some important lessons from our experience. Have a reliable map. Study your map and plan your path before you set out on a journey. Consult with a person who is knowledgeable about the area in which you are traveling, or have a reliable guide to lead you. Do not assume that a path that appears wide and easy is the best one to take. These lessons have a counterpart in finding direction in counseling.

The basic steps for counseling could be summarized in the three requirements for location: (1) Where are you? (2) Where do you need to be? (3) How will you get there? Counseling involves identifying the current position of an individual, family, or group, determining a goal or destination, and developing a plan to reach the goal.

Problems arise when confusing signals are given and there is disagreement over the exact location of a lost person. This issue is one of the fundamental problems in counseling where various theories and models clash in an attempt to identify how best to define the human condition and how to help a person in need.

Bernard O'Reilly and the Lost Airplane

On Friday, February 19, 1937, a Stinson Airliner with a pilot, copilot, and five passengers took off from Brisbane on the eastern coast of Australia, rose into the clouds, and disappeared. The plane was making a routine flight from Brisbane to Sydney with an intermediate stop in the town of Lismore to pick up additional passengers. When the plane failed to arrive in Lismore, a search was organized. Reports came in from people who claimed to have seen the plane enter a cloudbank over the McPherson Ranges south of Brisbane, but they later began to doubt themselves when word came in of sightings further south and closer to Sydney. A fruitless search continued over the following week by air, land, and even by sea after a reported sighting of the plane from a steamship. Newspapers clamored for information and gave updates on the search that now included both the Australian Air Force and civilian planes.

The assumption was made that the pilot had chosen to bypass Lismore, probably because of unfavorable weather conditions, and fly directly to Sydney. Yes, the plane had been seen and heard by people in the region just north of Sydney. Yes, floating plane wreckage had been observed from Palm Beach. Yes, the evidence was clear, according to both the press and the radio, "beyond doubt" the plane had come down in the wilderness area south of the Hawkesbury River, a few minutes by air north of Sydney.

By the end of the following week, newspapers and the radio were reporting the obvious conclusion, based on the convincing evidence. The plane had crashed either in the wild bush country north of Sydney, or, more probably, it had come down in the ocean and disappeared without a trace. Survival by this time was highly unlikely, and so the decision was made to abandon the search.

Nearly four hundred miles north of Sydney, high in the McPherson Ranges, one man examined the evidence and said no.

Bernard O'Reilly and his family lived in the largely uninhabited McPherson Ranges in an area now known as Lamington National Park. The people who settled in this area were hardy stock who grew to appreciate the rugged terrain and the thick jungle of rain forests that tested the toughest pioneers. O'Reilly was familiar with the tropical flora and fauna of the region. He knew the plants and trees and vines, the venomous snakes, the dingoes, wallabies, and tiger cats, the lyrebird and the many colorful parrots. He had explored the thick, largely impenetrable jungle where tall trees interlaced their branches and leaves to form a canopy so thick that sunlight cannot penetrate to the ground, and he had experienced the vicious pricks of the lawyer vine that positioned itself in places that provided inviting handholds to naïve bush walkers.

Bernard O'Reilly also possessed a basic Christian faith borne by a rural living that dealt in hard facts and realities, not in unsubstantiated theories and vague assumptions. He was not given to embracing current trends and restless speculations, and his intimate knowledge of the intricate and complicated natural world of the rain forest confirmed for him the irrefutable and logical conclusion that a Builder and Manager

37

God must exist. With this faith and reason in hand, O'Reilly examined the information on the mystery of the Stinson aircraft, eight days after its disappearance.

From a study of the contradictory evidence and the various theories surrounding the crash, O'Reilly determined two clear facts. The first fact was that the plane had made no apparent attempt to contact the Lismore airport to report a diversion down the coast and away from the ranges because of unfavorable weather conditions. O'Reilly believed that an experienced pilot like Captain Rex Boyden would have radioed his position and change of plans. The second piece of information was that hundreds of people, including O'Reilly's brother, had seen the plane flying toward the ranges and Lismore shortly before it disappeared into the clouds. He also remembered that on the day of the plane's disappearance a severe storm of hurricane-like proportions had swept through the ranges, producing downdrafts and damaging farms and properties in the region. Rains from the aftermath of the storm were still continuing in the area. Armed with these two facts, O'Reilly took the latest copy of an aerial survey map of the McPherson Ranges and with a ruler and pencil drew a straight line from the spot the plane was last seen to the town of Lismore. The line crossed four high mountain ranges.

O'Reilly's plan was to follow the line. The problem was that the ranges were located in over eighty thousand acres of jungle where visibility is often reduced to less than ten yards. O'Reilly believed that, even by following the line, it would take more than three lifetimes to complete such a search. Despite these overwhelming difficulties, he set out alone to find the plane and its occupants.

Nine days had now passed since the disappearance. O'Reilly took with him a few rations of bread, butter, onions, and tea, a snakebite kit and a cord to bind limbs. One of his feet had become infected from a rusty nail two days before, but he carried with him the encouragement of his family and the prayers of his mother.[2]

For hours O'Reilly hacked and slashed his way through dense and dark jungle, with its thorns and vines impeding his steps. His wealth of knowledge provided him with his tools of navigation. He knew the direction and the number of ridges; northern slopes have heavy growths of raspberry and lawyer vines; moss and lichen grow on the southern face of trees; certain species of trees will be going to seed at low altitudes, while at the same time they will be blooming at two thousand feet and beginning to bud at four thousand feet; a similar principle for altitude applies to the nesting patterns of birds; the prevailing winds from the south in the McPhersons meant that exposed trees would lean to the north. This bush compass provided by the Creator would be his only guide.

By the late afternoon of his first day, O'Reilly had reached the most distant point of earlier exploration in the region. The next morning he climbed the first of the four ridges. He waited for the clouds to lift along his plotted line of flight; and then in the distance, eight miles away, on the third ridge called the Lamington Plateau, he noticed a light-brown patch among the trees. Some trees turn brown in the spring, but this was late summer. A lightning strike might cause the discoloration, but natural fires do not burn well in soaking rain forests. Gallons of burning aviation fuel, however, might create such a brown area. Fortified by this hope, O'Reilly entered the soaking, thick rain forest. He walked blindly, relying solely on his bush knowledge. He would not see the brown tree again for eight hours when he arrived twenty yards from it, an amazing feat of navigation.

As he entered the vicinity of the tree, the cry of a human voice led him to the charred remains of an aircraft and to two men, John Proud and Joseph Binstead, who were barely alive after ten days. Both men were desperately in need of medical attention. The pilot and copilot, along with two passengers had died upon impact. Three men had survived. One of them, an Englishman by the name of James Westray, had decided to go for help. He was an experienced climber in the Scottish Highlands, but he was unfamiliar with the treacherous vegetation in the Australian bush. The giant Helmholtzia lilies appear to provide a safe handhold for descent to the bottom of the cliffs, but they will break away under the weight of a climber. O'Reilly would later come across a mass of torn lilies that would indicate the place where Westray had

39

fallen. He would find Westray's body seated on a boulder after he had crawled for miles down slippery boulders and four waterfalls in a valiant and sacrificial attempt to reach safety and bring help.

O'Reilly's trials and those of the two survivors were not over. He still had to get the men out, and neither one of them was capable of walking. Proud had a broken leg and was feverish, and Binstead was barely able to crawl. His first item of business was to develop a plan. It would take too long to return along the path he had made from his home. He did not know his exact location on the map, but experience told him that the gorge below was a southern branch of Christmas Creek and nine miles down its track would be a clearing and civilization. O'Reilly made the men as comfortable as possible and then he set out. It was half-past four in the afternoon.

For three hours O'Reilly traversed previously unexplored terrain, scrambling down a slippery gorge, at times running blindly along the creek bed, past the body of Jim Westray and through waist-deep pools of water, ignoring countless cuts and thorns and bruises, until he broke into a clearing and raised the alarm. O'Reilly was exhausted, but another forty-eight hours would go by before he slept.

A rescue plan was organized as dozens of volunteers made preparation to cut their way into the crash site over ground O'Reilly would later describe as "fourteen miles of soaking green hell." The rescue party, with Bernard O'Reilly leading, would take eight hours to retrace his steps back to the ailing Binstead and Proud.

In the meantime, news of the discovery and O'Reilly's incredible achievement was broadcast around the country. An army of reporters and photographers descended on the area and clamored for more information on the man who had found the plane and had led the subsequent rescue. People were puzzled about what would motivate a man to search for a plane four hundred miles from where the world had determined it had crashed. Reporters attributed the amazing feat to his knowledge of the environment and to intuition or a hunch, but O'Reilly rejected these explanations.

O'Reilly's response to these conjectures is illuminating. In his book *Green Mountains*, he stated that bush knowledge and instinct alone would be insufficient for finding a plane in the dense vegetation of the McPherson Ranges. Due credit, he said, must be given to the prayers of his mother that buoyed his hope and guided him.[3] Faith also countered the speculation that O'Reilly was driven by a hunch. He did not believe in hunches. Behind his human reasoning was the divine hand of God. In O'Reilly's words, God would not "inspire anyone with a blind unreasoning impulse to go and do His will, but it seems quite natural that he would inspire in a man the reasoning and initiative which would send that man out on his own accord; the fact that the man so chosen had spent most of his life in unwittingly fitting himself out for just such a job seems to further indicate a clear purpose behind it all."[4]

Important Principles for Location

The story of Bernard O'Reilly gives us a picture of our world and the role of the Christian counselor. Secular theories of counseling tell us that we are definitely located in a certain area. They describe our human condition and what we need to do to save ourselves. They contain some elements of truth and factual information, but in a fundamental way they conflict with the biblical picture of our location and where we must begin the search for truth.

Some principles in determining location are found in the O'Reilly story, and these guidelines are applicable to the Christian counseling process.

1. *Finding a person's location requires a careful study of the facts.* Accurate information must be separated from spurious conjecture. O'Reilly was able to sort through the contradictory bits of data and determine some essential truths. He was not swayed by the beliefs and speculations of other people, including the supposedly authoritative voices of the media and experts. Be cautious of the loud and dissonant voices that can lead you astray (Eccl. 9:17).

Christian counselors must sort out facts from the attitudes, speculation, theories, and emotions present in a counseling session. Look carefully at the evidence in a situation and avoid an uncritical acceptance of the world's interpretation of events. Avoid the mistake of Adam and Eve, who chose to replace reasoned faith with an arbitrary impulsiveness that succumbed to a distorted vision of life and fed their pride.

2. *Even with the best of intentions and considerable experience, people are not always able to help themselves or save others.* There are times when we need assistance. We may lack the resources or knowledge to solve a problem. Westray possessed a wealth of skill and practical know-how, but he was ill equipped to handle his problem because he had landed (or, in this case, crashed) in unfamiliar territory. Westray did not know the dangers he faced; consequently, in spite of his heroic intentions, he was doomed to failure.

Trained and skillful Christian counselors are in a position to help people in need. They can assist people to realize the size of their problems and help them accurately assess their personal capabilities. At the same time counselors must be cautious of their own limitations. They need to avoid the temptation to practice in areas beyond their knowledge, training, and personal skills.

3. *Do not expect or rely on support from the world, but look for encouragement and support from the Christian community.* O'Reilly was encouraged by the prayers of his mother and the support of his wife and family. He did not rely on the sometimes fickle sentiment of world opinion.

In biblical counseling there is no room for the Lone Ranger counselor who sets off impulsively on his own to rescue a person, but there is room for self-sacrifice under the guidance and direction of God. Christian counseling draws from the spiritual gifts and disciplines provided and nurtured by the Holy Spirit, the authority of Scripture, the prayers and encouragement of fellow believers, and accurate investigation and observation of God's creation.

4. *Listen and observe carefully, and respond to the inspiration and leading of the Holy Spirit.* O'Reilly said that he was not acting on a hunch. He relied on a reasoned faith that trusted God to guide and direct him.

Christian counselors must look for the hand of God in every counseling situation, expecting God to provide.

5. *Continue to develop your God-given gifts, skills, and abilities— you never know when you might need them.* O'Reilly pointed out that preparation for the rescue had taken a lifetime. His knowledge of the bush, the terrain, plants, and weather was nurtured and developed over many years, along with his commonsense attitude and his abiding faith in the Creator God.

Christian counselors need continually to develop their biblical knowledge, spiritual gifts, spiritual disciplines, and counseling skills.

6. *Helping people may require self-sacrifice.* The physical toll Bernard O'Reilly experienced must have been incredible. He went days without sleeping. The ground he covered would be impenetrable to most individuals, and he risked ridicule from other people. Doing the right thing is not always easy.

Christian counselors may be called upon to go above and beyond the normal call of duty in order to help people. The danger here is the temptation to violate ethical, moral, and even legal codes in counseling. "I have a higher calling," the reasoning goes. "Therefore, I'm not subject to human rules." Such tendencies should be rejected in favor of thoughtful planning and consultation with knowledgeable and wise people in the community of faith before taking any extraordinary or unusual steps.

7. *When your achievements are recognized, be sure to make the correct attribution for your success.* Bernard O'Reilly was careful not to let the adulation of a grateful world turn his head. He acknowledged that for all his skill and reasoning, his chances of finding the lost men were smaller than finding the proverbial needle in a haystack. His success was due to the grace of God.

Christian counselors occasionally receive sincere thanks (and criticism) in their ministries. There is a temptation to be self-congratulatory and boast of our accomplishments. The humble counselor recognizes that successful biblical counseling depends entirely on God's guidance and grace.

The Supreme Rescue

Jesus Christ provides us with the preeminent example of a successful and sacrificial search and rescue attempt. Christian counseling follows the model of Christ in helping lost people to find their way home. The biblical call to witness and share the gospel with a lost world is certainly part of the mandate for all Christians, and this message should be part of all work that Christians do, including the counseling ministry. But the biblical message is clear that we are not capable of finding our way by ourselves. God alone initiated the search and provided the way to salvation.

The Location of Secular Theories and Theorists

Of what value in determining our location are the counseling and personality theories of researchers like Freud and Rogers? There are countless theories of psychotherapy in print (some estimates range up to five hundred such theories), but for the sake of discussion I will use these two acknowledged pioneers in psychotherapy. They have attempted to study the "living human document" and report their findings. It is not possible to question or understand all their motives, but we can assume that both Freud and Rogers held the honorable goals of trying to help people who were experiencing mental anguish and turmoil. Beyond this observation, any consensus on their theories will be difficult. The differences between their two theories are obvious. Rogers has admitted that his theory was developed, in part, as a reaction to Freud's psychoanalytic theory. They cannot both be right, though they could be like the blind men who touched different parts of an elephant and subsequently gave contradictory descriptions based on their experience.

Books on biblical and Christian counseling tend to be critical of both psychoanalysis and person-centered therapy. The more critical works dismiss both of them as antibiblical and unworthy of any consideration in counseling.

I have already noted the failure of all secular theories in regard to Genesis, but I believe these theories can contribute information in two areas: (1) in observation and research and (2) in biography and location.

Theories have more value when they provide supporting evidence and clinically tested data. Observation and experimentation are generally preferable and far more accurate than speculative theories and interpretations of human behavior. Recent studies on the factors leading to divorce are a good example. Research is revealing that divorce is highly predictable and that particular beliefs and counseling procedures used in the past in this area are untrue or ineffective. The new findings, however, complement and illuminate some biblical truths and principles. The disingenuous argument is to claim that such research is unnecessary since we have the truth already available in Scripture. But rigorous and careful studies can reveal information about God's creative work through the common grace and reason available to all human beings. Just as a solid foundation in hermeneutics helps Christians draw correct guidance from Scripture, so too do appropriate empirical research techniques and statistical analyses help us draw more precise conclusions from sensory data. Wise biblical Christian counselors first test such research against biblical truth before using it in their counseling ministries.

The theories and hypotheses presented by counseling theorists can prompt investigation and testing and reveal some truths of God in his creation. Such research also has an additional benefit in that it can also expose the human errors in belief and judgment and force people to reconsider the evidence.

In 1927, Sigmund Freud published *The Future of an Illusion*. In this book he argued that religion was simply an obsessional neurosis derived from a distorted view of the father-son relationship arising in childhood. God is simply a projection of our own intense unconscious desires and childish needs for protection and security. In other words, religious people suffer from psychological and intellectual weakness. The implication of Freud's argument is that atheists are more psychologically normal and that they have a rational, no-nonsense view of the world. In contrast, Christians must suffer from pathological delusions based on irrational and immature needs and wishes.

The impulse among some Christians is simply to scoff at Freud and his associates and dismiss these ideas. It is possible to refute Freud fairly easily from the basis of the divine revelation of Scripture, but Freud's theory of religion is one that also attacks us on the level of empirical observation—he presents us with a measurable scientific challenge.

In the late 1990s, Paul Vitz, a Christian and a professor of psychology at New York University, took Freud's thesis as a legitimate research challenge. Vitz decided to study the evidence that God has provided in his creation. Does belief in God correlate with a healthy or an unhealthy personality? Freud claimed that believers were delusional. By implication atheists should exhibit the characteristics of a sound mind and should have healthy relationships, particularly with their fathers.

In his book *Faith of the Fatherless: The Psychology of Atheism*,[5] Vitz presented a biographical study of over fifty prominent atheists and theists over the past four centuries. His research covered such well-known atheists as Friedrich Nietzsche, David Hume, Bertrand Russell, John-Paul Sartre, Albert Camus, Sigmund Freud, and H. G. Wells. His comparison group of theists included Blaise Pascal, Edmund Burke, Moses Mendelssohn, John Henry Newman, Søren Kierkegaard, G. K. Chesterton, Karl Barth, and Dietrich Bonhoeffer. Vitz focused on the relationships that these people had with their fathers or surrogate fathers. Freud implied that believers would have dysfunctional relationships with their fathers. In comparison atheists should have healthy relationships. What did Vitz find?

Vitz's research revealed that the atheists had weak, bad, or absent fathers while the theists had good fathers or father substitutes. His findings imply that absent or deficient fathers predispose their children to practical if not philosophical atheism. Vitz has turned Freud's projection theory of religion on its head. Freud's theory suggested that belief in God is an illusion that derives from our childish need for protection and security; but Vitz has shown us that "the atheist's disappointment in and resentment of his own earthly father unconsciously justifies his rejection of God." [6] Rather than Christians, atheists are in need of good therapy.

In a world that is constantly trying to debunk Christianity and replace God with the idols of reason and science or some New Age experience, Vitz challenges us to meet the conflict head on. We worship a God who is the Creator of heaven and earth. He is the Author of time and history. God is not a vague idea or illusion that we need to satisfy our inner longings. When someone uses the language of science or reason to attack our faith, we must look for biblical responses and accept the challenge to respond in the same language as our adversary. If the challenge is scientific, we must use that language to investigate and to communicate to others the Author of nature and science. All true scientific observations, principles, and laws will support the biblical view of God.

Theory as Biography

Personality and counseling theories tell us something about the theorists and other people like them. A counseling theory inevitably will incorporate elements from the personal experience of the theorist, just as a book reveals something about its author. These autobiographical features may be covert or more openly acknowledged. They may be derived from favorable conditions and pleasant events, or they may be a reaction to negative past experiences. Theorists usually draw from additional observations, experimentation, and research to develop suppositions on human nature and effective psychotherapeutic treatments that they then assume to be universal to the human condition. Even theorists who are openly adverse to Christianity can provide insights, opportunities, and ideas for study.

A study of the various theories of personality gives us an opportunity to discover the location of the theorists, and it opens up additional possibilities for ministry. When I teach classes on counseling theories, I require my students to study the biographies of the theorists. In one sense, theory is a form of biography. This activity gives students insights into this connection. After a few of these studies, students are able to associate significant biographical events with subsequent beliefs and the personality and counseling theories presented by an individual.

I sometimes assign students to read the biographical information before they study the theory. I then ask them to predict and describe the view of human nature and characteristics of the counseling theory they would expect from someone with that particular background. Their descriptions are surprisingly accurate. They are able to connect events in a person's life with a belief system that is subsequently generated into a personality or counseling theory. The theorists have generalized their personal experiences, cultural conditions, and historical contexts into views they believe are universal or descriptive of all human beings.

A study of their theories helps us to understand the location of the theorists—how they think and feel, what they believe and hope, and where they believe solutions to problems lie. They also give us insights into people who share a similar worldview. Consequently, they may help some biblical Christian counselors connect with people who have a particular worldview or background. A functional equivalent of this use and benefit would be Paul's use of Stoic and Epicurean thought in communicating with the Athenian philosophers (Acts 17:18-34). Paul by no means accepted the pagan philosophies, but he did take advantage of the prose and concepts in those philosophies to direct his listeners to the truth. He located the people in terms of their beliefs, literature, and language; he began from their point of view, and then he led them to godly truths.

A brief and relatively simplistic summary of the lives of Sigmund Freud and Carl Rogers will serve as an example of the influence of biography upon theory.

The Location of Sigmund Freud

Sigmund Freud was born in the small town of Freiburg, Moravia, in the country of Austria. His official biography gives his date of birth as May 6, 1856, but town records indicate March 6.[7] The question over the date is significant when considered with the marriage date of his parents, which, with the revised date, would have been eight and not ten months before his birth. There may have been secrecy and cover-up even at this time in Freud's life. He was the first of seven children. His father Jacob was forty, and his mother Amalia was twenty when Sigmund was born. Jacob had two sons from a former marriage, both of whom were older than his wife Amalia. One of the sons, Philipp, was single and lived in a house directly opposite the Freud home for a time; and some scholars have questioned the relationship between this stepson and Jacob's young and attractive wife.[8] Jacob was a wool merchant, and to improve his business he moved his family to Vienna when Sigmund was four years old. Freud was the first of Amalia's seven children, and he was given special privileges, such as having his own bedroom in which to study. He excelled in school and was granted exemptions from examinations.[9] Freud was raised in an anti-Semitic climate. He experienced the prejudice of being considered "inferior and alien,"[10] and he recalled his shame in his childhood when he learned that his father had failed to defend himself against a racial attack and slurs.[11] He harbored ambivalence toward his Jewish heritage; in *Moses and Monotheism* he questioned some of the basic tenets of Judaism. Yet scholars have noted that his ideas on personality resemble a secularized version of Jewish mystical literature and the oral mystical tradition of Kabbala.[12] Kabbala tradition involves secret teachings and the oral transmission of information to one person at a time by hints and inferences rather than explicit explanations. We find a similar process in psychoanalytic training.

Because he was Jewish, Freud had only two professional options, law or medicine. He chose medicine. He worked with patients suffering from neurological disorders in the Viennese General Hospital. He spent a short time in Paris under the supervision of the French neurologist Jean Charcot, where he studied the conversion reactions of hysterical patients and learned hypnotic technique. (In conversion reactions, mental conflicts are expressed as physical symptoms.) With the support of the physician Josef Breuer, he studied the dynamics of hysteria. He believed that his patients' problems were caused by traumatic memories locked in the unconscious. He developed techniques, including free association, to overcome resistance to the recall of these traumas. The formal origins of his psychoanalytic theory are found in his medical work. He developed a model of illness rather than health; he studied people who were consumed by their problems.

Freud lived in a time and a culture that invited secrecy and deception. He was a Jew living in a Gentile world in nineteenth-century Europe, with all the accompanying prejudice and hypocrisy of that place and period. Jewish people in Vienna valued the importance of discretion, the detailed analyses of events, development of relationships over time, word plays and discussion on the meaning of words. The Victorian period also nurtured ambivalent and inconsistent attitudes toward sexuality.

His theory focuses on the keeping of secrets and the repression of childhood thoughts, sexual desires, and experiences. Unconscious and conscious forces in the personality compete for control of the self. The impulsive childlike id, which is driven by a pleasure principle, must be controlled by strengthening the ego, which functions on a reality principle. At the same time, the overbearing, highly moralistic superego must be held in check.

In his personal life, Freud dealt with issues of secrecy and with being an outsider in a society where the overbearing, supercilious, and moralistic social forces in medicine and culture sought to keep Jews in their place. His theory models these personal experiences and issues, including possible repressed memories and sexual matters from childhood.[13] Attempts to make the theory universally applicable to all human beings have run into problems since it was first proposed. The anthropologist Bronislaw Malinowski, for example, found no evidence supporting the presence of the Oedipus complex among the South Seas natives of the Trobriand Islands.[14] Freud's alienation from his father and strong attachment to his mother provide an obvious source for his development of this complex, which he then apparently assumed had a universal application.[15] The value of his theory may lie in helping us to understand Freud himself and people like him. Freud represents the type of person who is ambivalent about his personal life and his world, an outsider who has experienced prejudice and discrimination and who harbors secrets, underlying motives, ambiguous sexual feelings, and disturbing childhood experiences. This person is articulate, resistant to change, yet willing to analyze his or her life, both past and present, over a period of weeks or even years with a professional consultant.

Christian counselors must decide whether psychoanalysis and its revised manifestations such as Transactional Analysis and Object Relations Theory hold enough value and truth to warrant study and uses. For some counselors and people in need, they may offer a means of communication and assistance in determining the location of individuals. In their secular form, they will inevitably defer to the centrality of the self and social forces for understanding and for the power to change.

The Location of Carl Rogers

Carl Rogers was born on January 8, 1902, in Oak Park, Illinois. He was the fourth of six children, and he was raised in a strict Protestant family. His mother conveyed two messages to young Carl: Do not associate with other people who do not share your beliefs; and no person, even at his or her best, is ever really good enough. People who engaged in activities such as smoking, dancing, playing cards, drinking, and going to the movies were to be avoided. They could be tolerated since they were ignorant, but there should be no contact or communication with them. While he was in high school, his parents reinforced these beliefs by moving the family to a rural farm in Glen Ellyn, Illinois. Rogers became a loner with weak social skills. He had strange or bizarre thoughts and fantasies and only superficial social contacts.[16] Three of the six children in the household, including Carl, developed ulcers.[17]

Rogers experienced new freedom when he left his family to attend the University of Wisconsin. A trip to China in 1922 led to further philosophical separation from his strict religious roots. His values and goals in life took a permanent shift after his move to New York City, where doubts about his religious faith led him to transfer from ministry studies at Union Theological Seminary to Teachers College, Columbia University, where he completed a degree in psychology.[18]

In young adulthood Rogers lived in an era and a country filled with optimism. America in the 1940s and 1950s embraced a can-do spirit, and an individualistic ethic that nurtured economic progress and questioned authority. Roger's nondirective, person-centered therapy reflects his personal history and his social and historical context. He reacted to the overbearing and pontificating image of his parents and of Freud. Classic psychoanalysis demanded strict adherence to the precepts of its founding father. It assumed that the analyst had superior knowledge about the patient's condition and possessed the ability to interpret and diagnose the problem; patients were unable to understand or resolve their own problems without the direct help of the psychoanalyst. Rogers rejected this authoritative and directive position. He taught that experience is the highest authority. In *On Becoming a Person*, he stated that "neither the Bible nor the prophets—neither Freud nor research—neither the revelations of God nor man—can take precedence over my own direct experience."[19]

We can see Roger's reactionary response to his parents and to the dictates of Freud in his personality and counseling theory. The person in need is no longer called a patient but a client, on equal footing with the counselor. In fact, the client is in control of the counseling session. People are capable of self-directed growth, and the function of the counselor is to foster an environment that promotes personal growth, just as Rogers was able to do when he broke away from the stifling judgmental confines of his family.[20] Rogers will not tolerate any directive actions from a counselor that insinuate superiority, conditional love, advice, or moralistic judgment. Rogers wants a therapeutic world that values and affirms an open expression of feelings and attitudes, realness, genuineness, unconditional acceptance, and integration of the self without the need to put on a false front or mask any thoughts and emotions. He wants what he missed in his own childhood.

Rogers's approach appeals to persons whose past has been marked by a lack of genuine love and affection. To locate these people, a counselor will need to avoid directive approaches that conjure up images of judgmentalism and devalue the individual in need. Such people may be overly dependent on others for advice to the point of failing to take personal responsibility. Or they may exhibit a rebellious spirit whereby any issue of authority is met by resistance or flight; they may not return to counseling. These people have a particular need for secure and loving relationships. We find a biblical example of nurturing such relationships in the ministry of Jesus, who modeled therapeutic and redemptive care in his patient guidance, gentleness, and love, particularly with his disciples. In fact, recent research has revealed once again the importance of listening and developing an affirming relationship in the counseling encounter for therapeutic change to occur.[21]

The weakness of person-centered theory, of course, lies in the belief that ultimate hope is found in the self. Rogers clearly stated that personal experience was his highest authority, even above the revelation of God and Scripture. The goals of self-growth and self-actualization ignore the biblical reality of the fall and our need for relationship with God. Christian counselors seek to reveal the true nature of God's unconditional love in Christ and the genuine hope found in him. Attempts to pull ourselves up by our own bootstraps, though admirable, are doomed to failure.

Location and Relationship in Counseling

Biblical Christian counseling seeks to discover a person, a family, or a group's position in relationship to God, to self, and to others. Shattered relationships lead to broken communication lines; information on a person's location becomes distorted, and solutions fail. Effective counseling centers on the following basic questions of location and the three dimensions of relationship.

Current Location

- Where do you say that you are located? What do you believe is the problem?
- Where does your counselor say you are located? Where do your parents, siblings, other relatives, friends, and other people who know you well say you are located? What do they say is your problem?
- Where does God say you are located? What is the biblical view of your situation?

Goal, Destination, or Solution

- Where do you believe you want to be? What is the solution to your problem and what changes do you want? Where do you have control? What changes are you willing and able to make?
- Where does your counselor say you need to be? Where do others say you need to be? What do they suggest?
- Where does God say you need to be? What does Scripture say is the solution to your problem, and what changes does God expect?

Plan for Change

- How do you propose to get to your goal? What resources do you have?
- What suggestions do your counselor and others have for reaching your goal?
- What is God's plan for your life in this situation?

It is not necessary or even wise to ask these questions in a rote manner in a counseling session. The questions reflect areas that need addressing with the person in need; and the counseling conversation needs to be adjusted according to the language, concerns, temperament, and wishes of the counselee. The ideal situation in counseling occurs when there is congruence or complete agreement between the three perspectives and dimensions. Real difficulties arise when different and conflicting views occur between a counselee, counselor, and Scripture on the nature of the problem, the goals of therapy, and possible solutions, interventions, or treatments.[22]

Summary

1. The Bible reveals that we are created for relationship with God, with self, and with others. Disobedience has led to the destruction of our unique relationship with God our Creator. We are in a state of sin. Dissonance also exists in our relationships with others. God alone has the power to restore our relationship with him.
2. The location of a person is in current dispute in our world. Secular therapies present different, often conflicting views on human

nature and counseling theory. All secular therapies fail to address adequately our relationship to God. These theorists claim that their views were derived from observing other people, individuals in society, but they are also a reflection of the self. They are expressions of their own experiences and their personal history writ large. To their credit, some theorists acknowledge this influence. Christian counselors can disregard these theories and theorists, or they can study them as a means of identifying the location of some people and developing opportunities for ministry.

Where Do We Go from Here?

Locating a person is an essential feature of counseling; however, the process is not arbitrary. Biblical Christian counseling has a clear design and purpose. The next chapter will examine the defining characteristics of effective Christian counseling and connect its unique features to the historical church and a biblical worldview.

Questions and Exercises for Reflection

1. The metaphor of a map was used to describe the basic counseling process. What other metaphors or illustrations could you use to explain biblical Christian counseling?
2. Find and describe some additional biblical examples of God's leading lost people to safety.
3. How would you deal with counseling situations where the counselor and the counselees disagreed over their location and the nature of the problem?
4. How would you have counseled a young Sigmund Freud if he had come to you for help? What approach would you take in locating him and ministering to his needs? How would you have counseled Carl Rogers?
5. Study the biographies of one or two other counseling theorists and identify connections between their backgrounds and their subsequent theories.

References

Bakan, David. *Sigmund Freud and the Jewish Mystical Tradition.* Boston: Beacon Press, 1958.

Balmary, Marie. *Psychoanalyzing Psychoanalysis: Freud and the Hidden Fault of the Father.* Ned Lukacher, trans. Baltimore: The Johns Hopkins University Press, 1979/1982.

Fadiman, James, and Robert Frager. *Personality and Personal Growth,* 5th ed. Upper Saddle River, N.J.: Prentice Hall, 2002.

Freud, Sigmund. *An Autobiographical Study.* Authorized translation by James Strachey. New York: W. W. Norton & Company, 1952.

Freud, Sigmund. *The Interpretation of Dreams.* James Strachey, trans. New York: Avon Books, 1965.

Hubble, Mark A., Barry L. Duncan, and Scott D. Miller. *The Heart and Soul of Change: What Works in Therapy.* Washington, D.C.: American Psychological Association, 1999.

Jones, Ernest. *The Life and Work of Sigmund Freud: Vol. 1.* New York: Basic Books, 1953.

Malinowski, Bronislaw. *Sex and Repression in Savage Society.* Chicago: The University of Chicago Press, 1927/1985.

Milton, Joyce. *The Road to Malpsychia: Humanistic Psychology and Our Discontents.* San Francisco: Encounter Books, 2002.

O'Reilly, Bernard. *Green Mountains.* Annandale, NSW, Australia: Envirobooks, n.d. (originally published in 1940).

Rogers, Carl R. *On Becoming a Person: A Therapist's View of Psychotherapy.* Boston: Houghton Mifflin Company, 1961.

Schulz, Duane, and Sydney Ellen Schulz. *Theories of Personality,* 6th ed. Pacific Grove, Calif.: Brooks/Cole Publishing Company, 1998.

Van Belle, H. A. "Carl Ransom Rogers." In *Baker Encyclopedia of Psychology and Counseling,* 2nd ed. Ed. David G. Benner and Peter C. Hill. Grand Rapids, Mich.: Baker Books, 1999. 1046–47.

Vitz, Paul C. *Faith of the Fatherless: The Psychology of Atheism.* Dallas: Spence Publishing Co., 1999.

Vitz, Paul C. *Sigmund Freud's Christian Unconscious.* Grand Rapids, Mich.: William B. Eerdmans Publishing Company, 1988.

Endnotes

1 God uses a similar location question in Genesis 4 when he approaches Cain after he has killed his brother Abel. Cain's response to the question "Where is Abel your brother?" reveals his failure to accept responsibility ("Am I my brother's keeper?") and leads to his subsequent punishment. Cain clearly violated God's command to love one's neighbor (cf. 1 John 3:11–12).

2 Bernard O'Reilly, *Green Mountains* (Annandale, NSW, Australia: Envirobooks, 1940), 16.

3 Ibid, 50.

4 Ibid., 15.

5 Paul C. Vitz, *Faith of the Fatherless: The Psychology of Atheism* (Dallas: Spence Publishing Co., 1999).

6 Ibid., 16. Vitz calls this new theory of atheism the "defective father" hypothesis.

7 Ernest Jones, *The Life and Work of Sigmund Freud: Vol. 1* (New York: Basic Books, 1953), 1.

8 Paul Vitz, *Sigmund Freud's Christian Unconscious* (Grand Rapids, Mich.: William B. Eerdmans Publishing Company, 1988), 39–42.

9 For further discussion on Freud's early life and his relationship with his parents, see Marie Balmary, *Psychoanalyzing Psychoanalysis: Freud and the Hidden Fault of the Father,* trans. Ned Lukacher (Baltimore: The Johns Hopkins University Press, 1979/1982).

10 Sigmund Freud, *An Autobiographical Study,* authorized trans. by James Strachey (New York: W. W. Norton & Company, 1952), 14.

11 Sigmund Freud, *The Interpretation of Dreams,* trans. James Strachey (New York: Avon Books, 1965), 230.

12 See, for example, David Bakan, *Sigmund Freud and the Jewish Mystical Tradition* (Boston: Beacon Press, 1958).

13 See Vitz, *Sigmund Freud's Christian Unconscious.*

14 Bronislaw Malinowski, *Sex and Repression in Savage Society* (Chicago: The University of Chicago Press, 1927/1985).

15 Duane Schulz and Sydney Ellen Schulz, *Theories of Personality,* 6th ed. (Pacific Grove, Calif: Brooks/Cole Publishing Company, 1998), 40–41.

16 H. A. Van Belle, "Carl Ransom Rogers," in *Baker Encyclopedia of Psychology and Counseling,* 2nd ed., ed. David G. Benner and Peter C. Hill (Grand Rapids, Mich.: Baker Books, 1999), 1046; James Fadiman and Robert Frager, *Personality and Personal Growth* 5th ed. (Upper Saddle River, N.J.: Prentice Hall, 2002), 394–95.

17 Jerry M. Burger, *Personality,* 4th ed. (Pacific Grove, Calif.: Brooks/Cole, 1997), 322.

18 Carl R. Rogers, *On Becoming a Person: A Therapist's View of Psychotherapy* (Boston: Houghton Mifflin Company, 1961), 6–10.

19 Ibid., 24.

20 It is perhaps important to note that the negative perception Rogers had of his family, particularly his mother, which helped shape his theory, was not shared by his siblings. See, e.g., Joyce Milton, *The Road to Malpsychia: Humanistic Psychology and Our Discontents* (San Francisco: Encounter Books, 2002), 128.

21 See, for example, Mark A. Hubble, Barry L. Duncan, and Scott D. Miller, *The Heart and Soul of Change: What Works in Therapy* (Washington, D.C.: American Psychological Association, 1999).

22 The Bible has a number of examples of people who responded to God from a healthy spiritual location—an obedient "Here am I, Lord" position. See, for example, Abraham (Gen. 12:1–4; 22:1–19), Moses (Exod. 3–4), Samuel (1 Sam.3), and Isaiah (Isa. 6:1–8).

4

CHARACTERISTICS OF BIBLICAL CHRISTIAN COUNSELING

Defining Biblical Christian Counseling
Counseling as a Dynamic Process of Communication
Counseling Design and Purpose
Counseling Dimensions of Relationship
The Issue of Self-Esteem

Defining Biblical Christian Counseling

B iblical Christian counseling is a dynamic process of communication between a representative of God and a person, family, or group in need designed to achieve healing in the relationship of that person, family, or group to God, to self, and to others. Since we are relational beings, the process addresses the universe of interdependent relationships that influence us, and it draws attention to our roles and needs and our godly calling of service to others. Such counseling has a purpose of assisting people to live more fully and to deal responsibly with issues, problems, and relationships in life. It seeks progress and development toward health and wholeness in the will of God.

Counseling as a Dynamic Process of Communication

Biblical Christian counseling is a *process*. It is a procedure or course of action involving particular methods of operation. The process is not arbitrary, but the steps or stages of change are carefully chosen with a direction and specific goals or a plan in mind. It is time limited not open-ended. The counseling encounter is usually of a short duration as determined by an agreement between both the counselor and the person or group in need. This characteristic distinguishes biblical counseling from being exclusively a formal ministry of evangelism or discipleship. Evangelism, discipleship, and counseling are complementary, but they have distinct characteristics and purposes.

Evangelism is a call on the life of every Christian, whenever and wherever the opportunity arises; it is usually not a structured and formal enterprise. We need to be open to opportunities to share the gospel, but we must not be deceptive with people seeking our help and use the guise of counselor to trick or manipulate people. We must follow the example of Christ, who allowed people first to identify their needs and then addressed their concerns. He was a living manifestation of God's question, "Where are you?" He came to find us and, in so doing, direct us to God.

Discipleship is a process of growth and development in the Christian life, whereby a more spiritually mature mentor guides and teaches a person who is younger in the faith. Discipleship is more open than counseling. It usually involves mutual sharing and accountability with less concern over confidentiality issues, more informal contacts, discussion and study over a wide range of topics, and an ongoing relationship of peer support, teaching, and encouragement. Counselors need to evaluate the spiritual condition of their counselees and, when appropriate, encourage Christians to be involved in discipling relationships; but the counseling relationship will normally focus on a specific issue or problem, under more formal conditions and with different rules of interaction.

What then is the value of counseling? Biblical Christian counseling attempts to raise an awareness of the particulars of a counselee's current condition that allows the person to move from guilt to the means of forgiveness, from separation to the possibilities of restoration of home and family, from hurt to ultimate justice, from feelings of worthlessness to immeasurable value in the Lord.

Biblical Christian counseling is a *dynamic* process. The counseling relationship implies an expectation of change on the part of the person, family, or group in need. The word *dynamic* is derived from the Greek word *dunamis*, which means strength or power.

The counseling process involves assessing and employing the energy, power, or motion to produce positive and therapeutic change. The motivating energy may be vigorous and forceful or gentle and nuanced as it guides and directs alterations, modifications, corrections, or even transformations in life. A dynamic process also implies a motivating power in which the underlying drive for change, including the reasons and the needs, is addressed and the goals are identified. Counseling must address the issue of motivation or the incentives, inspiration, and stimuli that are necessary to produce change in the lives of people in need.

This power can be directed toward constructive and godly purposes, or counselors can abuse it and cause pain that has destructive consequences. The creative power that nurtures and produces healing is manifest most clearly and perfectly in the work of the Holy Spirit in our lives.

Counseling involves a dynamic process of *communication*. Biblical Christian counseling is connected to the concept of koinonia. The Greek word *koinonia* means fellowship. It is a gathering of individuals who share a common bond and a close relationship. It is a partnership of like-minded people who have a common purpose and seek agreement and communion together.

Counseling involves an agreement to meet together between the counselor and a client. In the New Testament the word *koinonia* is used in connection with seeking fellowship with the Spirit of God, his word, his life, and his sufferings (Phil. 2:1; 1:5; 3:10; 1 Cor. 10:16)—the point of unity for all Christians (1 John 1:3,6); and with other people, including our Christian brethren (Acts 2:42; 2 Cor. 8:4; Rom. 15:26). If there is no agreement, then there can be no fellowship, even as darkness and light are separated (2 Cor. 6:14). For Christians, koinonia means setting our mind in agreement with the mind of Christ.

An underlying component of koinonia is the concept of communication. Communion together or fellowship implies communication, a meeting of the minds, or mutual understanding. Koinonia communication involves a willingness to listen and to seek understanding and a desire to convey truthful and accurate information in a loving and supportive manner.

Communication also implies that both the counselor and the counselee participate in the process. It is not a one-way street, in which one person dictates to another; rather, it is a dialogue that requires skillful and accurate listening and measured and thoughtful therapeutic conversation.

Counseling Design and Purpose

Counseling has a *design*. Christian counseling has an overall purpose or a goal. It is not an arbitrary process; instead, it involves assumptions, plans, beliefs, values, and coordination and agreement between the counselor and people in need. The design has a beginning, a middle, and an end. As we have seen in the previous chapter (chapter 3), the planning must identify the location of persons, their intentions, and the means available for achieving their objectives.

The goal is to *achieve healing* or cure. The word *therapy* comes from the Greek word *therapeuo*, which means "care, heal, or restore." This word should not be understood in the secular naturalistic sense that we find in modern medicine and psychology where such "healing" is void of any spiritual force or connotation.[1] The biblical concept of healing can be traced through the historical church and into biblical times. The ancient practice of *cura animarum* or cure of souls is a comprehensive concept that covers the care and healing of the body, mind, and spirit. Greek philosophers often considered themselves physicians or healers of the soul, arguing that correct thinking and beliefs cure diseased souls in the same way that medicine cures a diseased body. Health includes not just the physical or material dimensions but also the mental, emotional, and spiritual well-being of the soul.[2] Such work is an essential part of Christian ministry. In fact, the word *minister* is derived from the Latin word *ministerium*, which is a translation of the Greek word *therapon* (the noun form of the verb *therapeuo*) meaning "servant, or one who helps, serves or cares for the needs of another, and heals."[3] Pastoral ministry includes the functions of healing, sustaining, guiding, and reconciling.[4]

Biblical expressions of healing cover multiple dimensions. There are healing of the land and nations (2 Chron. 7:14; Rev. 22:2); healing words (Prov. 1:18; 12:18); emotional healing (Ps. 147:3); healing from apostasy or lack of faith (Hos. 14:4); spiritual healing (Luke 8:2; Isa. 53:5; Jer. 17:14; Ps. 30:2); and physical healing (Ps. 103:3; Matt. 10:1; John 4:47). The healing may be physical, spiritual, mental, emotional, relational, or any combination of these. The overall focus and direction in biblically based counseling is toward health and wholeness. Yet counselors must constantly monitor their work and avoid iatrogenic problems.

Iatrogenic effects occur when a helper, rather than improving a situation, actually has exacerbated a problem and made it worse. The medical field has been dealing with this issue for decades. "The operation was a success, but the patient died" encapsulates this concern. One of the major dangers facing patients in hospitals is the problem of contracting opportunistic diseases from nurses and doctors who fail to wash their hands after they have been in contact with each patient. Health-care workers may cause harm when they are trying to heal the patient.

Counselors must constantly monitor themselves to make sure they are not allowing any unresolved personal issues to encroach on the counseling process and are engaging in wise and proven practices. Study, training, supervised practice, monitoring, consultation, and accountability play a role in quality evaluation, management, and improvement in counseling.

Counseling Dimensions of Relationship

God and Ultimate Healing. Ultimate healing is found in relationship to God. Biblical Christian counseling needs an absolute authority or a constant reference point upon which to determine truth and direction. For centuries navigators in the Northern Hemisphere have used the

North Star (Polaris) in the night skies as a reference to plot their course. Amid all the other stars that appear to rotate in the heavens, the North Star has remained the one constant that can be relied on to stay fixed in the same position with barely a perceptible movement for hundreds of years. God is the "North Star" for the Christian counselor, our reliable guide or reference point at all times. His Word provides us with the means of determining our position in relationship to him, and he reveals himself through his spirit and his general revelation in his creation.

Christian counselors are active representatives of God. They must communicate his healing message in the therapeutic encounter and look for his guiding hand in every counseling situation.

Healing of the Self. Christian counseling involves healing of the *self.* The original meaning of the word *psychology* was the study of, or a word about, the *psuche* or soul. The term *psychotherapy* literally means "soul therapy or soul healing." Well before the arrival of Freud and secular psychology, studies in biblical psychology were being published, particularly in Germany, where we find, for example, the book *Umriss der biblischen Seelenlehre (An Outline of Biblical Soul-Teaching)* by J. T. Beck appearing in 1843 and *System der biblischen Psychologie (A System of Biblical Psychology)* by Franz Delitzsch in 1855.[5]

These books examine the biblical concepts of the self, the ego, and the soul. Delitzsch devoted an entire chapter to a biblical understanding of the ego, which he distinguished from the spirit, soul, and body.[6] (His book was published one year before Sigmund Freud was born.) He considered biblical psychology to be one of the oldest sciences of the church.[7] Beck divided his work into an analysis of the soul life of humanity as soul (Hebrew: *nephesh*), the distinctiveness of the soul from the spirit (Hebrew: *ruach*), and how the soul is discerned in the heart (Hebrew: *leb*).

Scott Fletcher has noted that the concept of psuche has different shades of meaning in the New Testament. The word is translated as "life" in some passages and as "soul" in others, but Fletcher argues for four distinct senses in which the term is used, reflecting a logical development of thought: the soul (1) as embodied human life; (2) as the seat of feeling and desire; (3) as the self; and (4) as the spiritual part of man.

Four main terms describing the various aspects of a person's total life are found in the Bible: the *soul*, which is the subject of life or the bearer of the individual life, also called the ego or self; the *spirit*, which is the principle of life generally, higher than the soul, and connecting a person to God; the *heart*, which is the organ of life and the seat of all thinking, feeling, and willing; and the *flesh*, which is living matter and the medium of life's manifestation, not merely the body or its material substance. Fletcher expanded on these biblical psychological terms in *The Psychology of the New Testament*, published in 1912.[8]

Christian counseling addresses the process of healing in the individual and the importance of healthy self-evaluation and accurate biblical self-understanding. Accurate self-understanding accepts our worth and value as created by God, though fallen and in a state of sin. Since God loves us, we must do no less than love ourselves or we dishonor our Creator; however, this awareness must not be confused with the secular versions of self-esteem, which promote self-improvement without acknowledging our Genesis identity in God.

Our Relationship with Others. Counseling also addresses the need for healing in our *relationships with other people*, including spouses, children, siblings, relatives, church members, business associates, and, in fact, all our social contacts and acquaintances. The expression of godly self-love is our desire to love and serve others. The Bible has much to say about how we are to relate to other people and the appropriate valuing of self.

The Issue of Self-Esteem

The difference between the love of self in the Bible and the emphasis on self-esteem and self-acceptance in popular psychological literature today is significant. Biblical love is not selfish or egocentric. It does not encourage the philosophy of self-indulgence, the primacy of the individual, and the enhancement of self-esteem. The biblical love of self is based on an awareness of God's love for his creation and an acceptance that we were created in his image. If God loves us, then we in turn must honor that love, first by taking care of ourselves by repenting and finding forgiveness of sin in Christ and receiving the gift of the Holy Spirit (Acts 2:38–39). The highest expression of a godly self-love is found in accepting the love of God and being obedient to his will. An immediate expression of this type of self-love will be a desire to love and serve others. The sacrificial love of God in Jesus Christ gives us the preeminent example and the model to follow.

The self-esteem proposed in most self-help books presents a distorted picture that is not biblical, and, in fact, recent research is beginning to question the entire self-esteem industry. More than two thousand books have been published that deal with ways to help people raise their self-esteem. People are coached to repeat mantras and post notes around the house on self-acceptance. Therapists tell sociopathic clients to repeat the words "I adore myself" every day. When these approaches are examined and investigated, a troubling picture emerges.

Low self-esteem is not a cause of low academic performance in young people; although it has been connected with self-destructive behaviors and negative experiences such as depression, teen pregnancy, suicide attempts, and victimization from bullies. The assumption that higher esteem will ameliorate some of these problems is false. While low self-esteem may result in some problems for the individual, people with high self-esteem are far more likely to cause harm to others. High self-esteem people are more likely to embrace racist attitudes and engage in social activities that put other people at risk, such as reckless or drunk driving. They are more likely to administer pain and injury than timid people.[9]

High self-esteem people are significantly more likely to act aggressively toward other people than low self-esteem people. In fact prisoners may have a higher average self-esteem than the general population. An examination of self-esteem tests done by antisocial men reveals that there is no evidence for the old psychodynamic concept that these men secretly feel bad about themselves. They are driven by racism and violence, not by poor feelings about themselves. Low self-esteem is not a risk factor for racist attitudes, delinquency, and drug use or alcohol abuse. To teach antisocial men and sociopaths to have pride in themselves is dangerous since few of them know how to be humble and to value other people.[10]

Recent studies on self-esteem reveal that persons with high self-esteem pose a greater threat to other people than individuals with low self-esteem. High self-esteem people are more likely to have an unrealistic opinion of themselves that may lead them to act aggressively and cause harm to other people when they feel threatened. The problem is that the self-esteem industry is a multimillion-dollar enterprise that has become entrenched in our culture. There is little interest in replacing conferences and workshops on self-esteem with ones on self-discipline, self-control, and replacement of or death to self with identity and life in Christ (Rom. 6:1-11; Gal. 2:20).

The biblical approach to self does not focus on self-esteem and accepting oneself as a wonderful person; instead it challenges us to have an honest and accurate self-assessment (e.g., Phil. 2:3-8). We need to find our location. We need to evaluate our body, mind, and spirit in terms of our Genesis identity and the position of God. This self-appraisal is not about how good one feels but how faithful we are in pleasing God and ministering to significant others in all settings. Only from this perspective are we able to attain wholeness, true peace, and godly esteem.

The secular understanding of high self-esteem is closely related to the biblical meaning of pride and what the King James Version quaintly refers to as "a haughty spirit" (Prov. 16:18). Such people are filled with overconfidence, arrogance, pride, conceit, and an unrealistic self-importance, and their behavior may cause harm to others and ultimately to themselves. A cursory survey of Scripture will reveal that the Bible corroborates some of the recent research on self-esteem. It clearly informs us of both the dangers of pride and the value of humility. Pride prevents the wicked from turning to God or even thinking about him (Ps. 10:4). Rather than increasing a person's sense of worth and value, pride actually leads to shame; in contrast, wisdom seeks humility (Prov. 11:2). Pride is connected with foolish talk and behavior.

Prideful and covetous people persecute the poor and boast of selfish things (Ps. 10:2-3). Pride causes conflict and disharmony in relationships, and it prevents people from listening to sound and wise counsel (Prov. 13:10). Pride leads to foolish talk, while wise and sensible talk can save lives (Prov. 14:3). Selfish pride leads to dishonor and shame, but a humble spirit brings honor and respect (Prov. 29:23). Whereas secular counseling offers no clear, healthy alternative to the problems of low self-esteem and high self-esteem, the Bible gives us the therapeutic answer in the provision of Christ and godly esteem.

Christian counselors need to redefine the word *self-esteem* and infuse it with a biblical meaning or come up with a new term. Changing the meaning of a word is not an unusual occurrence. Witness the recent changes in meaning of words like *bad* and *gay*. The New Testament took the relatively sterile Greek word *agape* that carried a connotation of "fondness" and transformed its meaning into a powerful term for the regenerative, supernatural, personified expression of God's love. At a minimum, Christian counselors need to be clear about what they mean when they use such terms, and they need to be sure that their definitions are based on sound biblical truth and accurate research.

Summary

1. Biblical Christian counseling is a dynamic process of communication between a representative of God and a person, family, or group in need designed to achieve healing in the relationship of that person, family, or group to God, to self, and to others.
2. The counseling process is distinguishable from, though complementary to, evangelism and discipleship.
3. The design and purpose of counseling are directed toward comprehensive relational healing. Such healing is rooted in a biblical worldview that recognizes the spiritual dimension and is clearly distinguishable from contemporary secular definitions and expressions of therapy and healing. The cure of souls has been a basic component of the ministry of the historical church.

4. Both Scriptures and research reveal the dangers of misguided counseling on self-esteem and the relationship of high self-esteem to pride. Christian counselors need to have an accurate biblical understanding of the issue.

Where Do We Go from Here?

Without an understanding of the love of God and the importance of placing him first in our lives, we have no eternal hope. If we accept his love for us, then we are compelled to express it in love and service to others, in all places and at all times. The two tables that form the Greatest Commandment guide counselors to locate people and express biblical love.

Questions and Exercises for Reflection

1. What is your personal definition of Christian counseling? Give your definition and compare it with the one presented in this chapter.
2. Describe the relationship between Christian counseling and the concept of sanctification. Can Christian counseling function as part of the sanctification process? If so, how?
3. How does the biblical view of healing differ from secular definitions of therapy?
4. Find a definition of psychology in a college textbook and compare it to the meaning of the word found in biblical psychology and historical theology and philosophy. How might the different definitions affect a person's approach to counseling?
5. How has your understanding of self-esteem changed after reading this chapter?

References

Beck, J. T. *Outlines of Biblical Psychology.* Trans. from the 3rd enlarged and corrected German ed., 1877. Edinburgh: T. and T. Clark, 1877.

Clebsch, William A., and Charles R. Jaekle. *Pastoral Care in Historical Perspective: An Essay with Exhibits.* Englewood Cliffs, N.J.: Prentice-Hall, 1964.

"Clinician's Digest: Is Self-Esteem Snake Oil?" *Psychotherapy Networker* (November/December 2003): 22.

"Clinician's Digest: Low Self-Esteem and Aggression." *Psychotherapy Networker* (March/April 2002): 16.

Delitzsch, Franz. *A System of Biblical Psychology*, 2nd ed. Trans. the Reverend Robert Ernest Wallis. Grand Rapids, Mich.: Baker Book House, 1899, 1966.

Fletcher, M. Scott. *The Psychology of the New Testament*, 2nd ed. London: Hodder and Stoughton, 1912.

McNeil, John T. *A History of the Cure of Souls*. New York: Harper Torchbooks, 1951.

Nussbaum, Martha C. *The Therapy of Desire: Theory and Practice in Hellenistic Ethics*. Princeton, N.J.: Princeton University Press, 1994.

Oden, Thomas C. *Classical Pastoral Care. Vol. 3. Pastoral Counsel*. Grand Rapids, Mich.: Baker Books, 1987.

Slater, Lauren. "The Lowdown on Self-Esteem." *Fort Worth Star-Telegram* (25 February 2002): 3E.

Wuest, Kenneth S. *Wuest's Word Studies from the Greek New Testament*. Grand Rapids, Mich.: Eerdmans, 1984.

Zodhiates, Spiros. *The Complete Word Study Dictionary: New Testament*. Chattanooga, Tenn.: AMG Publishers, 1993.

Endnotes

1 In the nineteenth century regular, orthodox, or "allopathic" medical physicians engaged in sectarian wars with alternative medical philosophies, particularly homeopathy to gain control of the medical profession. The subsequent success in the West of a medical model based on naturalistic science has resulted in the medical community gaining a measure of social regulation and political control over social behavior and moral choice. Medical and psychiatric forces have applied their therapeutic models to the management of such areas as delinquency, drug abuse, and sexual deviation. In the process, the concept of therapy has changed in meaning in most secular literature to reflect a humanistic and secular scientific worldview. See Paul Starr, *The Social Transformation of American Medicine: The Rise of a Sovereign Profession and the Making of a Vast Industry* (New York: Basic Books, 1982), 93–102, 336–37.

2 John T. McNeill, *A History of the Cure of Souls* (New York: Harper Torchbooks, 1951), vii, 17–41; Martha C. Nussbaum, *The Therapy of Desire: Theory and Practice in Hellenistic Ethics* (Princeton, N.J.: Princeton University Press, 1994). Nussbaum (p. 49) notes: "In fact, an analogy between *logos* and medical treatment is extremely old and deep in ancient Greek talk about the personality and its difficulties. From Homer on we encounter, frequently and prominently, the idea that *logos* is to illnesses of the soul as medical treatment is to illnesses of the body. We also find the claim that *logos* is a powerful and perhaps even a sufficient remedy for these illnesses; frequently it is portrayed as the only available remedy. The diseases in question are frequently diseases of inappropriate or misinformed emotion." By *logos,* Nussbaum means speech and argument or persuasion, exhortation, criticism, and calming.

3 Thomas C. Oden, *Classical Pastoral Care. Vol. 3: Pastoral Counsel* (Grand Rapids, Mich.: Baker Books, 1987), 7; Kenneth S Wuest, *Wuest's Word Studies from the Greek New Testament. Vol 2: Philippians, Hebrews, the Pastoral Epistles, First Peter, In These Days* (Grand Rapids, Mich.: William B. Eerdmans, 1973), 71; Spiros Zodhiates, *The Complete Word Study Dictionary: New Testament* (Chattanooga, Tenn.: AMG Publishers, 1993), 2323–24.

4 William A. Clebsch and Charles R. Jaekle, *Pastoral Care in Historical Perspective: An Essay with Exhibits* (Englewood Cliffs, N. J.: Prentice-Hall, 1964), 32–66.

5 J. T. Beck, *Outlines of Biblical Psychology*, trans. from the 3rd enlarged and corrected German ed. (Edinburgh: T. and T. Clark, 1877); Franz Delitzsch, *A System of Biblical Psychology*, 2nd ed., trans. The Reverend Robert Ernest Wallis (Grand Rapids, Mich.: Baker Book House, 1899, 1966).

6 *Ego* is the Greek word for the first person singular pronoun "I."

7 As evidence that biblical psychology was one of the oldest sciences of the church, Delitzsch (pp. 7–11) identified Christian literature on the subject from the second and third centuries (e.g., Melito of Sardis, Tertullian), works in the fourth century (e.g., Gregory of Nyssa, Augustine), fifth through seventh century works (e.g., Nemesius, Cassiodorus, Johannes Philoponus, Aeneas of Gaza, Gregory the Great), the Middle Ages (e.g., Alexander of Hales, Peter de Alliaco, Erigena, William of Champeaux, Hugo of St Victor, Albertus Magus, Thomas Aquinas), and the Reformation (e.g., Melancthon). Following the Reformation, psychology was studied formally and debated in German universities, and Delitzch noted numerous authors and works from that time to the middle of the nineteenth century, including: Caspar Bartholinus, *Manuductio ad veram Psychologiam e sacris literis* (1629), which contains a sketch of biblical psychology; Vives, *De anima et vita* (1538); Melancthon, *Commentarius de anima* (1540) republished as *Liber de anima* in 1552; John Conrad Dannhauer, *Collegium psychologicum* (1627), which contains seven examples of academic disputations on psychology that occurred in German universities; Jacob Bohme, *Psychologia vera*, or *Forty Questions about the Soul,* and *Psychologiae supplementum: Das umgewandte Auge;* Magnus Friedrich Roos, *Fundamenta Psychologiae ex sacra Scriptura collecta* (1769), translated into German in 1857 by Cremer of Unna as *Gundzuge der Seelenlehre aus heiliger Schrift,* a careful research in anthropologic exegesis; J. G. F. Haussmann, *Die Biblische Lehre vom Menschen* (1848), a biblical anthropology; Gust. Fried. Oehler, *Veteris testamenti sentential de rebus post mortem futuris* (1846); Heinr. Aug. Hahn, *Veteris testimanti sententia de natura hominis* (1846); Bottcher, *De inferis rebusque post mortem futuris* (1846), a collection of biblical psychology materials; and additional literature that Delitzch mentioned but did not recommend due to "low rationalistic views," such as Friedr. Aug. Carus, *Psychology of the Hebrews* (1809) and Ge. Fr. Seiler, *Animadversiones ad Psychologiam Sacram* (1778–1787).

8 M. Scott Fletcher, *The Psychology of the New Testament*, 2nd ed. (London: Hodder and Stoughton, 1912), 27, 21.

9 Lauren Slater, "The Lowdown on Self-Esteem," *Fort Worth Star-Telegram* (25 February 2002), 3E; "Clinician's Digest: Low Self-Esteem and Aggression," *Psychotherapy Networker* (March/April 2002), 16; "Clinician's Digest: Is Self-Esteem Snake Oil?" *Psychotherapy Networker* (November/December 2003), 22.

10 Slater, "Clinician's Digest."

5

THE GUIDING COMMANDMENT IN BIBLICAL CHRISTIAN COUNSELING

Jesus and the Greatest Commandment
Crisis Counseling and the Greatest Commandment
Crisis Counseling in the Wedgwood Ministry

J esus identified the greatest commandment as the call to love God with all our heart, soul, mind, and strength, and to love our neighbors or other people as much as we love ourselves (Matt. 22:34–40; Mark 12:28–34; Luke 10:25–28). He summarized the message of the Ten Commandments into two distinct dimensions, our relationship to God (commonly referred to as the First Table) and our relationship to others (the Second Table).

The primary focus for Christian counseling is to help people examine the spiritual dimension and their relationship to God (our North Star). The spiritual dimension must also be expressed in our association with other people; however, this desire to converse with and assist others is not limited only to those people with whom we have some affinity. We are not simply to help people who share our racial or ethnic identity, socioeconomic level, or religious affiliation. Jesus made this abundantly clear when a theologian asked Jesus to define the word *neighbor* for him. Jesus told him the story of the good Samaritan. The story illustrated the point that we must not limit our definition of neighbor to people who share our views or are like us. We must help all people in need, both Christians and non-Christians. We will examine the context of this story a little further in this chapter since it provides some important lessons about finding the location of people in counseling.

Where are you? Where are you in relationship to God, and where are you in relationship to others? These two questions echo throughout the Scriptures. They are fundamental questions in Christian counseling. We see them clearly delineated in the Ten Commandments. The Decalogue begins with the commandments that address our relationship to God. God must be first in our lives. From this foundation comes the second table of the commandments, our relationship with family and neighbor. These commandments form a basis from which we engage in pastoral care and counseling.

Augustine (AD 354–430) recognized the importance of these relationships. He claimed that before a Christian is capable of ministering to another person, he must first recognize God as the supreme authority in his life. His primary purpose in life is to love and serve God. The second thing a Christian must do is to accept himself since it is "impossible for one who loves God not to love himself." Concern for our neighbors and others is derived from this foundation since there is "no surer step towards the love of God than the love of man to man."[1] All compassion and care given to or received from an individual should be directed toward the ultimate end of loving God. Such love may involve "suffering for the sake of others," choosing voluntarily to remain and support a neighbor, even though opportunities to leave and avoid such hardship are available.[2] Christians must seek to protect both the body and the soul of their neighbor. They are to help develop healthy minds for the treatment of physical needs, and they are to encourage a fear of and a love for God in the care for the soul.[3] The relational dimensions forming the Greatest Commandment help to locate people in need and prevent a superficial assessment of people's problems.

Jesus gives us the model to follow in dealing with the core nature of people and helping them to assess themselves and to find godly esteem, true peace, and eternal life. We see examples of his approach in his encounters with two men who both asked the same question but received different replies.

74

Jesus and the Greatest Commandment

Jesus discussed the Ten Commandments with two men, both times in response to the same question, "What must I do to inherit eternal life?" But he dealt with the commandments differently in each situation. In one case a rich young ruler approached him. "A ruler questioned Him, saying, 'Good Teacher, what shall I do to inherit eternal life?' And Jesus said to him, 'Why do you call Me good? No one is good except God alone. You know the commandments, "DO NOT COMMIT ADULTERY, DO NOT MURDER, DO NOT STEAL, DO NOT BEAR FALSE WITNESS, HONOR YOUR FATHER AND MOTHER." ' And he said, 'All these things I have kept from *my* youth' " (Luke 18:18–21).

Jesus began his response by first questioning the young man's use of the word *good*. He implied that, in its full meaning of perfection, only God is good. In reality, the word is an apt description of Christ, but the context suggests that the man was not fully aware of this fact. Also Jesus was drawing attention to a priority principle that he would return to later in his discussion.

The ruler had asked a reasonable question, and he was apparently honest and sincere with his inquiry. The response Jesus gave to the young man, however, is unusual. He did not summarize the commandments as he had done so on other occasions (e.g., Mark 12:29–33), nor did he begin with the First Table of the Commandments that addresses our relationship to God. Instead, Jesus listed the commandments from the Second Table. Do not commit adultery. Do not murder, steal, or bear false witness. Honor your parents. Why did Jesus begin with these commandments when he had always stressed the importance of the first commandments?

A lesser counselor would have pressed the man directly in an attempt to expose the true nature of his relationship to God and to others. An attack on his core problem could have easily turned the young ruler away or led to an argumentative debate. Instead, Jesus joined with the youth at the point of agreement. He found the location of the person in terms of the man's sincere, although perhaps naïve, self-assessment. Here was an honorable man who had tried since his childhood to live a godly life in his relationship to other people. As a ruler, his statement on his lifestyle was significant. In his position he controlled people's lives, and he had the power to produce good or evil in his social relationships. His ardent demeanor drew an obvious affection from Jesus (Mark 10:21).

By beginning with the Second Table of the Ten Commandments, Jesus had found a common ground. He was on the young man's side. He was a supporter and encourager who could now direct the man's attention to the crucial priority principle that would revolutionize his life and fully answer his question. "When Jesus heard *this,* He said to him, 'One thing you still lack; sell all that you possess and distribute it to the poor, and you shall have treasure in heaven; and come, follow Me.' But when he had heard these things, he became very sad, for he was extremely rich. And Jesus looked at him and said, 'How hard it is for those who are wealthy to enter the kingdom of God!'" (Luke 18:22–24).

At this point Jesus addressed the First Table, the young man's relationship to God. God must be first in his life, or he cannot inherit eternal life. Jesus knew the man's problem. In a choice between his personal wealth and God, he could not relinquish his riches on earth for the treasures of heaven. His problem was idolatry. God was not first in his life; and Jesus had revealed to him, in the most loving and supportive way possible, the true nature of his spiritual condition and need. The final decision was up to the young man.

In the second case, a scribe or lawyer asked Jesus the same question. The man was testing Jesus, but there is no indication that his tone or intentions were malicious. His inquiry was apparently an honest one. The man was a specialist in Mosaic Law, so Jesus connected with him by adopting a deferential attitude and asking for his expert opinion on the Law and how it addressed the question.

> And a lawyer stood up and put Him to the test, saying, "Teacher, what shall I do to inherit eternal life?" And He said to him, "What is written in the Law? How does it read to you?" And he answered, "You shall love the Lord your God with all your heart, and with all your soul, and with all your strength, and with all your mind;

and your neighbor as yourself." And He said to him, "You have answered correctly; do this and you will live" (Luke 10:25–28).

Once again in this brief conversation Jesus has joined with a person by matching his language and by starting with the particular problem or issue defined by the individual. The simple way in which Jesus engaged the scribe and led him to godly truths belies the complex and difficult nature of this skill. One of the hardest things to teach a trainee in counseling is the ability to listen carefully to a person on multiple levels. This skill requires listening to and understanding the actual words used; the thoughts, beliefs, meaning, and content behind the sentences; the tone of voice, the attitude, demeanor, and nonverbal behaviors of the speaker; and the broader context of gender, social status, education, and culture.

Jesus allowed the scribe to set the direction of the conversation, but his affirmation of the scribe's summary of the commandments appeared to contain a challenge. If you will only do this in reality, not just talk about it—that is, love God and your neighbor totally and completely—then you will inherit eternal life. In response, the scribe adopted a defensive posture and challenged Jesus to give his definition of the word neighbor.

Jesus had located the man's position in his relationship to God and to others. This man had no problem with the First Table of the Ten Commandments. He was a pious Jew and an expert on the Torah who, along with any priest or Levite, would defend to the death the primacy and worship of God alone (Deut. 5:6–11). Idolatry was not his problem. His failure lay with the Second Table, and Jesus would reveal the man's bigotry or ungodly attitude and answer his challenge by telling him the story of the good Samaritan.

> Jesus replied and said, "A man was going down from Jerusalem to Jericho, and fell among robbers, and they stripped him and beat him, and went away leaving him half dead. And by chance a priest was going down on

that road, and when he saw him, he passed by on the other side. Likewise a Levite also, when he came to the place and saw him, passed by on the other side. But a Samaritan, who was on a journey, came upon him; and when he saw him, he felt compassion, and came to him and bandaged up his wounds, pouring oil and wine on them; and he put him on his own beast, and brought him to an inn and took care of him. On the next day he took out two denarii and gave them to the innkeeper and said, 'Take care of him; and whatever more you spend, when I return I will repay you.' Which of these three do you think proved to be a neighbor to the man who fell into the robbers' hands?" And he said, "The one who showed mercy toward him." Then Jesus said to him, "Go and do the same" (Luke 10:30–37 NASB).

The Jews had a narrow definition of neighbor that excluded both the Gentiles and the half-breed Samaritans. Jesus used the medium of a story to communicate to the scribe a truth that was distasteful to him. The central figure and unlikely hero in his story was a Samaritan who offered genuine compassion, comfort, and aid to a robbery victim. The scribe's heroes, the priest and the Levite, avoided the suffering man.

Jesus made the scribe identify the true neighbor. His question brought into focus the underlying problem facing the scribe, and it is apparent in the answer he gave. Even after listening to such a compelling story, the scribe cannot bring himself to utter the word *Samaritan*. The word is so distasteful that he identified the man only as "the one who showed mercy toward him." Jesus had exposed the inadequacy of the scribe's understanding of the Second Table and his relationship to other people. His final challenge to the man was to embrace God's definition of neighbor and show love, compassionate concern, and self-sacrificial action toward all people, regardless of their ethnicity or social status.

Christian counseling must explore the spiritual condition of individuals in their relationship to God and to other people. The nature of this exploration should be determined by the situation and position of the people in need—in other words, by their location. In the two cases described, Jesus could deal immediately and openly with these relationships because they represented the subject on the hearts and minds of both of his inquirers. If they had brought him other problems, he would have begun his healing ministry with their understanding of the nature of the particular troubles they identified.

In some cases counseling begins with and focuses on personal and social relationships with other people, while at other times the relationship with God is examined first. Both dimensions should be covered, but the examples Jesus gave suggest that the person in need assumes much of the responsibility for the initiative, pace, and direction in these areas. In all circumstances the Greatest Commandment should be the guiding principle in competent Christian counseling. This truth was driven home to me when my associates and I were called upon to offer comfort and counsel to victims of violence in a church sanctuary.

Crisis Counseling and the Greatest Commandment

On the evening of Wednesday, September 15, 1999, a man entered the front doors of Wedgwood Baptist Church in Fort Worth, Texas. Underneath his coat he carried a 9 mm Ruger semiautomatic, a .380 caliber AMT handgun, nearly two hundred rounds of ammunition, and a pipe bomb. In the sanctuary at the time were four hundred mostly young people who had gathered for a praise concert.

Earlier in the day the pastor of the church, Dr. Al Meredith, had returned from preaching his mother's funeral in Michigan. He was tired and attempting to rest and recuperate when he received a phone call asking him what was going on at his church. Meredith arrived at the church to find a scene of carnage and tragedy. Larry Ashbrook had walked down the church hallway shooting people. He had entered the sanctuary and proceeded to spray bullets up and down the church aisles, and he had exploded the pipe bomb. His final act was to sit down in a back pew, put a gun to his head and take his own life. Around him lay seven people who were dead or dying and several others who were wounded.

Wedgwood Baptist Church is located in a quiet neighborhood about two miles from the campus of Southwestern Baptist Theological Seminary. A number of faculty and students attend the church, and most of the people who were killed had some connection to the seminary. When I arrived at the church a short time after the shootings, along with many of my colleagues from the seminary, we found people in a state of crisis. I will never forget walking down the hallway of the building opposite the church, where a command center had been set up, and looking across the street toward the sanctuary. The church had been sealed off by the police, spotlights lit up the building, barricades held back onlookers, overhead were media helicopters, and behind me were families searching for and being reunited with their loved ones. As the evening wore on, fewer families remained to be reunited, and those who remained were beginning to grasp the awful truth that their loved ones were still in the church sanctuary. They would not be coming home.

How do you minister to people in such crises? In the days that followed, there was plenty of advice and suggestions, both solicited and unsolicited, about how to help the church. "Organize crisis intervention teams." "Just give them the Word of God." "Let them know that they will be OK." "It's God's will." "We're experts in these matters; we can help." "Tell them not to make any important decisions or lifestyle changes right away." "Challenge their doubts with statements of faith." During this period I turned to the Bible to examine the responses of people to another crisis event—the crucifixion. The greatest tragic triumph in human history was not accompanied by any unified or consistent reactions. In fact, the diversity of behavior surrounding the events of the cross is surprising. People reacted to the traumatic event in a variety of ways.

- *Confusion* (Matt. 26:56). The disciples fled from the scene in bewilderment and fear, deserting Jesus.
- *Denial, Fear, and Guilt* (Matt. 26:69–75). Peter wanted to help Jesus, but when he was challenged about his identity, he denied even knowing Christ. The rooster's crow after the third denial brought

conviction and guilt upon Peter. Not only had he failed to help; he had also disowned his Master.

- *Suicide* (Matt. 27:1–5). Some people can become overwhelmed by the circumstances and become self-destructive. Judas hung himself when his sin and the awareness that he had betrayed innocent blood plagued him to the point of hopeless despair.
- *Anguish and Mourning* (Luke 23:27,48). Groups of people gathered at the cross, weeping and inconsolable in their pain and despair. They struggled and failed to make sense of the situation.
- *Mockery and Condemnation* (Matt. 27:27–30; Luke 23:35–37). Some observers and soldiers around the cross taunted Jesus, mocked him, and derided his faith.
- *Anger and Confrontation* (Matt. 27:39–43; Luke 23:39). One of the thieves, along with some priests, teachers of the law, and elders, hurled insults at Jesus and tried to humiliate him and dismiss his message.
- *Repentance* (Luke 23:40–43). Another thief on the cross admitted his own sin and recognized Jesus' innocence. Jesus accepted his repentance and told him that he would join him in paradise.
- *Onlookers, the Curious, and Distant Observers* (Matt. 27:55; Luke 23:49). Some people are just interested bystanders, and they choose to observe events from a distance. Some of the people who knew Jesus, including the women who had followed him from Galilee, kept a discreet distance from the cross, probably for their own safety and protection.
- *Intense Discussion of Events* (Luke 24:13–35). Some people want to engage in deep conversation and analyze the events. As they walked toward the village of Emmaus, two people reviewed the details surrounding the crucifixion, trying to make sense of what they had observed.
- *Hiding and Uncertainty* (John 20:19). Friends gathered in a room and hid, unsure of what to do next.
- *Practical Responses* (Matt. 27:57–60; John 19:38–42). Joseph of Arimathea and Nicodemus took care of the funeral arrangements,

the preparation and burial of the body. Such people have a practical mind-set, and they try to bring order to a situation and meet immediate needs.

- *Additional and Secondary Traumas* (John 20:11–14). Some people experience additional crises. Mary discovered that the body was missing. She showed classic signs of multiple trauma when she was unable to recognize a familiar voice. Her behavior was like someone in a daze or a trance, unable to process even basic information. Nothing seemed to make sense to her.

- *Demands for Information and Proof and a Struggle with Faith* (John 20:21–29). Some people refuse to believe what has happened until they have convincing evidence. Thomas did not believe the other disciples had seen the risen Lord. He would believe only if he could see Jesus and actually place his fingers and hand in the wounds. He was demanding incontrovertible proof, or he would not believe.

- *Lack of Concern* (John 19:23–24). Some people in tragic situations show no concern about what is happening. Such traumas are simply part of their everyday work. The soldiers at the crucifixion were just doing their jobs; they did not know Jesus, and they did not really care about him beyond deciding on an equitable distribution of his garments.

- *Morbid Satisfaction and Irrational Thinking* (John 19:7–16). Some people actually find pleasure in the suffering of others. The cry of the crowd for crucifixion, despite Pilate's finding that the charges against Jesus were baseless, showed a chilling predisposition toward irrational thinking and mob behavior.

- *Escape and Attempts to Return to the Familiar* (Mark 14:50–52; John 21:3). Some people want to run away and hide. They want to avoid talking or even thinking about the traumatic event, perhaps in an attempt to gain or regain control over their world. The disciples scattered at the time of the crucifixion, and later some disciples tried to return to their old, familiar lifestyle. They went fishing.

People react to crisis situations in a variety of ways. Some people experience no apparent difficulties at first, but later they struggle with the memories. A second group has initial difficulties but achieves an early resolution and moves on with their lives. A third group experiences ongoing struggle; they are chronically stuck, and their lives revolve around memories of the trauma and its aftermath. A final group consists of those people who are able to take the crisis in stride or refocus their energies in ways that diminish the negative impact of the crisis. These people usually have additional resources and experiences to draw from that give them strength. Some people who have simply chosen to ignore or deny the crisis might fit in this last group, but others may be a more appropriate fit in the first or third group.

Each of these responses requires a different counseling intervention. Examples of these various responses are evident in Jesus' postresurrection appearances. As I examined these occurrences more closely, I noticed the way Christ engaged people at their point of pain and concern and led them to a place of healing in their relationship to God and to others.

The Road to Emmaus

The two people walking the seven miles from Jerusalem to Emmaus were in an intense discussion over what they had witnessed. When Jesus joined them, they did not recognize him. He asked them what they were discussing—a variation on the question "Where are you?" Their response revealed the theological and biblical dilemmas that confounded them. They believed Jesus was a prophet and possibly the Messiah, but the chief priests had handed him over to be crucified. To add to the confusion, some of their friends were claiming that the burial tomb on the third day after the crucifixion was empty, and the women were reporting a vision of angels who said Jesus was alive.

The two companions wanted an explanation, so Jesus gave them a lesson from the Scriptures. He took them through the Law and the Prophets, connecting the Messianic promises with his life, death, and resurrection. Only after they asked him to stay with them and he took the bread at the table and broke it and gave it to them did they recognize him, and all the pieces of the puzzle finally fell together. They were now in communion with God, and their first action was to share the good news with others by returning immediately to Jerusalem. They had become ambassadors of the gospel and the Greatest Commandment (Luke 24:13–35).

The Appearance to the Disciples

The disciples were in a state of confusion when Jesus first appeared to them after the resurrection. They were startled and frightened as he stood among them and said, "Peace be with you." They thought he was an apparition. He immediately addressed their troubles and doubts by showing them his hands and feet. He then made one of the most physically human of all requests; he asked them for something to eat. He was not a ghost. After he had calmed their fears, Jesus shifted to theological and spiritual issues as he reminded them of all the predictions in the Law of Moses, the Prophets, and the Psalms that were fulfilled in him. He opened their minds to understand the Scriptures as he connected them with the plan of God and prepared them for their mission to others (Luke 24:36–49).

Thomas

Thomas represents the type of person who needs more than spoken words to reassure him. He wanted absolute and irrefutable proof. He did not believe the report of the other disciples, and he was adamant that he would believe only if he saw the nail marks in Christ's hands and he could put his fingers in his side. When Jesus appeared before the disciples a week later, he insisted that Thomas fulfill his requirements for proof. Thomas acknowledged his Lord and God. Jesus then shifted the focus to the needs of others and said, "Blessed are those who have not seen and yet have believed" (John 20:24–29 NIV).

Mary

Most of the male followers needed reasoned assurance from Scriptures along with visual confirmation of the resurrection. When Jesus came to Mary, he used a different approach. Mary at first responded like Joseph of Arimathea in a practical way, helping prepare the spices and perfumes to anoint the body (Luke 23:55–56); however, when she discovered an empty tomb, she was inconsolable (John 20:10–11). Mary exhibited signs of multiple traumas. Multiple traumas occur when additional experiences following an initial tragic event threaten to overwhelm a person. First, the crucifixion had occurred, and now the body had disappeared. Even the assuring presence of angels could not soothe her. She appeared to have difficulty processing information. When she became aware of someone standing nearby, she turned and, assuming it was the gardener, asked about the disposal of the body. The traumatic fog had engulfed her so much that even a familiar voice and figure could not penetrate it at first.

Jesus repeated the questions designed to locate her and minister to her needs. "Why are you crying?" "Who are you looking for?" (John 20:13–15 CEV). We can hear echoes in his words of God's question to Adam and Eve in the garden, "Where are you?" Mary was not interested in an extended conversation with anyone, much less a theological lesson; she just wanted to know what they had done with the body. Jesus then said only one word to her, "Mary." One can only imagine the tone of his voice, but it must have reached into the innermost depths of her being, cutting away the emotional despair and instantly healing a broken heart. She needed no further proof, no physical evidence of the crucifixion, no theological discussion, only the sound of her name spoken by her risen, visible Savior (John 20:10–18).

As part of his healing encounter, Jesus affirmed his identity and gave Mary an assignment. He connected his resurrection and return to the Father with the relationship of his followers to God. They would be identified with him, and he gave Mary a specific task of sharing this good news with the disciples.

The Transformation of Peter

In Matthew 26 Jesus predicted his crucifixion and the falling away of his disciples. He quoted Zechariah 13:7 as he described the death of the shepherd and the scattering of his sheep. He also predicted that Peter would deny him (Matt. 26:31–35; cf. John 13:37–38). Twice Peter said that it would never happen (Matt. 26:33, 35); but by the end of the chapter, he has denied knowing Jesus three times (Matt. 26:69–75; cf. John 18:15–18, 25–27).

Most commentaries see the threefold question Jesus asked Peter following his resurrection as a reinstatement of the disciple to a position of leadership and a mirroring of his threefold denial. These interpretations may be true, but I believe there is an additional dimension to the encounter that relates to crisis intervention and the Greatest Commandment. Peter was still living in the old paradigm, the old way of thinking and doing things; and Jesus was about to challenge him to become transformed into a new way of living.

One of the effects of the crucifixion trauma and the lack of spiritual leadership before the coming of the Holy Spirit (Acts 2) was that some of the disciples began to return to their old, familiar lifestyles, which provided comfort and security. Retreat and regression to earlier stages in life is common in trauma victims. One day Peter decided to go fishing (John 21). He took along six other disciples including his old fishing associates, James and John the sons of Zebedee (Luke 5:9–10). Jesus, as he had done before, appeared to them in their physical location and connected with them at their point of interest or concern. This time it was catching fish.

The disciples did not recognize Jesus at first, an indication that they had taken their eyes off God and were not looking for him. When they said that they had caught no fish, Jesus told them to cast their nets on the right side of the boat. They followed his instructions and were rewarded with an enormous catch of 153 fish. At that point John recognized the Lord.

After they had finished breakfast and their hunger needs had been met, Jesus turned to Peter and asked him, "Simon son of John, do you truly love me more than these?" Peter affirmed his love, and Jesus then asked Peter to feed or take care of his sheep. The question, response, and comment are repeated, with slight variations, three times. What was Jesus expecting of Peter; how does it illustrate a healing ministry; and how does it relate to the Greatest Commandment?

Jesus was asking Peter for a total commitment that involved a radical change in the fisherman's lifestyle and calling. Peter had organized and led others on a fishing expedition. Jesus had found them out at sea in a boat with empty nets, and he had met their needs. The natural language, the idioms and metaphors of conversation one would expect from Jesus during this encounter, should have been associated with fishing. After all, he had used fishing imagery when he had first met these disciples and called them to be "fishers of men." Peter at that time had "immediately left and followed" (Matt 4:18–19). They were now seated around the embers of a fire with the smell of cooked fish in the air. But Jesus does not speak of fishing. In words reminiscent of the original calling, Jesus does eventually ask Peter to "follow me" (John 21:19), but his metaphor switch to sheep and shepherding represented a revolutionary challenge and change to Peter's worldview. He was telling Peter to turn his back on his old lifestyle forever and accept a new mission.

The heart of the mission Jesus had for Peter is associated with the two requirements in the Greatest Commandment. Jesus wanted to know if Peter truly loved God "with all his heart and soul, mind and strength" and if he were willing to "love his neighbor as himself."

Jesus asked Peter, "Do you truly love me more than these [others do]?" (John 21:15 NIV). Here Jesus focuses on the First Table. "Where are you in relationship to God?" he is asking Peter. "Are you willing to put God first in everything you think, say, and do?" "Are you ready to renounce completely for me 'these others,' your old lifestyle and relationships?" "Are you ready to speak my language and my message, for me?"

Then "feed my sheep." "Take care of my Lambs." "Where are you in relationship to your neighbor, Peter? Do you really love others as much as you love yourself? Then do something about it. Express your love of God by following my example of caring for others and proclaiming the gospel. I want you to think in terms of my shepherding ministry not your old fishing lifestyle. Complete healing will come from your recent traumas when you embrace my vision and receive my Spirit."

The heart of Christ's message had been three years in incubation. Peter had walked with the Lord. He had heard him preach and teach, and he had seen him heal. Jesus was reminding Peter that God has a purpose for everything, and his intervention was a means of preparing Peter for his mission. The crucifixion and resurrection had a reality beyond just the prediction and fulfillment of Scripture, and Peter had a role in God's plan to spread the message of salvation. Jesus was telling Peter that his life had a postresurrection meaning and purpose.

A short time after the challenge on the beach, Peter would receive all he needed to carry out the task—Pentecost was coming. God's grace and faithfulness would be manifest in the presence and power of the Holy Spirit. Peter would face suffering. God does not always cover up the damaging effects of sin, and Jesus did not sugarcoat the dangers Peter faced. But he did give Peter the promise that, if he followed, he would be used to glorify God (John 21:18–19).

I find no evidence in Scripture after this time that Peter ever went fishing again or used the language of fishing. But I do find him using an interesting and familiar metaphor in 1 Peter 5:1–5, where he appealed to the elders of the church, as a fellow elder like him, to "be shepherds of God's flock that is under" their care, "being an example to the flock" until "the Chief Shepherd appears."

Crisis Counseling in the Wedgwood Ministry

Christian counselors minister to people in tragedies and crises by meeting them at their point of pain as they define it and by sharing the healing love of God as the caregivers discover ways to meet physical and spiritual needs. The counselors become living expressions of the Greatest Commandment.

One of the first questions from the media that Pastor Al Meredith had to address on the night of the Wedgwood shootings was, "Where was God while this tragedy was happening?" How can you explain a loving and caring God when a crazy man enters a church sanctuary and shoots people? Meredith was being asked a question of location, and the pastor's inspired response revealed the compassion and understanding of the Lord: "God was exactly where he was when his Son died on the cross." God knew the pain of unprovoked violence, and he knew the anguish of a parent who lost a child. Where was God? His healing Spirit was right there in the midst of all the pain. The Word of God became living flesh on earth; he had dwelled among us and had suffered for our sins. God understands our loss, pain, and suffering; and he invites us to join with him in ministering to a lost and needy world.

The people at Wedgwood had a variety of needs and concerns. Like the disciples of long ago, they experienced confusion and emotional distress. The counseling ministry was designed to locate these people at their point of need and assist them in finding healing and wholeness. The Christian witness from church members was evident from the beginning, and it was no more apparent than at the funerals and memorial services where faith, the grace of God, and the proclamation of his Word were central.

One of the people struck by bullets was Kevin Galey, the church counselor and a doctoral student at Southwestern Baptist Theological Seminary. He was shot twice when he encountered Ashbrook in the hallway to the sanctuary. Galey remembers thinking that the hits were paintballs and that the man was part of a church skit. He experienced a denial response; he could not conceive of a gunman entering his church and killing people. Galey survived the shooting and recovered from his physical wounds, but he admits that the emotional scars run deep. As a counselor, he could understand and describe the responses of a person in a crisis, but this knowledge did not protect him from actually experiencing the emotional reactions. He found the emotions, at times, overwhelming. He sought healing by focusing on the love and grace of God and by soliciting prayers from others. He did not seek answers to why it had happened; instead, he requested prayers that God would give him peace and grace to deal with the event.

"It is important for people to realize," said Galey, "that God didn't choose Wedgwood Baptist Church. A madman did. Yet God's promises continue. Where evil abounds, his grace is more abundant."[4]

At a corporate level, the pastor led the people to focus on God and to find ways to help others. Like Jesus in his postresurrection appearances, Meredith identified some specific tasks that accelerated the spiritual and emotional healing of the church body. One of the first goals he set was to hold worship services in the sanctuary the coming Sunday. The police and city officials demurred, saying it was not possible. The sanctuary was a crime scene, and evidence of the carnage was apparent in the bullet-ridden walls and ceiling and on the blood-soaked pews. Meredith insisted. He understood the importance of reclaiming the sanctuary as holy ground and drawing people's attention to the worship of God. The officials relented, the building was released as a crime scene, and the pastor's vision was embraced as people came to remove the carpet and some of the pews and prepare the building for worship. The hallway walls of the church building heralded the grace of God as they were covered with notes, cards, letters, e-mails, and pictures filled with messages of hope, sympathy, and prayer—further evidence of spiritual and koinonia support and care.

On the following Sunday the people gathered in the sanctuary while a church group from a neighboring state walked around the outside of the building praying for their Christian brothers and sisters, a visible expression of the love of God and neighbor. A sign of healthy healing in the church was revealed in the desire of many church members to share the message of God's provision and love to a fallen world. An informal memorial of flowers, cards, and messages appeared at the curbside near the church almost immediately after the shootings. The pastor arranged for his people and counselors to provide ministry to visitors at the memorial. Although the church body was wounded, it was not defeated, and evidence that it was on the path to healing could be found in specific efforts such as this one to share the Word of God with a needy world.[5]

Summary

1. The Greatest Commandment guides biblical Christian counselors to reveal the love of God and to express the love of neighbor.

2. The encounters with the scribe and with the rich young ruler il-lustrate how Jesus applies the two dimensions of the Greatest Com-mandment. He finds the relational location of the two inquirers, and he adjusts his responses to meet individual needs.

3. An examination of the response of people at the time of the cru-cifixion reveals that individuals react in many different ways to a crisis. Christian counselors need to develop the skills necessary to recognize the cognitive, affective, behavioral, and spiritual reac-tions of people in a situation and provide an effective therapeutic counseling ministry.

4. The shootings at Wedgwood Baptist Church in Fort Worth, Texas, provide an example of the crises that Christians may face in our world and the importance of applying the Greatest Commandment in the healing process of counseling.

Where Do We Go from Here?

Biblical Christian counselors examine a person's relationship with God, self, and others. They recognize the importance of finding a coun-selee's spiritual, psychological, and social location. The perfect model of one who embodies the Greatest Commandment is found in the love and sacrificial example of Jesus Christ, the Master Counselor and our Counselor of heaven on earth.

Questions and Exercises for Reflection

1. What is the primary focus of other counseling models you have studied, both secular and Christian? Examine these approaches and compare them with the emphasis in this chapter.

2. How do counseling and the Greatest Commandment relate to the Great Commission (Matt. 28:18–20) and the call to go and make disciples of all nations?

3. Find some examples in the Bible, in addition to the crucifixion, that reveal a variety of responses to an incident or situation. How might Christian counselors respond effectively in these situations?

4. Describe a contemporary example of ministry, preferably one related to Christian counseling, that illustrates the application of the Greatest Commandment.

5. What evidence do we see of expressions of the Greatest Commandment in Peter's ministry after Pentecost?

References

Crawford, Dan. *Night of Darkness, Dawning of Light*. Colorado Springs, Colo.: Shaw, 2000.

Kerr, Cindy. "Walking Again, Galey Seeks Emotional Healing." *Southwestern News: Special Edition*, 58:2 (1999), 12.

Schaff, Philip, gen. ed. A Select Library of the Nicene and the Post-Nicene Fathers of the Christian Church. Volume I: *The Confession and Letters of St Augustin*; Volume IV: *St Augustin: The Writings Against the Manichaeans, and Against the Donatists*. Buffalo, N.Y.: The Christian Literature Co., 1887.

Endnotes

1 Augustine, *Morals of the Catholic Church* 26.48, in A Select Library of the Nicene and the Post-Nicene Fathers of the Christian Church, ed. Philip Schaff, Volume IV: *St Augustine: The Writings Against the Manichaeans, and Against the Donatists* (Buffalo, N.Y.: The Christian Literature Co., 1887), 55.

2 Augustine, *Letters* 228.3, in A Select Library of the Nicene and the Post-Nicene Fathers of the Christian Church, ed. Philip Schaff, Volume I: *The Confession and Letters of St Augustin* (Buffalo, N.Y.: The Christian Literature Co., 1887), 577.

3 Augustine, *Morals of the Catholic Church* 28.56.

4 Cindy Kerr, "Walking Again, Galey Seeks Emotional Healing," *Southwestern News: Special Edition*, 58:2 (1999), 12.

5 For further information on the Wedgwood shootings, see Dan Crawford, *Night of Darkness, Dawning of Light* (Colorado Springs, Colo.: Shaw, 2000).

6

JESUS THE MESSIAH: THE COUNSELOR OF HEAVEN ON EARTH

The Spirit of Wisdom and Understanding
The Spirit of Knowledge and Power
The Spirit of the Knowledge of God and the Fear of God

The relationship of God to his creation reveals the nature of biblical Christian counseling, and the definitive demonstration of caregiving is the sacrificial life of Christ. Christ's character provides the basis for identifying the optimum qualities of a Christian caregiver, and God's grace in the gift of the Holy Spirit allows us to follow Christ's example as we engage in biblical counsel and caregiving.

What particular elements in Jesus' ministry are pertinent to the art of counseling? Rather than begin this discussion with a study of the life of Christ in the New Testament, I believe that we can find foundational principles that answer this question in the Old Testament. In fact, a description of Jesus the Messiah provides us with the ideal traits of a master counselor.

The nature of the Messiah is described clearly in the book of Isaiah. "For a child will be born to us, a son will be given to us; And the government will rest on His shoulders; And His name will be called Wonderful Counselor, Mighty God, Eternal Father, Prince of Peace" (Isa. 9:6).

The Messiah will come as a child, as a gift to the world. John 3:16 tells us that God loved the world so much that he gave us his Son. The

Son of God has the authority to govern all the forces in heaven and on earth, and his names identify essential attributes of his character.

The terms *Wonderful* and *Counselor* are often combined in commentaries and translations (e.g., RSV, NASB), allowing the former to act as an adjective describing the type of counselor. If separated (usually by a comma), as some translations prefer (e.g., KJV), "Wonderful" conveys a sense of the incomprehensible nature of God. The Messiah's nature is a marvel or mystery extending beyond any words we are capable of conceiving or uttering in description.

The term *counselor* (Hebrew *yaats*) means one who advises or consults. This is a more expansive term than the counseling we associate with formal psychotherapy in the twenty-first century. The Messiah will be able to discern what is good and what is the right thing to do in any situation, and he will be able to give guidance and direction in all of life's issues, without need of any human consultation. When connected to the term *wonderful* (Hebrew *pali*), the concept takes on an even more supernatural force. The Lord's counsel is so perfect, so exceptional, and so matchless that no human language is capable of describing it. It is beyond words; it is incomprehensibly marvelous. No person is capable of teaching and advising like Christ. Human counsel and wisdom by comparison appear as foolishness (1 Cor. 1:25; 3:19).[1]

As *mighty God*, the Messiah has the power of God. He is capable of controlling the heavens and the earth. He can change the course of history and the heart of an individual. He has the power to create and to destroy, and we are dependent on him for our creation and continued existence.

As *eternal Father*, the Messiah comes as both human child and eternal Father. Unlike earthly fathers and kings who are fallible and a temporary presence in our lives, the Messiah brings the comfort and assurance of a heavenly Father who will always be with us.

As *Prince of Peace*, the Messiah is the Great Mediator between a Holy God and sinful humanity. In him we find the eternal peace that enables us to deal with the storms in our present life and provides us with the promise of salvation and everlasting peace with God (Rom. 5:1).

The model for the Christian counselor is Jesus the Messiah/Christ. The description of the Messiah found in Isaiah 9:6 is elaborated on in Isaiah 11:2. This passage describes six characteristics or expressions of the Spirit of the Lord in the Wonderful Counselor, grouped together under three "spirits" or categories.

> Then a shoot will spring from the stem of Jesse,
>> And a branch from his roots will bear fruit.
>> The Spirit of the LORD will rest on Him,
>> The spirit of wisdom and understanding,
>> The spirit of counsel and strength,
> The spirit of knowledge and the fear of the LORD
> (Isa. 11:1–2).

Bible commentaries agree that Isaiah is not describing three or even six different entities or "spirits" in this passage.[2] The terms all refer to qualities that are an expression of the one Spirit of Jehovah. The descriptions give insight into the personal nature and the authority of Messiah. While the six terms should not be seen as independent, they also should not be considered synonyms.

Hebrew literature often uses parallelisms in which a concept is repeated using similar words. Hence, Proverbs 20:1 tells us that "wine is a mocker, strong drink a brawler, and whoever is intoxicated by it is not wise." The first two phrases repeat the same idea, that abuse of alcohol will bring serious problems into your life. The repetition or parallelism gives emphasis to the point. In Isaiah 11:2, however, the words used in the description of the Messiah are not parallelisms; rather, they have distinct or exclusive meanings. Yet the grouping into three pairs or "spirits" tells us that the terms are not completely discrete; the concepts are interconnected and have a degree of overlap in meaning. They are describing a single person—the Messiah.

The six characteristics of the Messiah are functionally manifested in the life of Christ. As a description of the Master Counselor, they also give us a model of caregiving and biblical counseling. The terms give us an insight into the basic features of an effective biblical Christian counseling ministry.

The Spirit of Wisdom and Understanding
Wisdom

Wisdom (Hebrew *hokmah*; LXX: *sophias*) is the ability to recognize the true relationship between things, in order to determine the correct decisions to make at the right time; to fully comprehend or correctly appraise a situation in complete detail to determine the appropriate way to proceed in the matter.[3] The Messiah will not engage in the superficial judgment of appearances, relying on the external senses of what he sees and hears (Isa. 11:3–4); instead, his judgment will be righteous and fair, based on a thorough and complete understanding.

> And He will delight in the fear of the LORD,
> And He will not judge by what His eyes see,
> Nor make a decision by what His ears hear;
> But with righteousness He will judge the poor,
> And decide with fairness for the afflicted of the earth;
> And He will strike the earth with the rod of His mouth,
> And with the breath of His lips He will slay the wicked.
> Also righteousness will be the belt about His loins,
> And faithfulness the belt about His waist (Isa. 11:3–5).

This is a theoretical wisdom that comprehends the true nature of things. In counseling, this involves the ability to perceive the correct relationship of the individual to others and the steps to take to produce healing. It is based on a deep and comprehensive awareness of human nature and the cognitive, behavioral, affective, and spiritual dimensions, and a Spirit-led insight that determines the optimum time to speak and to act.

Job makes clear that such wisdom does not come from an earthly source (Job 28:12–28). "Where shall such wisdom be found, and where is the place of understanding? Man does not know its value, nor is it found in the land of the living. Where does it come from? It is found in

God," says Job. Such wisdom and understanding are discovered in the fear and reverence of God.

Proverbs 8:1–36 gives an extended treatment of this wisdom. Wisdom is defined or personified, and its characteristics include possessing knowledge (*da'ath*), offering sound advice (*etzah*), and having understanding (*binah*) and strength (*geburah*). These four terms, as we shall see, are also found in our passage in Isaiah 11:2.

Jesus and Wisdom. Jesus learned the way of wisdom. As he grew in wisdom and stature, he found favor with God and man (Luke 2:52). There are numerous examples of his wise counsel; perhaps the most profound are found in his Sermon on the Mount (Matt. 5–7).

> Blessed are the poor in spirit, for theirs is the kingdom of heaven.
>
> Blessed are those who mourn, for they shall be comforted.
>
> Blessed are the gentle, for they shall inherit the earth.
>
> Blessed are those who hunger and thirst for righteousness, for they shall be satisfied.
>
> Blessed are the merciful, for they shall receive mercy.
>
> Blessed are the pure in heart, for they shall see God.
>
> Blessed are the peacemakers, for they shall be called sons of God.
>
> Blessed are those who have been persecuted for the sake of righteousness, for theirs is the kingdom of heaven.
>
> Blessed are you when people insult you and persecute you, and falsely say all kinds of evil against you because of Me.
>
> Rejoice and be glad, for your reward in heaven is great; for in the same way they persecuted the prophets who were before you (Matt. 5:3–12).

Here Jesus reveals the true nature of the kingdom of God. He stresses that the really fortunate people are humble in spirit and recognize their absolute dependence on God. These people understand their location and position in relationship to God. Blessed are the people who realize that they are intellectually, emotionally, and spiritually impoverished in comparison to the richness of God; who grieve over their sin and seek the saving grace of God. The craving for God will lead such people to show mercy toward their neighbors. Hearts cleansed by the blood of Christ will bring people into fellowship with God and lead them to share the gospel of peace with others.

Once again we see the close relationship between loving God and caring for our neighbors. The biblical counselor will seek such wisdom. "The godly man is a good counselor because he is just and fair and knows right from wrong" (Ps. 37:30–31 TLB). Such a counselor will possess an understanding of human nature and will be attentive to the motives and forces that lie beneath the presenting problem and the words and attitudes of the person in need.

An Example: The Use of Silence in Wise Counseling. One example of this wisdom is the ability not only to appraise a situation correctly but also to know the correct time to speak and to act and the time to be silent. A common feeling among immature counselors is the fear of silence in a counseling session. At such times the counselor is tempted to say whatever comes to mind in order to fill the void of silence. The wisest counsel given by the counselors of Job was probably in the first week of their ministry to him.

> Now when Job's three friends heard of all this adversity that had come upon him, they came each one from his own place, Eliphaz the Temanite, Bildad the Shuhite and Zophar the Naamathite; and they made an appointment together to come to sympathize with him and comfort him. When they lifted up their eyes at a distance and did not recognize him, they raised their voices and wept. And each of them tore his robe and they threw dust over their heads toward the sky. Then they sat down on the ground with him for seven days and seven nights with no one speaking a word to him, for they saw that *his* pain was very great (Job 2:11–13).

They located Job and joined with him emotionally, giving him consolation by their presence and actions. Their silence spoke volumes in support of their friend. Then they opened their mouths and spoke, and the counseling devolved into an argumentative debate. Their wrongheaded view that Job's problems were obviously due to sin in his life that required his confession and repentance brought more anguish rather than healing, more darkness and despair than light and hope. They could not comprehend that Job's righteousness was being tested and that his problems were connected to spiritual warfare. They lacked the wisdom to see the big picture. The falseness of the position of Job's counselors is revealed after God confronts everyone. He demands that the counselors offer a sacrifice, and he accepts an intercessory prayer from Job on their behalf for their folly (Job 42:7–9).

Wise counselors understand that there is a time to be silent and a time to speak (Eccl. 3:7b). Silence can provide time for people to gather their thoughts and ruminate. It leaves opportunity for the Holy Spirit to convict people or lead them into a new awareness of godly truths.

A group of Christians met with a counselor to talk about a recent tragedy in which some of their missionary friends had died. The counselor was aware that a few of the people were reluctant to come to the session, but they had been encouraged to do so by their fellow believers. A number of these people would need time to contemplate and consider the possibility of revealing some of their traumatic experiences and private thoughts. At the outset the counselor decided that listening and silence would be an important part of the counseling process.

After an opening prayer the counselor invited the group members to share their knowledge about what had happened and the role they had played in the events. One or two of the people who were more vocal and comfortable with sharing began to speak, but after they had finished, the group lapsed into silence. It was tempting for the counselor to speak up at this time, to encourage the group members to open up, and to ask questions designed to gather more information. The counselor did not want to appear incompetent, and the lack of conversation seemed to attest to his lack of counseling skills. Wisdom prevailed, and he kept silent. The silence lasted for several minutes, and then some of the quieter ones began to express their thoughts and feelings. As they shared their experiences, other members began to fill in additional information and answer questions that had been bothering some people in the group.

Slowly the fragmented stories came together, and like pieces joining in a jigsaw puzzle, a remarkable picture began to emerge. In the midst of discussing the tragedy, each member of the group was drawn into a realization that the hand of God had been guiding and comforting them. A phone call made at a precise time meant that necessary arrangements could be made and assistance given. One minute later and the person would have left the office, never receiving the critical call. The actions of another person had concerned and confused several members in the group. Now they understood his behavior and could see how God had used their friend to bring comfort in the confusion. In the midst of a tragedy, the group found the counsel of heaven.

Silence was an effective part of this counseling session. "Be still, and know that I am God," says the Lord (Ps. 46:10a). "Cease striving, relax, take comfort, be quiet, and listen to me." If the counselor had spoken up, he would have directed the counseling session on his own terms, meeting his own needs. They would have listened to him, and perhaps missed the voice of God speaking to them and affirming his presence.

Understanding

Understanding (Hebrew *binah;* LXX *suneseos*) is the ability to divide something into its various parts, the power to discern the true nature of a thing. It is the ability to see into the inner being, the heart, or the character of an individual. While the previous term deals with wisdom from a broad theoretical level, the word used here refers to a practical wisdom or understanding. It is the power to discern and discriminate between matters and to know how elements connect and relate to one another. While theoretical wisdom gives us a broad picture of the nature of things and our relationship to the world and to God, understanding addresses the psychological or inner dimension. Godly

understanding detects the motivations and the often-complex relationships that lead us to think and act in a particular way.

Solomon and Understanding. We find an example of this godly understanding in the life of Solomon (1 Kings 3:16–28). Two mothers lay
claim to the same baby. The case is brought before King Solomon, who
uses a paradoxical intervention to discern the true nature of the claim-
ants. He orders the child to be cut in two with a sword and the separate
parts given to the two mothers. The true mother immediately relin-
quishes claim to the child in order to save her son's life while the false
mother agrees to the king's edict. Solomon's practical wisdom has enabled him to discover the true relationship in the situation, beyond sight
and words, and the son is returned to its rightful mother.

Jesus and Understanding. Jesus was filled with this godly understanding. Christ did not need anyone to explain human nature to him,
for "He himself knew what was in man" (John 2:25). His insight enabled him to understand the motives behind the words and actions of
people. When the Pharisees brought a woman to him, caught in adultery, Jesus was confronted with a dilemma. How could he minister to
this woman in need and at the same time deal with both the motivations
of the Pharisees and the theological challenge they had placed before
him? Jesus was conscious of the people around him. He could detect
the tone of their voices and hear their condemnation and anger, but he
was also aware of the fear and the hurt in the woman before him. How
would it be possible to minister in such a situation?

The brilliance of the counseling response of Christ lies in his ability
to connect with both the accusers and the condemned woman and bring
a godly word of counsel to both parties. He had the ability to see beyond
the immediate situation into the hearts of the people around him and
minister on multiple levels (John 8:3–11).

The safest reaction in the situation would have been for Jesus to align
himself with the Pharisees in condemning the woman. After all, she
had violated the law, and the punishment was death by stoning (Lev.
20:10; Deut. 22:22–24). Defending the Word of God by attacking the

sinner would preserve his rabbinic reputation, and it would be a concil-iatory gesture toward the Pharisees.

It is easy for us in counseling to rush to judgment and condemn peo-ple for their actions without stopping to look at the context, the under-lying motivations, and the redemptive opportunities. We should not be soft on sin and excuse irresponsible behavior; however, we need to be asking ourselves what else is going on and how God might be work-ing in a situation. We want to be clearly associated with a righteous and biblical position in our counseling and avoid any taint of unholy contamination or spiritual weakness. Yet in the process of preserving our piety, we might miss the sacrificial model Jesus gives us, where the spiritual needs of others are placed ahead of our social status and religious reputation.

In this case Jesus understood that the Pharisees were testing him. They had seen his compassion toward others, particularly his loving concern for the poor and needy; and now they were intent on trapping him. Jesus was weak on sin, soft on the law, and his behavior was not biblical. "Choose," they challenged Jesus. "Choose between our inter-pretation of the law and your misplaced love for sinners. The punish-ment for this sin is death, and all godly people will stand in agreement with us. Accept that our way is the righteous way and that all other views deserve condemnation."

Jesus' response is a variation on the first question we should be ask-ing in counseling: "Where are you?" If he were to meet the challenge head on, his actions could lead to an intensification of the hostile emo-tions and make a dangerous situation even more perilous. Instead of matching the combative tone, Jesus began a process of locating and meeting with the adversaries from each of their perspectives, but on his own terms.

His initial step was to say nothing. He simply began writing on the ground with his finger. There are times to speak and times to be silent. "When there are many words, transgression is unavoidable, but he who restrains his lips is wise" (Prov. 10:19). They were motivated by hatred;

he was there to reveal the love of God. "Hatred stirs up strife, but love covers all transgressions" (Prov. 10:12).

Jesus was careful not to escalate the situation and increase the anger and abuse. His silence allowed time for thought and gave the accusers an opportunity to withdraw and drop the matter. Sometimes silence allows wiser heads to prevail, and tense situations can be defused. Three additional counseling principles are found within this passage.

First, Jesus did not let the Pharisees set the agenda on their own terms. His actions and later response would shift the focus of the problem. It would end in a way the Pharisees could never have foreseen. Wise counselors do not accept at face value the worldview or interpretation of a situation as presented by their counselees. The issues and expectations people bring into a counseling session provide clues about their location, but it does not follow that counselors should immediately respond and act in a manner that expresses complete agreement with these expectations and views. Their understanding of the problem may have led these counselees into their troubles in the first place.

In marriage counseling I often find that a husband, for example, will want to list the accumulated sins and errors he has discovered in his wife. It is important for him that I understand just how bad a wife she has been. His message is clear; he expects me to affirm his position and align myself with him in condemning his wife. I am there to tell his wife what she should do based on his interpretation of the situation. If he is a Christian, he may expect me to quote a few choice Scriptures as a seal of religious approval upon the reprimand I give her. If I proceed along the lines that this husband expects of me, there will be little chance of reconciliation. In fact, not only will I alienate his wife, but also any satisfaction he may get from having the marriage counselor agree with him will be short-lived, his bitterness will likely increase, and his feelings toward his spouse will harden even further.

Second, Jesus' silence illustrates the importance of allowing both counselors and counselees to gather their thoughts and decide how they wish to proceed in the situation. A rush to judgment and a failure to take some time out to think about matters has exacerbated many problems.

103

Silence is an effective tool in encouraging people to contemplate and weigh a situation. It forces people to question what is going on in an encounter. Did the person hear me? Did he understand what I said? What is he thinking? Why hasn't he agreed with me or answered me? Why doesn't he say something? What is going on?

Third, Jesus' initial actions were nonthreatening; he simply wrote in the sand. There is a great deal of speculation over what Jesus wrote. Was he just doodling to give the Pharisees second thoughts about what they were doing and give them the opportunity to withdraw? Was he gaining time to prepare his response? Or was he writing something significant in the sand that would catch the attention of the accusers, something that would challenge or confront them over their own guilt and sin? Regardless of what Jesus wrote, his action served to reinforce his silence and shift the focus so that the Pharisees were no longer in control of the situation. In tense confrontations, nonthreatening and even distracting actions may serve to diffuse hostilities and open the way for more constructive and redemptive dialogue.

When the Pharisees persisted, Jesus responded in a way that addressed the underlying agenda of the accusers and ministered to the woman. He straightened up and said, "Let the one among you who is free of sin be the first to throw a stone at her" (John 8:7). Both his eye contact and his statement were brief. His physical action lent emphasis to his statement, but its succinctness neutralized his opponents. He returned to a stooped position and continued writing on the ground.

The Pharisees were now forced to deal with their own spiritual condition. Who among them was willing to claim to be perfect, to be sinless? Even to acknowledge the possibility and step up first was to run the risk of expressing the sin of pride and, even worse, to blaspheme by implying equality with God, who, alone, is perfect. The older and wiser ones were the first to slink away, and then the others followed.

Jesus used a form of indirect confrontation with the Pharisees. He had revealed the incongruity and inconsistency of their position by forcing them to shift their focus from accusation and condemnation of another person to self-exploration and their own sins. He had upheld the

104

authority of the Word of God and had reminded them of their human inadequacy before God, joining them without directly opposing their position; but his actions had also allowed him to connect with and minister to the woman. She would not have been willing to listen to him if he had sided with the Pharisees in the beginning. But here was a Man who was different. He had single-handedly taken on men representing the epitome of Jewish religious piety in a theological battle with her life at stake, and somehow he had become her champion, her Savior. He did this while barely raising an eyebrow or his voice. After that she was willing to listen to anything he said.

Counselors sometimes talk about "earning the right" to speak with a counselee. We need to gain the trust of people in need by identifying with them. Again, this does not mean we condone a person's sin. Ignoring sin is never the biblical way. We need to convey a godly love and compassion toward them in such a way that they become aware of the presence of God.

What did Jesus have in common with this sinful woman? His point of contact was that both of them were being challenged or attacked by the Pharisees. Until this threat was gone, she would not be willing to listen to anyone.

"Where are your accusers? Has no one condemned you?" he asked.

"No one, Lord," she replied (see John 8:10–11).

He was able to join with the woman in dealing with this threat. His questions to her revealed that the danger was gone. No one had stayed to condemn her; the threat had disappeared. At this point Jesus shifted his attention to deal directly with the divine dimension, her relationship to God. Christ would not condemn her either; instead, he challenged her to give her life to God, to "go and sin no more."

Looking beyond the External and Superficial. What problem is uppermost in a counselee's mind? Does the person in need feel threatened? How will you join with the counselee in a way that enables you to bring a redemptive solution to the situation? The Messiah possessed a spirit of understanding that enabled him to connect with people and grasp the impulses and forces behind the thoughts and behavior of individuals. Our tendency is to judge on a more superficial level.

I stopped at a gas station near Carswell Air Force Base in Fort Worth early one morning. After fueling my car, I entered the shop to pay. I hesitated as I gave my money to the attendant. He was disheveled. His hair was oily and unkempt, he had not shaved in at least a day, his eyes were red and bleary, his speech was slurred, and his clothes were dirty. He fumbled with my money as he attempted to give me change from the register.

I knew immediately what his problem was. I had his number. He was obviously recovering from a night of drinking. Here was a man who lacked goals and a purpose in life; he was not going to amount to anything. He probably would not be able to keep his job much longer. He could barely stand up. The fact that he was from a different ethnic group from me only reinforced my feelings. It made me wonder why anyone would hire him in the first place.

He spoke and interrupted my thoughts.

"I'm sorry," he said, apologizing for his appearance and slowness. "They called me last night from the flight line at Carswell Air Force Base. They had a jet engine that they couldn't fix, and they needed my expertise. So I went out and worked on that engine all night before coming to my part-time job here. I haven't slept in more than twenty-four hours."

Sometimes our eyes and ears deceive us, and we rush to judgment. Eli the priest learned this lesson when he accused brokenhearted Hannah of being drunk. The priest had observed Hannah's behavior at the tabernacle of the Lord and had concluded from the movement of her lips and her physical demeanor that she was under the influence of alcohol. In reality she was weeping and grieving deeply over her inability to have children. In her despair she was turning in prayer to God with a promise that if she conceived, she would dedicate her firstborn son to the Lord. Eli's apology came in the form of a blessing of peace and a prayer that God would grant her petition. Hannah later conceived and gave birth to Samuel (1 Sam. 1:1–20).

Jesus looks into the heart of a person. He sees beyond appearances and discerns our true nature.

> And He will not judge by what His eyes see,
> Nor make a decision by what His ears hear;
> But with righteousness he will judge (Isa. 11:3–4).

Wisdom and understanding address the theoretical and intellectual aspects in counseling, and they have a particular application to how we should relate to others and the world. Knowledge and power shift our focus to the abilities and assets of the individual.

The Spirit of Knowledge and Power
Knowledge

Knowledge (Hebrew etzah; LXX boules). Knowledge is the awareness of truth, the ability to assess correctly a situation and determine the right way to proceed. The Hebrew word conveys the idea of giving counsel or advice. It is the ability to gather data for making wise plans and decisions. "Without consultation, plans are frustrated, but with many counselors (Hebrew *yaatz*) they succeed" (Prov. 15:22). All the decisions made by the Messiah constitute wise planning and counsel. The right means are chosen to arrive at the perfectly correct decision.

Rehoboam and Unwise Counsel. When Rehoboam came to the throne following the death of his father Solomon, he was confronted with a dilemma. The people were pressing for reform. They wanted the king to ease their burdens. Rehoboam sent the people away for three days so that he could consult with his counselors. He talked with the elder counselors who had served his father, and they recommended that he give the people what they had requested; and, in turn, they would be his faithful servants. The king then sought the advice of the young men who had grown up with him. Their advice to the king was that he should demand even more from the people than Solomon. In 1 Kings 12:13–14, we read of Rehoboam's fateful decision: "The king answered the people harshly, for he forsook the advice (*etzah*) of the elders which they had given him, and he spoke to them according to the advice (*etzah*) of the young men, saying, 'My father made your yoke heavy, but I will add to your yoke; my father disciplined you with whips, but I will discipline you with scorpions.' So the king did not listen to the people."

The advice of the elders carried an awareness of the dangerous mood of the people, and their knowledge led them to suggest a wise plan to the king. Instead, the king listened to the recommendations of the young men who lacked knowledge and foresight. These young counselors lacked insight into the hearts and minds of the people, and they appeared to have no interest in or desire to discover their true cognitive, sociopolitical, and spiritual location. Rehoboam would come to regret his decision when the people rebelled a short time later.

Wise counselors help people develop plans that consider the circumstances and address potential dangers in pursuing a course of action. The story of Rehoboam illustrates the hazards inherent in listening to poor counsel. Wise planning addresses the broader theory and context, acknowledges and seeks the guidance of God, and evaluates the immediate and practical concerns. "Many plans [thoughts and schemes] are in a man's heart, but the counsel (*etzah*) of the Lord will stand" (Prov. 19:21). Behind all the planning must be an awareness that God is still in control and the Christian's task is to seek the will of God. Our planning, calculating, and decision making come from our mind and heart, the book of Proverbs tells us. We make our own choices, but God is the One who ultimately decides what will happen (Prov. 16:9; 19:21). The person who fulfills the plans of the Lord and follows his directions is a true counselor of God (Isa. 46:11; literally: "the man of my *etsah*"). "Commit your works to the LORD and your plans will be established" (Prov. 16:3).

Christ's Mission Statement. The plan for the Messiah is spelled out in the mission statement Jesus made in Luke 4:18 where he quotes from Isaiah 58:6 and Isaiah 11:3–4. "The Spirit of the Lord has come to me because he has chosen me (1) to tell the good news to the poor. The Lord has sent me (2) to announce freedom for prisoners, (3) to give sight to the blind, (4) to free everyone who suffers, and (5) to proclaim that this is the year the Lord has chosen."

The good news to the poor is the message of salvation for all mankind (John 3:16). Jesus is the plan of salvation. He is the way, the truth, and the life. No person can approach God except through Christ (John 14:6).

Jesus announced freedom to prisoners. The Son of God would bring freedom from the law of sin and death (Rom. 8:2). "You will know the truth [I am the Truth], and the truth will make you free," he told them (John 8:32). His mission was to free us from our spiritual slavery (Gal. 5:1). If the Son sets you free, then you shall be free indeed (John 8:36). This freedom gives us compassion toward others and leads us to express our worship of the Lord by seeking to correct social injustice (Isa. 58:6).

Jesus brings light so that even the blind can see. This sight is available not just at a physical level but also at a relational and a spiritual level. His salvation would cleanse our hearts. "Blessed are the pure in heart, for they will see God" (Matt. 5:8 NIV). People who lack a heart for God will remain in a world of distorted spiritual vision and sound, where "seeing, they will not perceive, and hearing, they will not understand" (Matt. 13:14–17). His message brings sight to the repentant blind and spiritual blindness to those people who see themselves as righteous, having no need for Christ (John 9:35–41). Only people who pursue peaceful relationships and live in holiness will see God (Heb. 12:14).

The Messiah will free all suffering people. His freedom will be comprehensive. No area in life will be overlooked in Christ's mission. For Christians this freedom does not mean that all pain and difficulties will disappear for the remainder of their pilgrimage on Earth. In fact, acknowledging Christ in the world may invite persecution; but this pain, although it could last for the remainder of your earthly life, will be just temporary in comparison to an eternity living in the presence of God (Rom. 8:17–18; 1 Pet. 4:12–19).

The Messiah will proclaim the year of jubilee—the year of salvation when all debts will be forgiven. John the Baptist recognized this mission in Jesus. "Behold the Lamb of God," he said, "who takes away the sin of the world!" (John 1:29). Jesus identified himself as the resurrection and the life (John 11:25). He is the planner or author of salvation, the one who retires all our debts of sin (Heb. 5:9), and he has brought us the day of salvation (2 Cor. 6:2). "I am come that they may have life, a full and abundant life" (see John 10:10).

In Acts 10:36–43, we read that Jesus completed his mission.

Christians' Mission Statement. Christians are called to a living relationship with Christ, not to enslavement to a dead dogma. The Father wants everyone who sees the Son to have faith in him and have eternal life. He gave his followers a Great Commission (Matt. 28:18–20). Our motivation to complete this mission is drawn from a personal relationship with God, not just a code for living. Jesus told his followers: "I have been given all authority in heaven and on earth. As you are going, disciple people in all the nations, baptizing them in the name of the Father, Son, and Holy Spirit, teaching them to observe everything that I've told you and I will be with you always [i.e., His authoritative presence will be with us] till the end."

We have the promise of Christ's power, presence, and authority. As we obey Christ's command, we will be guided by the Holy Spirit, the *Paraclete* or comforter and counselor, who will help us. The Spirit of Truth will reveal to us the true nature of things, teaching us, reminding us, and helping us to witness for Christ (John 14:15–17,26; 15:26–27). All Christian counselors are blessed with at least one of God's many wonderful gifts to be used in service to others and to the glory of God (1 Pet. 4:10–11), and God has given us a Spirit of power and of love and of a sound mind to care for others (2 Tim. 1:7).

Your Personal Counseling Mission. Counseling is a part of a caregiving ministry and service to others. It assists in the sanctification process with Christians. It is a means of helping Christian brethren grow and develop a deeper and more mature relationship with God and with other people.

Counseling the non-Christian provides us with the opportunity of representing Christ in the therapeutic encounter. This witness may be overt and direct or more subtle and indirect. There is no single method or rule except that of being responsive and open to the leading of the Spirit and the guidance of his Word. The Bible shows us that we should start where people are located in their spiritual, mental, emotional, and physical lives. We may be part of a larger plan for the person in need whereby we will be used of God to give someone a glimpse of the ultimate healing possibilities to be found in Christ, or we may be fortunate enough to participate directly in presenting the message of salvation. If a person accepts Christ, discipleship and counseling can work hand in hand as the process of sanctification or growth in Christ begins. If not, then the Christian counselor should continue to pray for the person and seek to be used by God as a means of planting seeds of grace through the healing encounter.

Two concerns arise in this area. At one extreme is the position where spiritual issues are ignored or disregarded in counseling. From a Christian counseling perspective, this attitude could be considered therapeutic negligence, and it is certainly unbiblical. The position of avoiding any discussion on faith has been the attitude of many secular counseling approaches in the past although more recent training programs, under the influence of New Age and spiritualist movements in particular, have begun to address spiritual issues. A more benign expression of this position is the deliberate attempt by counselors to evade the topic in order not to offend a counselee.

The other extreme position is one in which a counselor insists on addressing religious issues, regardless of the wishes of the counselee. The counselor may speak in a theological jargon and expect the counselee to listen to quotations from Scripture. I have observed a variation of this approach in immature Christian counselors when they find themselves at a loss for words in a counseling session. Since they are not sure what to say or to do next, they simply quote a Bible verse they have memorized; or they present a standard, ritualized plan of salvation. No attempt is made to convey God's Word in a meaningful way to the person in need. Clients in this situation may believe that the counselor has no interest in understanding their concerns and fail to sense any godly love or care. They are not likely to return for further counseling.

The problem with these techniques is that they serve more to meet the needs of the counselor, not the counselee. The actions assuage any guilt over personal inadequacy and allow counselors to claim they have "shared the Word of God." The message to the counselees is that if they want help, then they must be prepared to learn the language of and address the issues determined by the counselor. They must find the counselor's location, rather than the counselor searching for their position and needs. God can use even our weaknesses and clumsy actions to bring glory to his name, but the Bible tells us that we are to go into the world and locate people at their point of need. Christian counselors must be good Samaritans not inflexible Pharisees.

Counselors must carefully consider how to communicate the Word of God, and they should allow the Spirit to work in his own time in a counseling context. Jesus never made acceptance of himself as the Son of God a precondition of his healing ministry. He allowed people to define their problem and pain and ministered at their point of need. His actions of healing on a physical level revealed the possibility of divine healing on an eternal level. Any assistance we are able to give a person in need can be used by God to reveal his active plan of salvation. Invariably, a Christian counselor's loving concern, commitment to the truths of Scripture, and sensitivity to the Spirit of God will lead to openness from a client and an eventual willingness to explore issues of faith and biblical hope.

Christian counselors must seek the Spirit of knowledge, but wise planning is not enough to ensure that changes will take place in a person's life. There must be a source of power strong enough to execute the plan and produce change.

Power

Power (Hebrew *geburah;* LXX *ischuos*) is the strength or might to produce change, the ability to execute a plan, and the capacity to remain firm and constant in a situation, despite any opposition.

The word is used in connection with physical strength. Gideon is described as rising up in might or physical strength and slaying two men (Judg. 8:21). The psalmist tells us that the days of our years are seventy, unless by physical strength we are able to endure for eighty years (Ps. 90:10). Power is identified with the reign of David (1 Chron. 29:30). Here the term is used in a broader sense than mere physical strength. David's power incorporated political astuteness and military leadership, as well as dependence on God.

Jesus and the Power of God. The Bible associates power, in particular, with the character of God. We are to acknowledge and sing praises to God's strength and power (Ps. 21:13); his powerful deeds save us (Ps. 20:6); there is no wisdom, no insight, and no plan that can succeed against God (Prov. 21:30). Job describes God as possessing wisdom (*hokmah*) and strength (*geburah*) and having forethought or plans (*etzah*) and understanding (*binah*). In other words, God understands Job completely; he has insight into the man's personal nature, his current situation and dilemma, and his ability to deal with his problems. In addition, he knows what needs to be done, and he possesses the power to determine Job's future (Job 12:13).

Jesus possessed this power. In his earthly ministry he worked in the power of the Holy Spirit (John 4:14); and following his resurrection, he proclaimed that he had been given all power and authority in heaven and on earth (Matt. 28:18).

Perhaps the most telling example of the power of the Messiah is found in John 10:17–18. Jesus informs his followers that his decision to sacrifice his life for others is voluntary. No person has the power to force him to die, unless he allows it to happen. At this point Jesus is no different from any other human being. We all have the power to sacrifice our lives for others, and the Bible acknowledges that such actions are honorable. "Greater love has no one than this, that one lay down his life for his friends" (John 15:13). But in the second part of John 10:17, Jesus makes a startling claim. He tells us that he is willing to lay his life down for us, but he also has the power to take it up again. Does any other person have that kind of power? The power that Jesus offers is the power that can overcome death. Jesus not only had a plan for salvation; he also possessed the power to implement the plan.

Assessment of Power in Counseling. Developing goals and objectives without the power to execute the plan is useless. We need to examine and assess the power level of our counselees. Pressing them to act when they lack the motivation, training, experience, and resources will only result in frustration, resignation, and even anger. Research has revealed that people can fall into a condition of habitual or learned helplessness.[4] After suffering constant defeat in their lives, these people simply give up. They are unable to deal with even minor problems. Ultimately all of us are driven to this state before God. We are incapable of saving ourselves. We are in a position not just of helplessness but hopelessness without God. Helplessness is closely connected to a loss of hope. Where there is no hope, the people perish, and scientific research has also revealed this principle. People who lose hope give up and die.

When we are at our wit's end, our only hope lies in the discovery of the wisdom and power of God. In the words of Oswald Chambers, "All our vows and resolutions end in denial because we have no power to carry them out. When we come to the end of ourselves, not in imaginations, but really, we are able to receive the Holy Spirit."[5]

Counselors need to assess the power level of their counselees, and they need to access the power available in Christ. Paul prayed that the Ephesian Christians would have the Spirit of wisdom and revelation to enable them to experience the hope and power available in Christ.

I ask the glorious Father and God of our Lord Jesus Christ to give you his Spirit. The Spirit will make you wise and let you understand what it means to know God. My prayer is that light will flood your hearts and that you will understand the hope that was given to you when God chose you. Then you will discover the glorious blessings that will be yours together with all of God's people.

I want you to know about the great and mighty power that God has for us followers. It is the same wonderful power he used when he raised Christ from death and let him sit at his right side in heaven. There Christ rules

114

over all forces, authorities, powers, and rulers. He rules over all beings in this world and will rule in the future world as well. God has put all things under the power of Christ, and for the good of the church has made him the head of everything. The church is Christ's body and is filled with Christ who completely fills everything (Eph. 1:17–23 CEV).

The Spirit of the Knowledge of God and the Fear of God
Knowledge of God

The Knowledge of God (Hebrew *da'ath*; LXX *gnoseos*) is a perfect understanding of the will of God. In its infinitive form the word means "to know, to have insight, realize, recognize, experience, and be acquainted with." This comprehension is a correct knowledge that sees a situation from God's point of view and reveals the way God wishes you to proceed. Jehovah is a God of knowledge, and by his justice and power, our actions are weighed (1 Sam. 2:3). God has an infinite understanding; he knows everything in the most perfect manner.

In Proverbs 2, we are told to bow our ears to wisdom (*hokmah*) and extend our hearts to understanding (*binah*). If we cry out and seek discernment (*binah*) and lift up our voices for understanding (*binah*), we will understand the fear (*yir'ath*) of Jehovah and the knowledge (*da'ath*) of God. Worship of God as the source of all wisdom and truth leads us to call upon God for all our needs. The more we know and the more we learn about God, the more his presence and knowledge overwhelm us.

Illustrations of the Knowledge of God. In 1 Kings 7:14, we find the three words, "wisdom" (*hokmah*), "understanding" (*binah*), and "knowledge" (*da'ath*), used in a single verse in reference to an artisan. The context is the construction of the temple. King Solomon has sent for Hiram from Tyre. Hiram is a skilled worker in bronze. He is described as being "filled with wisdom (*hokmah*) and understanding (*binah*) and expert knowledge (*da'ath*) for doing any work in bronze. So he came to King Solomon and performed his work."

115

Bronze is an alloy of copper and tin. The metal requires special skill and knowledge to cast. Portions of other elements can be added to the alloy, along with adjustments in heat, to produce different strengths and variations in the degrees of resistance to corrosion. The alloy was considered scarce and costly in the time of Solomon.

Our worker possessed the knowledge (*da'ath*) to do all the work in bronze. His knowledge was comprehensive and complete. He could correctly assess the steps to take in working with the metal. In other words, he had a comprehensive insight into the process of casting the bronze. He also had an understanding (*binah*) of the true nature of the metal. He knew its capabilities. He knew how to strengthen and weaken the bronze, and he was aware of its susceptibility to corrosion. In addition, he had the technical skill or wisdom (*hokmah*) to work with it (1 Kings 7:14). He understood the theory of metallurgy; he knew how to shape the bronze, and he was aware of the loads it could tolerate.

The worker in bronze with his comprehensive knowledge reminds us of the omniscience of God as the Potter who works with human clay (Job 10:9; 33:6; Isa. 29:15–16; 45:9). "But now, O LORD, You are our Father, we are the clay, and You our potter; and all of us are the work of Your hand" (Isa. 64:8). The wisdom and knowledge of God shapes and directs both individuals and entire nations (Jer. 18:6). He knows what we are capable of, and he knows our strengths and weaknesses. We have no right to challenge his wisdom and knowledge any more than a piece of clay has the right to question a potter over the design, shape, and purpose of its creation (Rom. 9:20–21).

The three Hebrew words also appear in reference to Bezalel who was appointed by God to do the intricate designs, the cutting of stones, and the carving of wood for the tabernacle and its furnishings: "I have filled him with the Spirit of God in wisdom (*hokmah*), in understanding (*binah*), in knowledge (*da'ath*), and in all kinds of craftsmanship" (Exod. 31:3). The knowledge of God enabled Bezalel to plan and design and construct key features of the tabernacle or residence of God on Earth. The words of Exodus 31:3 are repeated in Exodus 35:31 with the additional information in verse 33 that Bezalel would "perform in every inventive work." The description of Bezalel, working as master crafts-man in the power of the Spirit and knowledge of God, creating and producing designs and furnishings for the tabernacle, brings to mind another Master Carpenter (Mark 6:3)—the Messiah who would create a path to and prepare a place for all believers in an eternal tabernacle (John 14:2–3).

Jesus and the Knowledge of God. The Messiah knew and possessed the mind of God. "By His knowledge (*da'ath*) the Righteous One, My Servant, will justify the many, as He will bear their iniquities" (Isa. 53:11). Christ, the Suffering Servant, had the knowledge of saving power. He embodied the knowledge of the way, the truth, and the life (John 14:6).

We have access to the knowledge of God through our relationship to Jesus Christ and our complete dependence on the work of the Holy Spirit in our lives. The Spirit is the presence of God in us, bringing us spiritual insight as we dialogue without ceasing with him (1 Thess. 5:17). We also have the divine revelation of Scripture to reveal the knowledge of God to us.

Fear of God

The *fear of God* (Hebrew *yir'ath*; LXX *eusebeias*) is a sense of holy reverence of and respect or honor toward God. It is the loyalty and duty that we owe God by placing him first above everything else. The fear of God in its fullness represents a perfect relationship with the Creator.

"The fear (*yir'ath*) of the LORD is the beginning of knowledge (*da'ath*); fools despise wisdom (*hokmah*) and instruction" (Prov. 1:7). Wisdom and knowledge begin when God is placed first in our lives, and our entire world revolves around our worship of him. When we recognize the Lord as the Alpha and Omega, the entire alphabet, in knowledge and in power, for all time—past, present, and future (Rev. 1:8)—then we are overwhelmed by his absolute holiness and our total inadequacy (Isa. 6:3–5).

An Example from Ecclesiastes. The writer of Ecclesiastes came to understand the importance of the fear of God. He set out to study and explore all the wisdom in creation (Eccl. 1:13), but his search led him to existential despair. Everything proved to be meaningless, including the paths of pleasure and hedonism (2:1–11), intellectualism and madness or folly (2:12–16), toil and labor (2:17–26), social status (4:13–16), wealth and prosperity (5:8–12), and philosophy and science or the "scheme of things" (7:25–29 NIV). He decided that wisdom was to be preferred over physical power (9:16), but a little folly could overwhelm wisdom and honor (10:1). He learned that accumulating a wealth of human wisdom and knowledge simply increases the grief, pain, and confusion in life (Eccl. 1:13–18). His despair was alleviated by one single truth found in the final two verses of the book. If these two verses are omitted, then the writer of Ecclesiastes is left floundering in the gloomy vision we find in the agnostic and atheistic existential and postmodern philosophies of our recent history. What is the only way out of our misery and desolation? Only by fearing God, and obeying his Word or commands are we able to make sense of this world (Eccl. 12:13–14).

Jesus and the Fear of God. "The fear of Jehovah is to hate evil; I hate pride and conceit (self-love) and the evil way (deeds), and the perverse mouth" (Prov. 8:13). Godly people express their fear of the Lord by refusing to engage in sinful attitudes and actions. Jesus lived a perfect and sinless life. As such, he personified the fear of God. He was in the Father and the Father was in him (John 14:10). He was in his very nature God (Phil. 2:6–11). "I and the Father are one," he said (John 10:30). His entire life reveals to us the model of a person who never takes his eyes off the Father, an acknowledgement of the absolute holiness of God and a perfect expression of the fear and holiness of God. Christians must conduct themselves in reverence and fear of God in all their work and activities (1 Pet. 1:17–18).

True Fear Versus False Fear. The fear of God is not the same as the emotional reaction we get to creaking doors at night or childhood worries over possible monsters under the bed. Those responses trivialize godly fear. Blaise Pascal distinguished between true fear and false fear. True fear, he said, is the fear of losing God. False fear is the fear of finding God. "True fear comes from faith; false fear comes from doubt. True fear is joined to hope, because it is born of faith, and because men hope in the God in whom they believe. False fear is joined to despair, because men fear the God in whom they have no belief. The former fear to lose Him; the latter fear to find Him."[6]

False fear is found in the attitude of some people who live their entire lives as though God does not exist (Pss. 14:1; 53:1). Their behavior, attitudes, and entire lifestyle reflect an utter disregard for God. They live as though he does not exist, but they fear that perhaps he does and that eventually they will have to face him. They have a false fear of God that leads them to despair for their future. They do not believe in God, but they fear that one day they will find him and have to face his judgment.

True fear seeks God. Spirit-filled Christians cannot abide being out of the presence of God. They have a faith in God that he will always be there to meet their needs as long as they seek and obey him. When my son was about four years old, he became separated from us one day in a department store. He wandered off on his own, and for a while he was happy to get up to some mischief in a store aisle while I observed him from a distance. It did not take long for him to realize that he was alone and lost. His cry of despair conveyed a message that he was not able to put into intelligible words: "I've lost sight of my daddy." His security and his future were in jeopardy. True fear is the fear of losing sight of the Father.

In counseling we need to help people distinguish between true and godly fear and the false fears that mislead and debilitate. Fear is normally associated with distress rather than delight; however, believers who keep their focus on God and seek to obey his will find that the true fear of the Lord produces joy, happiness, and blessing (Pss. 112:1; 128:1, 4). The fear of God is life sustaining (Prov. 10:27); it leads believers to walk with integrity, confidence, and hope (Prov. 14:2, 26; 23:17–18), and it is one of the benefits of humility (Prov. 22:4).

The terms used to describe the Messiah reveal the comprehensive nature of God and provide us with a complete vision for a caregiving ministry. Wisdom and understanding address the theoretical and intellectual aspects in counseling, and they have a particular application to how we should comprehend and relate to *others* and the world. Knowledge or counsel and power deal with practical matters and the more internal and personal issues of the individual or *self*. The knowledge and fear of God focus on our dependence on *God* and emphasize his absolute authority and ultimate importance in every situation.

Summary

The Messiah provides counselors with a comprehensive and perfect model of caregiving. Jesus is the Master Counselor and the focal point of Christian counseling. The Messianic model and the example of Christ in his earthly ministry give us insights into a counseling ministry that addresses the relationship of the individual to God, self, and others. Biblical Christian counseling has six elements:

1. Biblical Christian counseling has a complete theory of human nature that covers time and history, the temporal and the eternal, and the spiritual and the material. Christian counselors seek the wisdom of God and recognize that each person has value in the sight of God, and each action or behavior can have eternal significance.
2. Biblical Christian counseling seeks to understand the unique elements, individuality, and interconnecting influences related to the person in need. It looks beyond superficial and surface observations and addresses the heart and character of individuals and the role of visible and invisible forces at work in a given situation.
3. Biblical Christian counseling develops plans and looks for the design and counsel of God in every situation. It accurately evaluates conditions and events and assists counselees to develop and implement a therapeutic and redemptive course of action. It accepts that the only successful course of planning and treatment is the one that follows the will of God.
4. Biblical Christian counseling assesses the power level or the ability to produce change in the counselee, and it seeks connection with the power of God. Treatment plans are matched with the spiritual, intellectual, cognitive, behavioral, and affective capacities of the individual in need.

5. Biblical Christian counseling is dependent on divine guidance and knowledge. Christian counselors seek the will of God in every counseling situation, and they rely upon the empowering leadership and control of the Holy Spirit.

6. Biblical Christian counseling acknowledges our complete and unconditional dependence on God for our existence and continued survival. Christian counselors worship God and desire communion with his Spirit. They live in a reverence of God and in holy fear of ever losing sight of him. They desire to represent and to reveal him in their caregiving ministry.

Where Do We Go from Here?

Biblical Christian counseling has a specific structure. It is based on the model of Christ, and it seeks to express the Greatest Commandment. The contents of the counseling process must also be addressed in terms of communication skills and the maintenance of a biblical perspective in which problems and situations are viewed through the eyes of faith. The next chapter will examine some of these issues.

Questions and Exercises for Reflection

1. In what ways is modern counseling different from the use of the term *counselor* in Scripture?

2. Identify and describe some additional examples of the six counseling elements in the ministry of Jesus.

3. What are some other principles or foundations for models of counseling that could be derived from Scripture? Identify and describe them.

4. What do you believe are the essential features in a counseling treatment plan?

5. How would you describe the six features of counseling to a non-Christian? Give a brief description of the way you might communicate the meaning and purpose of biblical Christian counseling to the person.

References

Alexander, Joseph Addison. *The Earlier Prophecies of Isaiah*. New York: Wiley & Putnam, 1846.

Chambers, Oswald. *My Utmost for His Highest*. New York: Dodd, Mead & Company, 1935.

Pascal, Blaise. *Pensèes and the Provincial Letters*. New York: The Modern Library, 1941.

Martin E. P. Seligman. *Helplessness: On Depression, Development, and Death*. San Francisco: W. H. Freeman & Company, 1975.

Young, Edward J. *The Book of Isaiah: The English Text, with Introduction, Exposition, and Notes*. In the New International Commentary on the Old Testament. Edited by R. K. Harrison. Grand Rapids, Mich.: William. B. Eerdmans, 1965.

Endnotes

1 One Jewish version of Isaiah 9:6 transliterates the name in the verse as "And his name is called Pele-joez-el-gibbor-Abi-ad-sar-shalom." The footnote giving an English translation captures the counseling focus of the verse: "That is, *Wonderful in counsel is God the Mighty, the Everlasting Father, the Ruler of Peace.*" See *The Holy Scriptures According to the Masoretic Text: A New Translation* (Philadelphia: The Jewish Publication Society of America, 1917).

2 See, e.g., Joseph Addison Alexander, *The Earlier Prophecies of Isaiah* (New York: Wiley and Putnam, 1846), 220; and Edward J. Young, *The Book of Isaiah: The English Text, with Introduction, Exposition, and Notes,* in the New International Commentary on the Old Testament, ed. R. K. Harrison (Grand Rapids, Mich.: William B. Eerdmans, 1965), 380–81.

3 LXX refers to the Septuagint, a Greek translation of the Old Testament.

4 Martin E. P. Seligman, *Helplessness: On Depression, Development, and Death* (San Francisco: W. H. Freeman and Company, 1975), 21–44.

5 Oswald Chambers, *My Utmost for His Highest* (New York: Dodd, Mead & Company, 1935), 5.

6 Blaise Pascal, *Pensèes and the Provincial Letters* (New York: The Modern Library, 1941), 92 (Pensèe #262).

7

COMMUNICATION AND BIBLICAL
CHRISTIAN COUNSELING

Reading the Signs and the Language of Counseling
Communication and Gender
Biblical Principles in Communication
Communication and the Use of Scripture in Counseling

The language you use as a counselor and the focus of your attention in the counseling encounter will either strengthen or undermine the healing process. Wise counselors carefully observe both verbal and nonverbal messages as they learn the language of the person in need. They are also competent students of Scripture. They communicate the Word of God in ways that counselees clearly understand.

The Bible reminds us of the importance of carefully choosing our words in order to avoid problems (Prov. 21:23). "Make your words good—you will be glad you did. Words can bring death or life! Talk too much, and you will eat everything you say" (Prov. 18:20–21 CEV). The ability to observe and read an individual can lead to significant changes, for good or evil, in that person's life. The book of Proverbs describes a woman who was adept at discerning the needs and weaknesses in a man, and she used her knowledge and skill with words to lead him astray.

From the window of my house, I once happened to see
    some foolish young men.
It was late in the evening, sometime after dark.

One of these young men turned the corner and was walking by the house of an unfaithful wife.

She was dressed fancy like a woman of the street with
only one thing in mind.

She was one of those women who are loud and restless and
never stay at home,

who walk street after street, waiting to trap a man.

She grabbed him and kissed him, and with no sense of
shame said:

"I had to offer a sacrifice, and there is enough meat left
over for a feast.

So I came looking for you, and here you are!

The sheets of my bed are bright-colored cloth from
Egypt.

And I have covered it with perfume made of myrrh, aloes,
and cinnamon.

"Let's go there and make love all night. My husband is
traveling, and he's far away.

He took a lot of money along, and he won't be back home
before the middle of the month."

And so, she tricked him with all of her sweet talk and her
flattery.

Right away he followed her like an ox on the way to be
slaughtered,

or like a fool on the way to be punished and killed with
arrows.

He was no more than a bird rushing into a trap,

without knowing it would cost him his life (Prov. 7:6–23
CEV).

The woman had a clear mission in mind, and she dressed to attract the
man she desired. Notice how her actions and her choice of words reinforced her intentions. She kissed him provocatively, and she shamelessly
offered herself to him. She used male language and thought processes

effectively to manipulate the man. "The way to a man's heart is through his stomach" the saying goes, and so she promised him the finest food. Her words are blunt, explicit, and erotic. They are the speech of a woman in a male's sexual fantasies. She flattered him as she stroked his ego and told him how special he was. Her final enticement was the promise of secrecy and safety. This woman was an expert in male communication. She persuaded the man to follow her by connecting with him in all his vulnerable areas: food, sensual and provocative words, sexual imagination and actions, flattery, and the promise of something forbidden along with security from discovery. Her speech was not that of a formal, austere, academic discourse. She spoke the man's language in the bluntest possible terms. Unfortunately, she used her communication skills for sinful rather than moral purposes.

Reading the Signs and the Language of Counseling

Counseling textbooks are filled with theories, concepts, techniques, and technical terms describing the process of psychotherapy. The person in need is called a client, a counselee, or an identified patient. Theories are divided into psychodynamic, behavioral, existential or phenomenological, cognitive, systems, social constructionist, and postmodern. Techniques are categorized as directive, nondirective, person centered, problem centered, and solution focused. An entire vocabulary of technical terms and concepts has been developed along with the institutionalization and professionalization of the caregiving industry.

The important thing to remember is that the textbooks on psychotherapy are written for counselors, and they speak a formal language appropriate for an academic world. These words and phrases are not in the vocabulary of the average person coming to you for counseling. The concepts behind this formal language reflect beliefs, research, and ideas about how best to help people in need and how to locate people and intervene effectively to produce a desired change. But these terms are not the language of counseling for the person in need, and it is the language of the people who are seeking your help that should determine the words and idioms you use in a counseling situation.

Counselors must read the signs that tell them how to communicate most effectively with people in need. Some of these signs include background and occupation, interests and hobbies, educational level, age, gender, economic status, marital status and family, emotional and rational state, physical health, spiritual condition and faith development, time orientation, decision-making abilities, stress indicators and reactions, and ability to handle change.

How would you counsel the man in the following case?

A Case Study on Communication

You are counseling a man who holds the highest political office in the land. You are aware that the man is engaged in immoral behavior. As a representative of God, you believe that you must address the sin, but you are also aware that the man has the power to destroy you professionally and possibly even to take your life. How do you proceed? What signs and clues do you look for that will help you to locate the man and communicate in a language that is therapeutic and redemptive? The prophet Nathan faced this dilemma.

King David had become enamored with Bathsheba. His infatuation led him to conspire to have her husband killed in battle, freeing her to marry him. His actions displeased God, so he sent Nathan to counsel and rebuke him (2 Sam. 11–12). Nathan had to decide how he was going to broach this delicate, potentially dangerous subject with David.

Nathan could have charged into the king's presence with his verbal guns blazing and confronted David with his sin. He could have taken a position of righteous indignation as he quoted from the Law and the Decalogue and exposed the adultery and the murderous plot. Nathan chose not to take this approach.

Was Nathan being weak, unbiblical, and indecisive by not dealing with the issue in a frank and straightforward manner? Nathan had obviously studied David's history and personality. The king's actions, including his deceit and adultery, told the prophet that he might not be willing to listen to reason. A direct approach could lead to anger and a violent response from David. Instead the prophet used his wisdom, knowledge, and communication skills to tell the king a story.

Nathan told a tale about a wealthy man in a village who possessed large holdings of sheep and cattle. In the same town lived a poor man who had only one ewe lamb that he had raised and cared for as though it were one of his own children. One day a traveler visited the rich man. A feast was prepared, but rather than take from his own livestock, the rich man took his poor neighbor's only lamb to provide a meal for the visitor.

The story and the injustice outraged David, as Nathan knew it would. The prophet understood David's nature. He was aware of the king's basic integrity. David had always tried to deal fairly with Saul and his family and give wise leadership to his people. Nathan also knew that as a young boy, David had tended his father's sheep (1 Sam. 16:11). David was acquainted with the life of a shepherd, and he could empathize with a family who had a pet lamb. Nathan used this knowledge to full effect in the story he told.

David declared that the rich man deserved to die for his unjust actions and lack of pity and that the poor man should be repaid fourfold. At this point Nathan revealed that David was the man, and he spelled out in detail the nature of the king's sins and the penalty determined by the Lord. David confessed and repented of his sin. He would not die, but his actions would have consequences.

Nathan's approach reveals some important counseling skills. He was able to connect with the king on a number of levels. He used the language of storytelling to convey a volatile message to David in a way that allowed the king to indict himself. His story used imagery that was familiar to David and made him comfortable. No terms or concepts needed an explanation. His approach revealed an awareness of David's emotional state and his sensitivity, as well as his sense of justice and fairness. This method might not have worked with another king like Ahab or a queen like Jezebel, although one prophet did use a story and a disguise to have Ahab pronounce judgment upon himself (1 Kings 20:37–43).

Paul's Advice on Communication

Another example of the importance of language and style of communication is found in Paul's epistle to Timothy (1 Tim. 5:1–2). Paul's instructions to Timothy contain some wise counseling tips about age, gender, and manner of speech in pastoral ministry. Timothy is a young minister, and his age is a factor in effective communication with other people. Paul tells him that he should allow no one to demean or dismiss him because of his age and that he should be a godly model for others in his speech, lifestyle, love, faith, and purity. He also tells Timothy that age and gender are important factors in selecting his manner of speech.

Paul was older than Timothy, and he often wrote in a manner that was direct and challenging to the members of the church, but he did not advise the younger man to adopt this style of communication in his own ministry. In fact, Paul intimated, in an epistle to the Corinthians, that his confrontational style in his letter writing was not always characteristic of his approach when he talked to the brethren in person. Some of Paul's opponents had criticized him for being too timid when he was with the church members. Paul reminded the Corinthians that he preferred to emulate the meekness and gentleness of Christ when he was face-to-face with them although, when necessary, he could be bold and direct (2 Cor. 10:1–2,10; 11:6).

Don't use confrontational language with an older man, he tells Timothy; rather speak to him as you would your father, using words of encouragement and support. Paul uses the word *parakaleo* to describe the speech to use with the elderly. The term conveys the image of a counselor drawing alongside an older man and making comments that suggest rather than demand change. In contrast, a more informal, familiar, and easygoing language is implied in Paul's advice that Timothy treat the younger men like his brothers. Older women should be addressed with the words of deference and the respect reserved for a mother while younger women should be treated with the same honor and familial love and concern you would express toward a sister.

Communication and Gender

One example of the differences in communication style that counselors need to be aware of is in gender. Men and women use different words, mean different things when they speak, and have different motives in their conversations. It is true that most men do not like to ask for directions, and most women do not understand why men don't like to ask for directions. In fact, most men probably are unable to explain this dislike.

Research has revealed that men tend to see everyday encounters as competitive situations. Asking for help places the man in a subordinate position; the other person is one-up on him. Consequently, a man will go to great lengths to avoid the one-down position, the subordinate status that historically reflects the female in our culture. This observation also explains why women are more likely than men to seek out counseling. Women are socialized into the subordinate position, and they are expected to ask for help. Women will even ask for assistance when they don't need it.

There are other differences between men and women in communication style.

Men are more likely to interrupt, talk over the other person, and ignore others' words. They speak authoritatively regardless of the subject. Women are interrupted more in conversation. They tend to be super-polite ("Could you possibly pick up a few items for me after work?"); they use hedge words or speak in tentative terms (e.g., "maybe," "sort of," "I think," "I guess"); and they tend to question rather than command ("Would you help me with the laundry, please?" not "Wash the clothes").

Men are taught the language of power, control, and domination. Men use commands to get what they want. They communicate to persuade, argue, control, or impress. Women learn the language of negotiation and the importance of seeking solidarity and consensus. Women use requests to get what they want. They communicate to share, inform, support, or ingratiate.

Men use more active sentence construction. They use pauses in sentences for emphasis. Women use more passive sentence construction. They use intensifiers (e.g., so, very, really) for emphasis.

Men emphasize talking rather than listening in conversations. They are more likely to use complete sentences. Women emphasize listening and sharing in conversations. They tend to let sentences dwindle to incompletion. This tactic leaves them an out should their view or opinion be unpopular; and it has the effect of granting another person the same right to speak—not dominating a conversation.

Men speak mostly in monotone. Women use a variety of tones of voice to convey emotion and meaning.

Men display feelings indirectly. Women verbalize feelings directly.

Some jargon and specialized vocabularies are male oriented. The language of business reflects its competitive nature and the concern for one's own well-being (e.g., taking a power lunch, hostile takeover, aggressive). Some jargon and specialized vocabularies are female oriented. The language of nursing is mostly female, reflecting compassionate care and concern for the other's well-being. Doctors fight a disease; nurses care for a patient.

Men talk to other men about "external" matters (e.g., business, music, politics, sports, facts). Men stress how-to elements in their conversations. Women talk to other women about internal matters (e.g., emotions, feelings, relationships, love life).

Men are action oriented; they use and respond to actions and use factual language when communicating. Women are verbally oriented; they rely on and respond to emotional and evaluative words when communicating.

Men call someone if they have something in particular to say or discuss. Women call their friends for no particular reason, just to chat.[1]

The differences between men and women in gender-role socialization and language are significant, and counselors need to be aware of their own language development and predisposition, as well as the communication styles and idiosyncrasies of the people who come to them for help.

Biblical Principles in Communication

The Bible warns us about the volatility of language and the difficulty we have in controlling our tongue. "It takes only a spark to start a forest fire! The tongue is like a spark. It is an evil power that dirties the rest of the body and sets a person's entire life on fire with flames that come from hell itself. All kinds of animals, birds, reptiles, and sea creatures can be tamed and have been tamed. But our tongues get out of control. They are restless and evil, and always spreading deadly poison" (James 3:5b–8 CEV). Our tongues are capable of both blessing and cursing, of praising God and cursing other people who are created in his image (James 3:9–10). Restraint and cautious words are far more likely to lead to a happy life than devious talk. For "whoever would love life and see good days must keep his tongue from evil and his lips from deceitful speech" (1 Pet. 3:10 NIV).

The Scriptures provide us with some additional guidance for improving our communication skills.

1. Be an attentive listener, and do not interrupt or answer until the other person has finished speaking. When we were children, we were taught to speak, but few of us have been trained to listen to other people and fewer still to listen to the Spirit of God. Yet these two dimensions of listening are essential to effective counseling. "He who gives an answer before he hears, it is folly and shame to him" (Prov. 18:13). "My dear brothers, take note of this: Everyone should be quick to listen, slow to speak and slow to become angry" (James 1:19 NIV).

2. Pay particular attention to people who are seeking God. Listen for indications that a person desires to communicate with the Lord and depend on him. "I love the Lord, for he heard my voice; he heard my cry for mercy. Because he turned his ear to me, I will call on him as long as I live" (Ps. 116:1–2 NIV).

3. Be slow to speak. Think first. Don't be hasty in your words. Speak in such a way that the other person can understand and accept what you say. "There is more hope for a fool than for someone who speaks without thinking" (Prov. 29:20 CEV). "Good people think

before they answer, but the wicked speak evil without ever thinking" (Prov. 15:28 CEV). "Without good advice everything goes wrong—it takes careful planning for things to go right. Giving the right answer at the right time makes everyone happy" (Prov. 15:22–23 CEV). "Watching what you say can save you a lot of trouble" (Prov. 21:23 CEV).

4. Listen to all sides in a situation before making up your mind. "The first to present his case seems right, till another comes forward and questions him" (Prov. 18:17 NIV).

5. Listen for evidence of wisdom. Does the person learn only through fear of punishment, or is the counselee an apt pupil who exercises creative thinking and prudent judgment? "An ignorant fool learns by seeing others punished; a sensible person learns by being instructed" (Prov. 21:11 CEV).

6. Do not mislead or lie in your conversation. Always speak the truth in a loving way. "Instead, speaking the truth in love" (Eph. 4:15 NIV). "Therefore each of you must put off falsehood and speak truthfully to his neighbor" (Eph. 4:25 NIV). "Do not lie to one another, since you laid aside the old self with its evil practices" (Col. 3:9 NASB). "Simply let your 'Yes' be 'Yes,' and your 'No,' 'No'; anything beyond this comes from the evil one" (Matt. 5:37 NIV).

7. Avoid disputes and arguments. It is possible to disagree without quarreling. "The start of an argument is like a water leak—so stop it before real trouble breaks out" (Prov. 17:14 CEV). "It makes you look good when you avoid a fight—only fools love to quarrel" (Prov. 20:3 CEV). "Let us behave decently . . . not in dissension" (Rom. 13:13 NIV).

8. Avoid angry responses that trigger emotional outbursts. Use words that are kind and supportive. "It's smart to be patient, but it's stupid to lose your temper" (Prov. 14:29 CEV). "A fool gives full vent to his anger, but a wise man keeps himself under control" (Prov. 29:11 NIV). "Don't get so angry that you sin" (Eph. 4:26 CEV). "Stop being bitter and angry and mad at others. Don't yell at one another or curse each other or ever be rude" (Eph. 4:31 CEV). "A kind answer

soothes angry feelings, but harsh words stir them up" (Prov. 15:1 CEV). "Patience and gentle talk can convince a ruler and overcome any problem" (Prov. 25:15 CEV).

9. When you are wrong, admit it and ask for forgiveness. Not only is this the right thing to do; it also provides a positive model for others. Use the language of godly love and forgiveness. "If you have sinned, you should tell each other what you have done. Then you can pray for one another and be healed. The prayer of an innocent person is powerful, and it can help a lot" (James 5:16 CEV). "Instead, be kind and merciful, and forgive others, just as God forgave you because of Christ" (Eph. 4:32 CEV). "Bear with each other, and forgive whatever grievances you may have against one another. Forgive as the Lord forgave you" (Col. 3:13 NIV). "Most important of all, you must sincerely love each other, because love wipes away many sins" (1 Pet. 4:8 CEV).

10. Avoid faultfinding, blame, and criticism. Instead, focus on restoration, encouragement, and edification in your language. "Therefore let us not judge one another anymore, but rather determine this—not to put an obstacle or a stumbling block in a brother's way" (Rom. 14:13). "My friends, you are spiritual. So if someone is trapped in sin, you should gently lead that person back to the right path. But watch out, and don't be tempted yourself" (Gal. 6:1 CEV).

Communication and the Use of Scripture in Counseling

Christian counselors are ambassadors representing God in caregiving. Successful ambassadors must be able to understand both the context and the nature of the people they address and the message they bring. In other words, counseling ambassadors for Christ are expected to know God and his message of reconciliation (2 Cor. 5:20), be in constant communication with him (1 Thess. 5:17), identify people's needs, communicate clearly and appropriately, and render therapeutic aid (Luke 10:25–37). Knowing the Word of God is crucial to this enterprise.

Be living letters of God. Christian counselors must be living letters of God. You may be the only letter from God that a person has the opportunity to receive and read (2 Cor. 3:3). Christian counselors must walk in the Word of God and speak and act in a godly manner. They must be models of a healthy Christian life.

Memorize the Word of God. More importantly, hide it in your heart. What is the difference? Sometimes students study for tests by trying to remember a word or a phrase, but they have no understanding of the meaning, concept, context, or purpose underlying the word or phrase. Such students are like people who have "eyes to see but do not see, ears to hear but do not hear" (Ezek. 12:2; Mark 8:18). Successful counseling in the eyes of God is not measured by how often you are able to quote a series of words from a translation of the Bible (or even cite them in Hebrew, Aramaic, or Greek) in a session (although God can even use our blunders and mistakes for good [cf. Gen. 50:20)]). To hide God's Word in your heart is to have it continually present with you as a motivating power under the direction of the Holy Spirit, not as outward show drawing attention to your personal piety. "Your Word do I hide—treasure up—in my heart, that I may not sin against You" (Ps. 119:11). "I have not strayed from God's commands," said Job. "I have treasured His words—they are more essential than my basic need for food" (Job 23:12). The message you convey from God reaches into the hearts of people, just as it has been written on your own heart (2 Cor. 3:2). We must always be sensitive to the direction and intercession of the Holy Spirit, recognizing that communicating with God and revealing him to others may require more than spoken words (Rom. 8:26–28).

Translate the healing message of God into the language of the people. Learn the language of the people in need. Be willing to do the adjusting yourself, rather than expecting counselees to change to meet your needs (1 Cor. 9:19–23). Speak words they understand at their point of need as they define it.

Examine alternative views and translations of Scripture. As you study the biblical and theological resources and various translations and interpretations of Scripture, you will increase your understanding and avoid lapsing into spiritual smugness and boasting. Don't just listen to and read other people who support your opinions on counseling and then commend yourself for measuring up so well to them (2 Cor. 10:12–13). Become a thorough student of the Word with competent hermeneutical skills. Consult and use concordances, Bible dictionaries, and lexicons in your Bible study, and compare observations from different commentaries when possible.

Do not confuse personal interpretations, preferences, and agendas with the Word of God. Books on biblical and Christian counseling contain a wealth of insights and helpful materials on caregiving. The value of these resources must be tempered by an awareness of the temptation to lock into a particular theory, technique, theological perspective or view of a particular author and allow it to become the arbiter of truth and fellowship. One effect of this tendency is that the Bible is used to support the "law" or the acceptable counseling criteria of an individual, and freedom in Christ is lost.

Oswald Chambers warns us to beware of people who use the Bible for their own ends. He challenges us to "stand fast therefore in the liberty wherewith Christ hath made us free" (Gal. 5:1).

> A spiritually minded man will never come to you with the demand—"Believe this and that;" but with the demand that you square your life with the standards of Jesus. We are not asked to believe the Bible, but to believe the One Whom the Bible reveals (cf. John 5:39–40). We are called to present liberty of conscience, not liberty of view. If we are free with the liberty of Christ, others will be brought into that same liberty—the liberty of realizing the dominance of Jesus Christ.
>
> Always keep your life measured by the standards of Jesus. Bow your neck to His yoke alone, and to no other yoke whatever; and be careful to see that you never bind a yoke on others that is not placed by Jesus Christ. It takes God a long time to get us out of the way of thinking that unless everyone sees as we do, they must be wrong. That is never God's view. There is only one liberty, the liberty of Jesus at work in our conscience enabling us to do what is right.

Don't get impatient, remember how God dealt with you—with patience and with gentleness; but never water down the truth of God. Let it have its way and never apologize for it. Jesus said, "Go and make *disciples*," not "make converts to your opinions."[2]

Competence and adequacy in Christian counseling ultimately come from God. Focus on relationship with God and his presence, not on rules and the letter of the law. We are to reflect God's glory and lead people into freedom not bondage. Be competent guides in that enterprise (2 Cor. 3:5–6).

In addition to skills in communication and biblical competence, Christian counselors must learn to look for the activity of God in people's lives. Discernment and sensitivity to the Spirit of God will enable counselors to look at situations that appear to be hopeless and help them to extract the precious from the worthless.

Summary

1. Christian counselors need to develop therapeutic communication skills. Counselors must be conversant not just with the technical language of their counseling field but, in particular, with the vocabulary of the person in need.
2. The Bible warns against intemperate language, and it gives some basic principles and examples of good communication skills in counseling.
3. Competent Christian counselors live godly lives. They memorize Scriptures, and they thoroughly study the Word of God. They carefully and accurately communicate it, using words that are clearly understood.
4. Christian counselors avoid using the Bible to further their personal interests and preferences. Rejecting legalism, they lead people into a living relationship with God.

Where Do We Go from Here?

Christian counselors help people to find their location in relationship to God, self, and others. They try to model the example of Christ, the

Master Counselor, as they engage in the theory and practice of care-giving. The Greatest Commandment gives them guidance as they seek to serve others by learning the idiosyncrasies and particular forms of communication unique to the person in need. They carefully study and share the Word of God. The next chapter will help counselors to develop a biblical perspective or focus in counseling by learning to "extract the precious from the worthless."

Questions and Exercises for Reflection

1. What are the most important communication skills in Christian counseling? Identify and describe five skills necessary for effective counseling. Give biblical references where appropriate.
2. Find a biblical example of communication skills other than the ones described in this chapter. Discuss the skills and explain how they can be applied in Christian counseling.
3. Under what conditions would you pray or read Scripture with a person in counseling? How would you pray or read the Scripture? Give some examples. What guidelines would you be careful to employ, and what would you avoid?
4. Identify some examples of inappropriate or incorrect interpretations of Scripture that might lead to poor counseling.
5. List ways that you plan to avoid legalism in counseling and, instead, lead people into freedom in Christ.

References

Chambers, Oswald. *My Utmost for His Highest.* New York: Dodd, Mead & Company, 1935.

Tannen, Deborah. *You Just Don't Understand: Women and Men in Conversation.* New York: Ballantine Books, 1990.

Endnotes

1 Deborah Tannen, *You Just Don't Understand: Women and Men in Conversation* (New York: Ballantine Books, 1990).

2 Oswald Chambers, *My Utmost for His Highest* (New York: Dodd, Mead & Company, 1935), 127.

8

EXTRACTING THE PRECIOUS
FROM THE WORTHLESS

Developing a Biblical Perspective
Freedom and Our Identity in Christ
Learning to Search for the Hand of God
Examples of Extracting the Precious from the Worthless

I n addition to skills in communication and biblical competence, Christian counselors must learn to look for the activity of God in people's lives. Discernment and sensitivity to the Spirit of God will enable counselors to look at situations that appear to be hopeless and help them to "extract the precious from the worthless."

Developing a Biblical Perspective

Jeremiah was upset. This attitude was not unusual for the prophet. An entire book of the Bible is filled with his lamentations, and his personality has been recognized in English literature with the term *jeremiad,* coined as a description of a sad and melancholy complaint. Jeremiah had been proclaiming the word of the Lord, and now he was depressed. In Jeremiah 15, he protests to God about his situation. He states that he has acted honorably, yet everyone opposes him. He has obeyed God, but instead of praise and peace, all he receives for his efforts are curses and grief. His very birth has become a questionable event (Jer. 15:10).

Jeremiah has a suggestion and a solution for God. First, God should remember how much he has suffered for him. He has spent his time devouring the words of God, all alone, while other people went to parties and engaged in revelry. He is filled with righteous indignation. He feels the pain of an apparently incurable wound, and he wonders if God really cares. Jeremiah contends that if God really does remember him and does care for him, then he will do something about the situation. Jeremiah's solution, and the sign of care that he wants from God, is that his persecutors will be destroyed (Jer. 15:15–18).

The response Jeremiah receives from God is unexpected. Rather than agree with Jeremiah's assessment of the situation, God tells him to repent. Jeremiah is no longer acting as a prophet of God. In the New American Standard Bible (1995), an interesting turn of phase in Jeremiah 15:19 captures the expectation God has for his prophet. God tells Jeremiah that he must "extract the precious from the worthless"; only then will he allow him to be his spokesman again. What does this phrase mean, and how do we "extract the precious from the worthless" in life?

The image used in the passage is of refining metal where the pure metal is separated from the other elements that taint it. But what is this pure or precious metal? The phrase does not mean Jeremiah has failed to deliver God's message to the people. The context tells us that the prophet has been faithful in proclaiming the word of the Lord. Also, God is not telling Jeremiah that he must limit his message only to people who are responsive to his word and that the godly people must be separated from the sinners. Another possible interpretation is that Jeremiah has been mixing God's word with man's word, but there is no evidence supporting this conclusion. "The idea that Jeremiah presented man's word for God's word, or God's word mixed with spurious, human additions, is utterly foreign to the context; nay, rather it was just because he declared only what God imposed on him that he was so hard bested."[1] In fact, the problem Jeremiah is having that has led to God's withdrawing his mantle as prophet is not due to any failure at all to deliver God's message to the people.

Jeremiah's problem is that he has lost his focus. He has begun to define his current condition in terms of his horizontal relationship with others, and his relationship to God has shifted to one of secondary importance. Consequently, his words and his suggested solution to his problem are imprudent at best and show a lack of faith in God.

Impatience and anger have replaced the godly virtues of patience and love as Jeremiah has defined his world in terms of his problems and selfish desires. He was failing to see the precious things of God working in the sinful world around him.

God is giving Jeremiah the formula for freedom from pain and anxiety in his life. C. F. Keil interprets the meaning of the phrase as, "If you will have freed the things precious in you from the filth that was mixed with them, if you will have freed the virtues which you have from the stains of impatience and wrath."[2] Like a prospector separating precious gold from worthless dross and an assayer determining the quality of the treasure, Jeremiah must draw out the empowering and valuable truths of God and distinguish them from the frivolous and distracting elements. He must learn to seek out and focus on God in the midst of his problems. When we focus on God, we discover the things that are precious to God; and we find the godly qualities, virtues, and attitudes necessary to overcome. We are able to understand fully this perspective only if we have exchanged the identity of the old Adam for the identity of Christ, the new Adam, which brings new life and new power and freedom to deal with formerly impossible situations.

Freedom and Our Identity in Christ

"Therefore if anyone is in Christ, *he is* a new creature; the old things passed away; behold, new things have come" (2 Cor. 5:17). Our identity in Christ enables us to look at situations in an entirely new light. We find all our needs met in him. "And my God will supply all your needs according to His riches in glory in Christ Jesus" (Phil. 4:19). We discover a peace that soothes the soul and unites us in fellowship with God and with one another. Christ came to produce peace and unity in the Spirit, a peace that can overcome the storms and tribulation in life (Eph. 2:14–18).

The new self in Christ enables us to share his likeness and prompts us to share truth with others in an attitude of loving-kindness that encourages holy living. We are instructed by his Word that "in reference to your former manner of life, you lay aside the old self, which is being

141

corrupted in accordance with the lusts of deceit, and that you be renewed in the spirit of your mind, and put on the new self, which in the likeness of God has been created in righteousness and holiness of the truth. Therefore, laying aside falsehood, speak truth each one of you with his neighbor, for we are members of one another" (Eph. 4:24–25). The deceit that has been practiced since the time of Adam is set aside, and our new identities and godly wisdom lead us to seek the precious truth of God in every situation and motivate us to serve our neighbor. We are able to extract the precious from the worthless.

Learning to Search for the Hand of God

We learn to extract the precious from the worthless by looking for the hand of God in every situation. In his book *The Responsible Self*, H. Richard Niebuhr put it this way: "God is acting in all actions upon you. So respond to all actions upon you as to respond to his action."[3] In other words, when you find yourself confronted by a difficult situation, remember that God is present and that any response that you give will be directed toward God, whether you intend it to or not. This truth can have a profound effect when presented in marriage counseling and in times of conflict.

A Marriage Counseling Example

The couple were constantly bickering and arguing. "What have you done with all the money I gave you for groceries?" he demanded. "Turn sideways and look at yourself in the mirror," she retorted, "and then you'll see where all the grocery money has gone." The fighting continued over big things and small things. Occasionally, they would attempt to talk about their problems, but the discussions inevitably led to more arguments. By the time they came to the counselor, they were already talking about divorce. Both of them said that they were Christians, but their faith was not expressed in their attitudes and behavior. After they shared their problems and both said they were willing to make a commitment to build a godly marriage, the counselor made a few observations.

"You appear to have forgotten your first love," said the counselor. They had read their Bibles, and they understood that the counselor was referring not only to their first love for each other but also to their first love for God, mentioned in Revelation. The message to the church at Ephesus was blunt. The people had worked hard and persevered, but somewhere in the process of all their activities, they had lost sight of God. He was no longer the priority in their lives; they had forsaken their first love (Rev. 2:1–5). "Where are you?" God was asking this couple. "Where are you in relationship to me, and where are you in relationship to each other?"

How could this couple learn to shift their focus from the problems that beset them and begin to rebuild their relationship with God and with each other? One of the exercises the counselor asked them to do was to begin to recognize God in every conversation.

"When the tension begins to rise," he said, "I want you to remember that God is present there with you. Even if someone is yelling in your face, I want you to remember this truth and do the following exercise. Look slightly above the other person's shoulder, if it helps, and acknowledge the presence of Christ. He is looking at you, listening for your reply. He is asking you to extract the precious from the worthless. So when you respond and speak back to the other person, talk to God also, and say the words to your spouse that you believe the Lord wants to hear from you."

The Example of Paul

When Christian counselors are in the center of the will of God, they will be constantly looking for the actions of God in a situation. Paul understood this principle. After his conversion his focus shifted. Whatever things he considered valuable in the past he now viewed as worthless for the sake of knowing Christ (Phil. 3:7). "In all things," said Paul, "God works for the good of those who love him." He works in every situation to help us to grow into Christlikeness (Rom. 8:28–29 NIV). This focus enabled him to deal with people who were preaching about Christ as a means of provoking him and stirring up trouble. By keeping his eyes on God, Paul could say sincerely that he could rejoice because, regardless of the sincerity of the motives of others, Christ was still being proclaimed (Phil. 1:15–18). Paul had learned to extract the precious from the worthless.

Paul encouraged the Philippians also to focus their attention on "whatever is noble, whatever is right, whatever is pure, whatever is lovely, whatever is admirable, anything excellent or praiseworthy" (Phil. 4:8). A focus on these godly virtues can have profound, life-changing, and even life-saving implications.

Part of God's work in times of conflict and crisis is to create something new in a situation. Christian counselors must not focus only on the cause of problems and overlook the redemptive possibilities whereby God is revealing his grace and creating a new vision of hope for those people who love him (Rom. 8:28). God's message to Isaiah is appropriate here: "Do not call to mind the former things, or ponder things of the past. Behold, I will do something new" (Isa. 43:18–19).

There are numerous cases of people who have learned to extract the precious from the worthless. The following section will give you a few examples from Scripture, church history, and more recent times.

Examples of Extracting the Precious from the Worthless
A Story of Elijah and Elisha

Our perception of events in our lives shapes our emotions and our responses. What we believe will direct the path we take. In a comparison of life-threatening events in the lives of Elijah and Elisha, we see an example of how our view of the world can change when our perspective shifts and we fail to listen to God.

In 1 Kings 19 we find Elijah running in fear from Jezebel, who has threatened to kill him. In the previous chapter we read that Elijah had triumphantly beaten the prophets of Baal on Mount Carmel, by calling upon God to consume with fire his water-soaked sacrifice on the altar. Now we find him fleeing into the desert and begging to die. Elijah exhibits signs of emotional flooding and catastrophizing as his problems overwhelm him. What has brought about the sudden change in his attitude in the course of just one chapter in the Bible?

144

The context makes clear that God has not abandoned Elijah. He provides food and water for the prophet in response to his needs, but Elijah still does not feel safe, and so he hides in a cave. While he is in the cave, God comes to him and asks him why he is hiding there (1 Kings 19:9). Elijah's response gives us an insight into someone who has shifted focus from the precious provision of God and now feels engulfed and consumed by the evil and worthless in the world. Elijah highlights all that has gone wrong in his life (v. 10):

- "I did my best." (But it wasn't good enough.)
- "The people are still disobeying." (They won't listen to me.)
- "The have killed everyone like me." (I'm all alone.)
- "They are going to kill me" (The situation is hopeless.)

He is catastrophizing his situation. God reveals his presence and again asks Elijah why he is there (vv. 11–12). Elijah repeats his fears and his reasoning: I did my best. Nobody listened to me. They kill people who take my position. They will kill me.

In response God presents his view of the situation (vv. 15–18), and in the process he provides a model of crisis intervention.

1. *Identify the facts.* God gave Elijah the facts: You are not alone; seven thousand have refused to worship Baal.
2. *Set a realistic goal.* God gave Elijah a goal of returning from where he had come and destroying his opponents.
3. *Develop a practical plan and identify power resources.* A plan is included with the goal. Elijah will anoint Hazael king over Aram, Jehu king over Israel, and Elisha to succeed him as prophet. Together these people will rid the country of the idolaters.
4. *Implement the plan.* This step emphasized the importance of action. Elijah leaves the cave and sets out on his mission.
5. *Have a support system.* God has displayed his support for Elijah in practical ways, and he gives him Elisha for further assistance (v. 21).

Elijah had shifted his focus from God to the genuine dangers that threatened his life. His faith in God slipped as his fear increased. He lacked food and water—the essentials of physical survival, which exacerbated his weakened physical and emotional state—and his sense of isolation led him to exaggerate his conditions and to believe that he was all alone. He feared that his situation was hopeless.

The intervention was designed to shift the prophet's focus back to God and increase his sense of security and safety. Elijah was challenged once again to extract the precious things of God—his blessing, presence, protection, plan, promises, and provision—from the worthless and corrupt forces in the world that would seek to destroy him. His shift in perspective brought him peace of mind and a renewed purpose in life and additional spiritual and social support.

Elisha joined Elijah in his prophetic mission. The strength of Elisha's support is revealed when God prepares to take Elijah up to heaven. At least three times Elisha swears that he will stay with Elijah and never abandon him (2 Kings 2:1–6). As Elijah is taken into heaven, Elisha seeks and receives a double portion of his spirit (2 Kings 2:9–15). This double empowerment will be put to an important use when Elisha finds himself caught in a life-threatening situation similar to his predecessor's (2 Kings 6:8–23). This time the perspective and the outcome will be different.

The people of Dothan awoke one morning to find their city surrounded by Syrian troops (2 Kings 6:8–23). The king of Aram or Syria had discovered that Elisha was responsible for warning the king of Israel about the position of his military camps and the plans of his army. The enraged king sent his best troops out to surround the city at night and capture Elisha. Like Elijah before him, Elisha found himself pursued by a mortal enemy. Most people in his position would be quaking in fear. He knew that the king was coming for him and that his adversaries encircled him, but he did not respond in the same way as Elijah.

One person did panic in the situation. Elisha's servant saw the troops and rushed to report to his master. He wanted to know what they could do about the threat to their lives. Elisha's servant was focusing on the dangers around him, and he was unable to see the precious provision of God in the circumstances. Elisha responded out of his faith in God and prayed for the Lord to open the servant's eyes. When the servant saw the problem through the eyes of the prophet, he must have been astounded. The surrounding hills were full of heavenly horses and chariots of fire. The armies of God were standing between Elisha and his enemies, protecting him and ready to respond to divine command. In the eyes of man, Elisha had a problem; but through the eyes of God, the Syrians were the ones in trouble.

As the Syrian army attacked, Elisha prayed, and God answered by blinding the soldiers. Elisha led the blind troops to Samaria where their eyes were opened and they were captured by the king of Israel. Elisha directed the king to show compassion for the soldiers by giving them food and water and allowing them to return home. Following this action, the raids on Israel ceased.

A comparison of Elijah and Elisha reveals that Elisha responded much differently to the threats of an enemy. Both Elijah and Elisha were targets of an evil plot. A violent and dangerous enemy pursued both men, but one viewed the problem through the human eyes of fear while the other saw the provision for the problem through the eyes of faith. Elijah hid in a cave; Elisha remained in his home, refusing to flee. Elijah experienced weakness and depression. Elisha was not afraid and showed a resolute faith. Elijah looked for signs of the enemy's strength and victories. Elisha looked at the signs of God's presence and protection. Elijah required the direct intervention of God to recuperate and turn defeat into victory. Elisha envisioned the victory before the enemy attacked. He was able to extract the precious from the worthless.

A Story of John the Apostle

A story about the apostle John, recorded centuries ago by the historian Eusebius, reveals the character of a man who had learned to "extract the precious from the worthless." John endured persecution and exile on the island of Patmos. After suffering for his Lord for years, he had good reasons to be discouraged, and he certainly deserved some quiet years of retirement toward the end of his life. Yet Eusebius records that the first thing John did when he returned from exile on Patmos was to travel around the region of Ephesus appointing bishops and reconciling churches.

In one city John placed a strong and enthusiastic youth under the care of the local bishop. The bishop raised the boy in his own house and eventually baptized him; however, soon after the baptism the bishop relaxed his care for the lad. He assumed that baptism would somehow protect him from evildoing. How wrong he was.

Without the strict care and guidance from the pastor, the young man became involved with the wrong crowd. He fell into a life of crime. He began to believe that he had lost his salvation, and he formed a gang of robbers. As a bold bandit leader, he surpassed them all "in violence and bloody cruelty."[4]

When John returned to the city, he was informed of the situation. It would have been easy for John to lapse into a cantankerous depression over the failure of all his hard work. He could have been angry with God for not protecting the young man. He could have joined with other church members in a discussion about all the terrible things the youth had done. I'm sure there were a number of fellow believers who were willing to share their suspicions about the lad and point out that they had predicted he would fall away. "He was just no good. I knew it when I first saw him. Rotten to the core."

Instead of analysis and recriminations, John did something remarkable that no other members of that church had attempted. He set off to find the boy. Imagine the picture: John, a giant in the church, now an old man, riding off on his horse along robber-infested trails in search of this rebellious youth—a man the local church considered worthless and had given up on. You can predict what happened next. John was set upon and captured by the robbers. He was brought before the youth, who, upon recognizing John, turned to flee in shame. But John, ignoring his own age and infirmities, ran after him, calling out: "Why are you running away from me, child—from your own father, unarmed and old? Pity me, child, don't fear me! I will give account to Christ for you and, if necessary, gladly suffer death and give my life for yours as the Lord suffered death for us. Stop! Believe! Christ sent me."[5]

The young man turned, threw down his weapons, and began to weep. John embraced him as he confessed his sins. John assured him of forgiveness, prayed with him, and kissed the lad's right hand, hidden behind his back, an instrument of so much bloodshed that he deemed it unworthy of forgiveness. "Then he led him back and did not leave him until—through prayer, fasting, and instruction—he had restored him to the church: a great example of true repentance and regeneration, the trophy of a visible resurrection."[6]

Is it any wonder that this was the disciple whom Jesus loved in particular? John, one of the Sons of Thunder, who as a young follower of Jesus selfishly desired a position of power and prestige in God's kingdom (Mark 10:35–37), grew in faith and spiritual maturity to the point where he modeled the life of Christ in separating the precious from the worthless. His values had changed. Here is an active ethic of care engaged in by a follower of Christ who did not understand the meaning of giving up, who was willing to attempt the impossible and sacrifice his own life, if necessary, for the sake of the kingdom. John was able to see the precious things of God in a young man and separate them from the worthless things of the world that were ruining his life. John gives us a picture of risk and sacrifice in caregiving, and a challenge to look at people in need through the eyes of faith and see the redemptive, therapeutic possibilities.

Martin Luther's Story

Martin Luther (1483–1546) recognized the important relationship between a healthy mind and a healthy body. He believed that Christians should be joyful people, and he was concerned about those who allowed the devil to breed negative thoughts in their minds that led to psychosomatic complaints. Luther had a solution for their problems that required them to learn to extract the precious from the worthless. His answer was to focus on the provision of God as a means of assisting in recovery.

149

One day Luther was informed of a man who had fallen ill and had become confused and depressed. Luther suggested that the man's mind and imagination had contributed to his problems. He instructed the man to change his thoughts, concentrate on Christ, and make positive, joyful statements about the Christian life, such as: "Christ lives." "I have been baptized into Christ, and raised to walk in newness of life" (Rom. 6:3–4). "The devil is defeated." Luther based his advice on the Word of God, and he reminded the man that the Lord is a compassionate God who is faithful in caring for his children.[7]

Luther admitted that he applied this positive approach to his own life. Luther believed that negative thoughts were a sign of the temptation of the devil since God desires his people to experience peace and have a joyful heart. When Luther experienced such temptation, he used a two-step approach to deal with his depression. His steps provide us with a simple exercise in learning to extract the precious from the worthless.

1. *Challenge your thoughts.* Luther's first step was to challenge his negative, ungodly thinking. For each destructive thought, he would say, "Das ist nit Christus" ("That is not Christ").
2. *Replace your unhelpful thoughts with godly ones.* After challenging each thought, Luther would make positive affirmations of faith. These affirmations can take a variety of forms, including repeating memorized verses of Scripture, prayer, poems, and statements of faith. In Luther's case, he usually sang a hymn of praise. I like to imagine him loudly singing his own hymn "A Mighty Fortress Is Our God."[8]

Alan's Story

How do you find hope after being victimized and betrayed by the unethical and criminal behavior of a counselor? Alan worked in a college setting where, as part of his Christian witness, he would post brochures on the sanctity of life on his office door. One day he received a note from a student that began by informing him that he was partially responsible for the birth of her baby. The initial shock of those opening lines was alleviated by the information that followed in the letter.

Dear Alan,

I enclose a photograph of a beautiful baby boy—THAT
IN PART—you are responsible for giving life to.

When my marriage was in trouble, I sought counseling and in my vulnerable condition fell victim to an
unethical therapist who seduced me with trust then betrayed me when I was pregnant with his child.

Some months before that, I had picked up some material from your door and for the first time became aware
of the physiology of early embryos and their developing
stages.

My therapist tried every means of persuasion to influence me to terminate the pregnancy. He promised the
moon, threatened suicide, threatened to murder me, and
terrorized me with a gun. He even lied to the police and
claimed I broke into his office, and I was jailed.

But with the knowledge that the tiny living baby in
me had a heartbeat and could feel pain, etc., I had the
courage to hang in there through those dark months.

My little baby thanks you and I do too.

Keep up the good work.

In the middle of all the pain and betrayal, a broken marriage, victimization and threats from a therapist, unwanted pregnancy, terror, lies
and false accusations, this woman was given a glimpse of the value of
life through the eyes of God. As a result, she was able to extract the
precious from the worthless and overcome the oppressive forces of evil.
The problem pregnancy was transformed into a gift from God.

Stan's Story

I first met Stan Jones in the lobby of a campus dormitory. He had
just flown into Fort Worth, Texas, with his wife Stephanie from the
other side of the world where he worked. Only hours before he had
learned from the television news that that there had been a shooting at

Wedgwood Baptist Church, and later it was confirmed that his beautiful daughter Kim had been shot to death in the church sanctuary in an apparently senseless killing. He and his wife were now preparing to go up to their daughter's room, which had remained closed since Kim left it the previous Wednesday evening. If there were ever a time for a person to be angry with God, this was it. A daughter who exuded the joy of Christ, who lit up a room when she entered, whose diary, they later discovered, was filled with prayers and praises to God, was gone. In her last journal entry two days before her death, Kim wrote: "I don't want to ever lose the passion of being totally in love with you alone! God, please continue to stir my heart, make me passionate now and always."[9] Now she had been murdered in a place of worship. Stan had a right to be enraged at the world and questioning God.

I will never forget the words he said to me as he prepared to go up to Kim's room. "You know," he said, "if anyone had asked me a week ago where I was in relationship to God, I would have to say that I was about 80-percent committed to the Christian life. But I want you to know that today I am 100-percent sold out to God."

Here was a man at a major crossroad in life. He had a choice to make: bitterness and anger or faith and hope. He chose to extract the precious from the worthless and cast himself upon the mercy and grace of God. In the midst of devastating loss, he was reaching out in absolute dependence for the hand of God to comfort and carry him through the dark hours.

Stan's choice has led to a ministry in which hundreds of people have been introduced to the gospel through a message of hope from his daughter videotaped only months prior to her death. The voice and faith of Kim Jones have not been quieted or stilled. They live on through the work and the faith of Stan, Stephanie, and Tim Jones (brother of Kim), who chose to find the precious comfort of God in the midst of the worthless and destructive forces of evil in our world.

To extract the precious from the worthless does not mean that Christian counselors offer shallow and insincere platitudes. We are not talking about a grinning-fool syndrome where a person expresses a lobotomized optimism in every situation. A superficial "Praise the Lord, anyhow" attitude denies the reality of the sin and depravity in the world and the gut-wrenching emotions that threaten to overwhelm people as they are confronted with tragedies in life. A healthy attitude acknowledges the depths of the pain and calls upon God to bring the healing power necessary to overcome. You will find such an attitude in another story from the Wedgwood shootings.

Kathy Jo's Story

If you pull back the new carpet in the sanctuary of Wedgwood Baptist Church, you will find the concrete floor covered in messages. The prose, poetry, Scriptures, comments, and letters express the hearts of the people during the dark hours of September 1999. Just outside the entrance to one of the doors to the sanctuary, you will find the following words written with red and blue markers at the place where Shawn Brown, a seminary student aged twenty-three, fell after being shot to death: "I am my beloved's and my beloved is mine" (Song 6:3) and "Peace I leave you, My peace I give to you; not as the world gives do I give to you. Let not your heart be troubled, neither let it be afraid" (John 14:27 NKJV).

The words were written by his wife of less than two years, Kathy Jo, and they communicate a memorial message from her to her husband and a word of comfort to her from God. Kathy Jo could have responded with bitterness and anger. In fact, she experienced a roller coaster of emotions, including grief and depression for several months. But she chose to extract the precious things of God from the worthless and destructive elements in the world. Her faith and hope enabled her to depend on God in her crisis.

In her words: "I believe the most beneficial aspect of my grief is to know that the whole gamut of my feelings is normal, and that God understands each and every emotion. He has carried me, even when I forget to ask. He speaks, even when I forget to listen. When I become overwhelmed with questions and despair, I have learned to cry out again and again, 'Lord, I trust you.'"[10]

"The Lord is close to the brokenhearted and saves those who are crushed in spirit" (Ps. 34:18 NIV).

The tragic loss of her husband led this young woman through a testing of her faith; but in the midst of her grief, she focused on God and expressed a concern for her neighbor. In an open letter to her seminary family, Kathy Jo revealed how God was enabling her to extract the precious from the worthless:

> I am so thankful for the blessing of being Shawn's wife, and I rejoice in the fact that I will get to be with him again one day. Thanks to God's awesome faithfulness, and His promise in Romans 8:28, many others will be with us in Heaven as well—those who have come to know Christ through this tragedy. May we continue seeking God and leading others to Christ, so as to not let the loss of our Shawn be in vain. It is my prayer that we would "run with perseverance the race marked out for us" (Hebrews 12:1–3) as Shawn desired to share at an upcoming youth rally.[11]

Summary

1. A biblical perspective in counseling means learning to extract the precious from the worthless. The words of God to Jeremiah (15:19) serve as a basis for assisting us to reframe problems into godly provisions and opportunities.
2. Identity in Christ enables a Christian to seek the truth and will of God in every situation.
3. We must learn to look for the hand of God working in all events. Consequently, we must remember that our actions affect not only other people, but they also represent our personal response to God.
4. We find examples of people who learned to extract the precious from the worthless in Scripture, church history, and contemporary situations.

Where Do We Go from Here?

Biblical Christian counselors try to find the provision and goodness of God in every situation. Attempts to extract the precious from the worthless require godly discernment and a personal relationship with God. One area that is unique to biblical Christian counseling is the spiritual empowerment and resources that are available. The next chapter will examine the role and gifts of our current Counselor of heaven on earth, the Holy Spirit.

Questions and Exercises for Reflection

1. What are some other terms, phases, or metaphors that capture the idea of extracting the precious from the worthless?
2. Find an example from the Bible, history, or a contemporary situation that illustrates extracting the precious from the worthless.
3. Describe an example from your own experience where you discovered the hand of God working in a difficult situation.
4. What are some constructive or therapeutic ways you could introduce the idea of extracting the precious from the worthless to a person who appeared to be engulfed by his or her problems?

References

Hailey, Cory J. "Shawn Brown: Braveheart, Big Heart." *Southwestern News, Special Edition.* Vol. 58, no. 2, 1999: 4–5.

Jones, Ian F. "Ministry to the Grieving: Care Giving after the Wedgwood Tragedy." *Southwestern News: Special Edition.* Vol. 58, no. 2, 1999: 16–17.

Keil, C. F. *Jeremiah, Lamentations.* Trans. James Martin. In Commentary on the Old Testament in Ten Volumes by C. F. Keil and F. Delitzsch. Grand Rapids, Mich.: William B. Eerdmans Publishing Company, 1978.

Little, Robyn. "Kim Jones: From a Good Life to Life Transformed." *Southwestern News, Special Edition.* Vol. 58, no. 2, 1999: 6–7.

Luther, Martin. *D. Martin Luthers Werke: Tischreden.* Vol. 1. Weimar: Hermann Böhlaus Nachfolger, 1912.

Maier, Paul L. *Eusebius—the Church History: A New Translation and Commentary.* Grand Rapids, Mich.: Kregel Publications, 1999.

Niebuhr, H. Richard. *The Responsible Self: An Essay in Christian Moral Philosophy.* San Francisco: Harper & Row, 1963.

Endnotes

1 C. F. Keil, *Jeremiah, Lamentations*, trans. James Martin, in Commentary on the Old Testament in Ten Volumes by C. F. Keil and F. Delitzsch (Grand Rapids, Mich.: William B. Eerdmans Publishing Company, 1978), 266.

2 Ibid., 266. Keil's original words are in Latin.

3 H. Richard Niebuhr, *The Responsible Self: An Essay in Christian Moral Philosophy* (San Francisco: Harper & Row, 1963), 126.

4 Paul L. Maier, *Eusebius—the Church History: A New Translation and Commentary*, (3.23) (Grand Rapids, Mich.: Kregel Publications, 1999), 111.

5 Ibid., 112.

6 Ibid.

7 Martin Luther, *D. Martin Luthers Werke: Tischreden*, vol. 1 (Weimar: Hermann Böhlaus Nachfolger, 1912), 243.

8 Ibid., 243.

9 Robyn Little, "Kim Jones: From a Good Life to Life Transformed," *Southwestern News, Special Edition,* 58:2 (1999), 7.

10 Ian F. Jones, "Ministry to the Grieving: Care Giving after the Wedgwood Tragedy," *Southwestern News: Special Edition*, 58:2 (1999), 16.

11 Cory J. Hailey, "Shawn Brown: Braveheart, Big Heart," *Southwestern News, Special Edition*, 58:2 (1999), 5.

9

THE HOLY SPIRIT AND THE SPIRITUAL GIFTS IN BIBLICAL CHRISTIAN COUNSELING

The Holy Spirit's Role in Counseling
The Gift of the Spirit
The Fruit of the Spirit
The Gifts of the Spirit
An Example of the Spirit's Work

> "But the Counselor, the Holy Spirit, whom the father will send in my name, will teach you all things and will remind you of everything I have said to you" (John 14:26 NIV). The Holy Spirit is our indwelling Counselor of heaven on earth.

The Holy Spirit's Role in Counseling

Our Advocate

Jesus Christ, the Counselor of heaven on earth, continues his ministry through the person and work of the Holy Spirit in us. Jesus revealed that God would provide "another Counselor" to be with us forever, the "Spirit of truth" (John 14:16). "I will ask the Father, and He will give you another Helper, that He may be with you forever; that is the Spirit of truth, whom the world cannot receive, because it does not see Him or know Him, *but* you know Him because He abides with you and will be in you. I will not leave you as orphans; I will come to you" (John 14:16–18).

Jesus promised to provide for us after his resurrection and ascension to heaven. His presence would remain through the Holy Spirit, "another

Helper." The Greek word for "helper" is *parakletos,* and it means "one called or summoned along the side of another to help; comforter; advocate; or intercessor." The most accurate rendering is probably *advocate*, although Paraclete, a transliteration of the original term, is now in common usage. Early English translations of the Bible used the word *comforter*, but this word is a little misleading. *Comforter* conveys the impression of someone who tries to soothe or placate and who attempts to cheer up a sorrowful and troubled person. Comfort has a passive connotation in its contemporary meaning, whereby the consolation directed toward the person in need carries no promise and no power to change the current conditions.

J. Oswald Sanders has pointed out that when John Wycliffe used *Comforter* in his English translation at the end of the fourteenth century, the word had a distinctly different meaning. Wycliffe understood the word in terms of its original Latin derivation *confortare*, meaning "with fortitude" or "strengthen." The Holy Spirit strengthens and empowers us in our weakness. A consoling element still remains in the term, however, since the Lord promised that he would not leave us as orphans.

The Holy Spirit is the Advocate, the Divine Barrister, who provides help against an accuser or judge. Sanders has observed that the traditional role of the barrister was to represent his client, defend his name, and guard and administer his client's property. The Holy Spirit is not our Advocate, available to serve us when we decide to summon him; rather, he is the Advocate of Christ (John 15:26). His work is to represent Christ on earth, to plead his cause, defend his name, and guard and administer the work and interests of his kingdom.[1]

Jesus said that he would send "another *Parakletos*." Christ was our Advocate and Helper on earth until his departure, and he is now our Advocate before the Father in heaven (1 John 2:1). The people who had known his earthly physical presence would not be abandoned like orphans. "But I tell you the truth, it is to your advantage that I go away; for if I do not go away, the Helper will not come to you; but if I go, I will send him to you" (John 16:7). The disciples could not see any advantage in Jesus' leaving them, but when the Holy Spirit came, they entered into a relationship with God that transcended physical boundaries. The Holy Spirit is not limited by a human body; he is an internal Presence who reveals Christ and continues his work through believers. The Holy Spirit is now the Paraclete of Christ on earth; he is the presence of God and the Spirit of Christ in us (Rom. 8:9), "Christ in you, the hope of glory" (Col. 1:27).

Our Counselor and Intercessor

The Spirit is our Counselor. The word *counselor* comes from the Latin *consilium*, meaning "consultation or advice," and its equivalent term in Hebrew is *yaats*, the word used in reference to the Messiah in Isaiah 9:6 (see chapter 6). The Spirit is now our Wonderful Counselor, our Consultant, who advises us and equips us for the ministry of soul care and counseling.

The Spirit provides his presence, his power, consultation, leadership and direction, and intercession in the Christian life and in the ministry of Christian counseling. The traits attributed to the Messiah in Isaiah 11:2 (wisdom, understanding, knowledge, power, the knowledge of God, and the fear of God) are now expressed through the Holy Spirit. All Spirit-filled Christians have access to the mind, love, will, gifts, and activities of the Spirit (Rom. 8:27; 15:30; 1 Cor. 12:1–11) who unites all believers into one body (1 Cor. 12:13,27). The Amplified Bible has attempted to capture the multifaceted ministry of the Spirit in its translation of John 14:26. "But the Comforter (Counselor, Helper, Intercessor, Advocate, Strengthener, Standby), the Holy Spirit, Whom the Father will send in My name [in My place, to represent Me and act on My behalf], He will teach you all things. And He will cause you to recall (will remind you of, bring to your remembrance) everything I have told you" (John 14:26 AMP).

Although Paul does not use the term *parakletos* in his epistles, he does stress the intercessory work of Christ and the Holy Spirit. The Spirit, in accordance with the will of God, helps us in our weaknesses and searches our hearts. He is able to intercede for us and translate and transform our prayers into language that is holy and acceptable to God

(Rom. 8:26–27). Paul tells us that Christ also intercedes for us before God (Rom. 8:34). We are bound together in his love, and nothing in heaven or on earth can separate us (Rom. 8:35–39).

The One Who Convicts

The ministry of the Holy Spirit is to convict people of sin, of righteousness, and of judgment (John 14:8–11). Counselors must be sensitive to the convicting work of the Holy Spirit in the lives of people in need. They must not be judgmental and accusatory in counseling. The Spirit is the One who illuminates the sin in a person's life. The Spirit reveals the extent of our personal inadequacy before God. All our human efforts for good, our moral creeds for living, and our attempts to live a virtuous life are insufficient in the eyes of God. In fact, all our righteousness is the equivalent of filthy rags in comparison to the righteousness of God (Isa. 64:6). The Spirit also convicts the world of judgment. Christ has defeated the evil one's power of death (Heb. 2:14), and the Holy Spirit reveals this truth to us.

The Gift of the Spirit

Christian counselors are filled with the Spirit (Eph. 5:18) and bear the fruit of the Spirit (John 15:16; Gal. 5:22). They must be sensitive to the prompting of the Spirit as they engage in the ministry of caregiving. Counselors who learn to depend on the inspiration and motivating work of the Spirit find that their ministry will be filled with rich and occasionally unanticipated blessings, as the following example reveals.

A Case Example

The question from the young man surprised me at first. I was not prepared for it. My lack of preparation was not in the way that you might think. The inquirer had asked me about faith and the necessity of finding a reason for every problem that occurred in life. He mentioned Job in a tone of voice that queried whether I had considered Job's dilemma. My surprised reaction, though not outwardly noticeable to him, was genuine. It was not due to the question itself but to the timing. Only hours before I had been prompted, in my morning devotional, to read the book of Job in its entirety, all forty-two chapters. The reading was outside of my normal plans and schedule. I was just not expecting the Spirit to use my study so soon and in such a practical way. Such was my lack of faith.

I was able to point out to the young man that after all his oppression and adversities and his final restoration, Job spent the remainder of his life never really knowing why it had all occurred. He never received a full explanation. He did not have the privilege, like us, of being able to read the first two chapters of his book, where the cause and nature of his testing are described. The Bible gives us no indication that Job ever discovered the full details of the spiritual conflict that shaped his life. All he could do was trust in God, despite his predicament. One of the most important messages in the book is that some problems and tragedies are inexplicable this side of heaven, and we must simply place our faith and hope in God.

The episode was a reminder to me that the Spirit prompts us at opportune times not only in actual counseling situations but also in the preparation stages. All mature Christian counselors have similar stories of the work of the Holy Spirit in their ministry. The biblical message is clear that we must be open, at all times, to the leadership and direction of the Holy Spirit.

The Bible distinguishes between the gift of the Spirit, the fruit of the Spirit, and the gifts of the Spirit. Mature Christian counselors understand the differences between these three areas and the essential function each plays in an effective biblical Christian counseling ministry.

Jesus promised his disciples that they would receive baptism in the Holy Spirit and be empowered to witness (Acts 1:5,8). This gift from God came at Pentecost, when they were all filled with the Holy Spirit and began to speak with other tongues provided by the Spirit (Acts 2:4). The gift enabled Christians who lacked education, eloquence, and confidence to proclaim God's message with clarity and boldness.

The filling with the Holy Spirit has a number of characteristics.

Evidence of Faith

We receive the Holy Spirit by hearing with faith (Gal. 3:2,14). Those people who believe or have faith in Jesus Christ receive the Holy Spirit (John 7:39) and are equipped to do his work.

Boldness and Authority toward Others

Peter, filled with the Holy Spirit following Pentecost, was given the words to say and the power to speak with divine authority to others (Acts 4:8). The Spirit enabled the believers to speak the word of God with boldness and heal the people. The Spirit brought a new confidence to believers, and they were empowered to perform his redemptive activities (Acts 4:29–31). Boldness of speech and personal healing are also connected with the filling of the Spirit in the life of Paul (Acts 13:9–11; 9:17).

Intercessory Prayer to God

The Spirit not only provides believers with the competence to deal with other people and the world; he also enables us to converse with God. "In the same way the Spirit also helps our weakness; for we do not know how to pray as we should, but the Spirit Himself intercedes for *us* with groanings too deep for words; and He who searches the hearts knows what the mind of the Spirit is, because He intercedes for the saints according to the will of God" (Rom. 8:26–27).

Service to Others

When a need arose in the early church, people who were filled with the Holy Spirit were selected to serve others (Acts 6:3). One expression of the presence of the Holy Spirit is the ability to express a divine love and assistance to our neighbor.

Godly Focus or Divine Perception

The Holy Spirit allows us to look at situations from God's perspective. Stephen, full of the Holy Spirit at his martyrdom, was able to keep his gaze on God's glory and on Jesus standing at God's right hand. The Holy Spirit enabled him to extract the precious from the worthless, even at the point of death. He died, not in bitterness and anger, but filled with eternal hope (Acts 7:55).

A Joyful Attitude

Joy is associated with the filling of the Spirit. The disciples were continually filled with joy and with the Holy Spirit (Acts 13:52). Christians are able to maintain an attitude of joy because they have the peace of God. The peace of God protects our thoughts and emotions from extreme anxieties as the Spirit reminds us of the promises, provision, and presence of God (John 14:27; Phil. 4:7; Col. 3:15). The inward peace and the outward expression of joy draw other people to God.

Prompter and Provider of Speech

The Holy Spirit prompts us and brings to mind what we need to say in difficult and even life-threatening situations (Matt. 10:18–20; Luke 12:11–12). The Holy Spirit is there to prompt us and teach us what to say when we confront problems that, under normal circumstances, would provoke consternation and leave us at a loss for words. At such times we need to relax and let the Spirit within us speak. A significant requirement for this provision is that we be in the will of God and our difficulties have arisen as part of our calling and service for him.

All effective Christian counselors will recall times when they were at a loss as to how to proceed in a counseling session. The person's problems may seem overwhelming, the situation may appear hopeless, and the future may appear bleak. The individual's despair may trigger personal doubts in the counselor. The wise counselor will pray in his spirit, resting on God's assurance and provision. In those moments the Spirit will prompt a thought, a comment, a memory, a word, a story, or a verse that will open up a new direction for healing.

The Fruit of the Spirit

The fruit of the Spirit is love, joy, peace, long-suffering, gentleness, goodness, faithfulness, meekness, and self-control (Gal. 5:22–23). These nine character qualities are common to all true Christians since they are expressions of the one indwelling Holy Spirit in the believer's life.

They are evidence of the Spirit's continuing presence and active work in a believer's life. The fruit is present in all believers, unlike the gifts which are given according to the will of the Spirit. There are a number of different gifts, but not a variety of fruits. The diversity of gifts comes from the same Spirit (1 Cor. 12:6), but there is only one fruit, the spiritual quality common to all who possess the one Spirit.

The fruit grows and develops within the believer over time. In the process of sanctification, believers are purified and cleansed in their nature and renewed in the image of God. They grow in grace through fellowship with the saints and ministry to others as the fruit is nurtured and strengthened. Believers are comforted and strengthened through the personal experience of love, joy, and peace. They grow in their relationship with others as they develop patience, gentleness, and goodness. Their outward conduct becomes more like Christ in faithfulness, meekness, and self-control. All these expressions of the fruit are important and necessary features of the mature Christian counselor.

The Gifts of the Spirit

The indwelling Spirit is revealed through the manifestation or shining forth (Greek: *phanerosis*) of his gifts, and the ministry of Christian counseling depends on this spiritual equipment. Exercising spiritual gifts blesses the individual and the church body, the believer and the unbeliever. For example, believers who have a hymn, a word of instruction, a revelation, or a word of interpretation must use their gift to strengthen the church (1 Cor. 14:26). One purpose of the Holy Spirit and the gifts is to provide spiritual capabilities far beyond any natural human abilities. The Spirit empowered Paul, for example, to do things beyond his personal talent and ability (Rom. 15:18–19).

The gifts reveal God and the eternal presence of his Spirit, and they minister to and edify the believer and others. Paul identified nine gifts in 1 Corinthians 12:8–10: the word of wisdom, the word of knowledge, special faith, healing gifts, the working of miracles, prophecy, discernment between spirits, tongues, and the interpretation of tongues. Paul clearly stated that the gifts were not distributed equally and that certain Christians were blessed with particular gifts of the Spirit.

> Now there are distinctive varieties and distributions of endowments (gifts, extraordinary powers distinguishing certain Christians, due to the power of divine grace operating in their souls by the Holy Spirit) and they vary, but the [Holy] Spirit remains the same.
>
> And there are distinctive varieties of service and ministration, but it is the same Lord [Who is served].
>
> And there are distinctive varieties of operation [of working to accomplish things], but it is the same God Who inspires *and* energizes them all in all.
>
> But to each one is given the manifestation of the [Holy] Spirit [the evidence, the spiritual illumination of the Spirit] for good *and* profit.
>
> To one is given in *and* through the [Holy] Spirit [the power to speak] a message of wisdom, and to another [the power to express] a word of knowledge *and* understanding according to the same [Holy] Spirit;
>
> To another [wonder-working] faith by the same [Holy] Spirit, to another the extraordinary powers of healing by the one Spirit;
>
> To another the working of miracles, to another prophetic insight (the gift of interpreting the divine will and purpose); to another the ability to discern *and* distinguish between [the utterances of true] spirits [and false ones], to another various kinds of [unknown] tongues, to another the ability to interpret [such] tongues.
>
> All these [gifts, achievements, abilities] are inspired and brought to pass by one and the same [Holy] Spirit, Who apportions to each person individually [exactly] as He chooses (1 Cor. 12:4–11 AMP).

Additional gifts include service to others and helping, teaching, encouragement, giving, leadership, mercy, apostleship, missionary evangelism, and pastoring (Rom. 12:6–8; 1 Cor. 12:28; Eph. 4:11). Each believer has been blessed with at least one spiritual gift, and the Bible tells us that we are to use our gifts to serve others and to honor God. We are expected to speak the words of God accurately and to work in the power of the Spirit as we minister to others with our gifts (1 Pet. 4:10–11). The exercise of our free will means that the gifts can be abused. Paul encouraged the Corinthians to follow the way of godly love and seek the higher gifts that strengthen, encourage, and support others rather than the lesser gifts, like tongues without interpretation, that only edify the individual (1 Cor. 14:1–5).

The gifts and the calling of God are irrevocable (Rom. 11:29). God does not remove a gift once it is given. We may be puzzled by the expression of gifts in a person whose private life shows a wanton disregard for God. How can a person act in such a way when he seems to have this wonderful gift? Our mistake is to use gifts as a sign of righteousness and an indication that other areas in that person's life are in the will of God. Gifts may be genuine, or they may be imitations of the real thing or demonic counterfeits. Jesus made clear that we were to identify believers not by gifts but by their fruit. Some who prophesied, cast out demons, and performed miracles would not enter the kingdom of heaven (Matt. 7:15–23). Godly character is revealed through a heart that expresses the good fruit of the Spirit, not just a particular gift (Luke 6:44–45).

Spiritual gifts, exercised correctly, reveal the power and the presence of God; they are a blessing from God. Some of these gifts are useful in counseling. They are all given by the one Spirit of Jehovah: (1) the Spirit of wisdom and understanding, (2) the Spirit of counsel and power, (3) the Spirit of knowledge and of the fear of the Lord (Isa. 11:2). The spiritual gifts are expressions of these three dimensions of the Holy Spirit.

The Spirit of Wisdom and of Understanding

The gifts of the word of wisdom and the message of knowledge are clearly identified in 1 Corinthians 12:8, and they have an obvious connection to the character of the Messiah (Isa. 11:2). The Bible instructs us to seek wisdom and understanding (Prov. 4:7), and Christian counselors should desire these gifts. The Spirit, through wisdom and understanding, gives us the right words to say in difficult situations (Matt. 10:19b–20).

Paul gives us an extended discussion on the role of the Spirit in understanding the mind of Christ and spiritual blessings (1 Cor. 2:6–16).

> God's Spirit has shown you everything. His Spirit finds out everything, even what is deep in the mind of God. You are the only one who knows what's in your own mind, and God's Spirit is the only one who knows what's in God's mind. But God has given us his Spirit. That's why we don't think the same way that the people of this world think. That's also why we can recognize the blessings that God has given us.
>
> Every word we speak was taught to us by God's Spirit, not by human wisdom. And this same Spirit helps us teach spiritual things to spiritual people. That's why only someone who has God's Spirit can understand spiritual blessings. Anyone who doesn't have God's Spirit thinks these blessings are foolish. People who are guided by the Spirit can make all kinds of judgments, but they can't be judged by others. The Scriptures ask, "Has anyone ever known the thoughts of the Lord or given him advice?" But we understand what Christ is thinking (1 Cor. 2:10–16 CEV).

As the word of wisdom is manifest in counseling, there is a sense that something supremely right has been revealed. The people present become aware of the presence of the Spirit of God and conscious of a transcendent mind prompting the thoughts and utterances and directing the encounter toward wholeness and healing. Spiritual wisdom involves the application of the correct words and knowledge at the right time for the spiritually prepared person to hear and receive it. "If you obey the Lord, you will always know the right thing to say" (Prov. 10:32a CEV).

People in the early church spoke a Spirit-prompted language and made prophetic utterances when they were filled with the Spirit (Acts 2:4; 19:6). These gifts enabled believers to communicate the gospel to others and to understand and explain the current times and conditions. Christian counselors need to explore how God might use these gifts in their ministry of caregiving. Certainly the capacity to read a situation in order to predict possible outcomes and the gift of discerning and interpreting God's work have important application in counseling.

We must remember that these gifts are not an abiding state or a static character quality. The Spirit grants a word of wisdom at the opportune time. There is no storage facility where spiritual wisdom is collected and dispensed at the whim and will of the counselor.

Wisdom and discernment are hallmarks of a mature Christian who has learned, practiced, and developed the ability to distinguish good from evil (Heb. 5:14), but these abilities are distinct from the Spirit's word of wisdom. Although spiritual gifts, moral reasoning, and intellectual maturation are not the same thing, they are not mutually exclusive; nor are they conflicting elements. Christian counselors who hold the attitude that they don't need to study and prepare for counseling because the Spirit will give them the words to say when the time comes are being unwise and immature. This pseudo-pious position does not reflect the biblical teaching on growing in wisdom, as reflected in the wisdom literature of Scripture in general and the book of Proverbs in particular. This attitude may be a cover for laziness and an excuse for avoiding rigorous scholarship.

The Spirit of Counsel or Knowledge and of Power

God has not given us a spirit of fear or timidity but of power and of love and of a sound mind (2 Tim. 1:7). Counsel or knowledge is expressed in the gift of discernment and in prophetic insight that enables a Christian to understand the will and plans of God. Power is evident in the gift of special faith, the gifts of healing and miracles.

God possesses the perfect insight to judge and evaluate a person and a situation. He searches every heart and understands the motive behind every thought (1 Chron. 28:9; Ps. 139; Jer. 17:10). Nothing is hidden from his eyes (Heb. 4:13), and we have access to this knowledge through his Word (Heb. 4:12) and the gift of discernment.

Jesus revealed his supernatural ability to discern the nature and heart of people in his conversations with Nathaniel (John 1:47–50) and the woman at the well (John 4:16–19). We see evidence of this gift in Peter, who exposed the deception of Ananias and Sapphira (Acts 5:1–11) and the mercenary heart of Simon the sorcerer (Acts 18:18–24). One important characteristic of this gift is the ability to distinguish between the divine and the demonic forces at work in a situation. Paul showed this discernment in dealing with a slave girl who was shouting to the people that he and Silas were "servants of the Most High God, who are telling you the way to be saved." Her words were accurate, but Paul recognized them as coming from an evil spirit, which he commanded, in the name of Jesus Christ, to leave (Acts 16:16–18).

Christian counselors should not confuse the gift of discerning the spirits with having a critical spirit or the possession of acute perception or insight into human nature. Pointing out another person's faults and weaknesses is not a sign of good counseling or evidence of a spiritual gift. This gift allows counselors to recognize spiritual activity in a situation and perceive the heart of individuals.

Prophetic utterance is manifest most perfectly in the inspired and infallible "prophecy of Scripture" (2 Pet. 1:20). The gift of prophecy is for the edification, "strengthening, encouragement, and comfort" of our neighbor (1 Cor. 14:3–4). The gift enables a believer to speak under momentary inspiration and reveal the mind of God in an event. At such times people are instructed and encouraged in the way of God. Paul cautioned the church to "weigh carefully" any prophecies (1 Cor. 14:29–33).

There are times when believers receive a special infusion of faith that enables them to triumph when confronted with overwhelming odds. Such was the case with Elijah on Mount Carmel when he stood before 450 prophets of Baal. Elijah soaked the offering and the wood on his altar with four large jars of water three times until it ran down into the trench, and then he stepped up and prayed for God to consume the sacrifice (1 Kings 18:30–39). A gift of special faith has the power to call down God's consuming fire and to move mountains (Matt. 17:20). This gift of faith also appears to be connected to extraordinary healing. Peter stated that it was by "faith in the name of Jesus" that he was able to heal the crippled beggar at the temple gate. "It is Jesus' name and the faith that comes through him that has given this complete healing to him, as you can all see," he said (Acts 3:16 NIV). Peter saw a clear relationship between the healing and the faith of Jesus, and such faith is a gift of the Spirit who manifests Christ on earth.

Physical healing was part of the ministry of Jesus (e.g., Matt. 4:23–25; 8:7,16; 9:35; Mark 3:10; Luke 5:15; 9:1,6), as well as healing in spiritual warfare and demon possession (Matt. 8:16; Mark 1:34; Luke 6:18b; 9:1). Jesus instructed his disciples to heal the sick, raise the dead, cleanse the lepers, and drive out demons (Matt. 10:8). The people tried to touch Jesus because of the healing power that emanated from him (Luke 6:19).

In 1 Corinthians 12:9, Paul talks about the "gifts" of healing. The word is in the plural, indicating that healing may take a variety of forms. Such healings are divine in origin; they are beyond the scope and ability of natural powers and medical science.

The Bible describes healing in the spiritual sense, such as healing from sin (Ps. 41:4); God heals our transgressions through the sacrificial death of Christ (Isa. 53:5; 1 Pet. 2:24). There is supernatural healing of relationships and emotions; God heals the brokenhearted and binds up their wounds (Ps. 147:3). There is the divine healing, peace of mind, comfort, and guidance that leads to godly worship and praise (Isa. 57:18–19). There is also the gift of healing and cure for spiritual rebellion that comes through the call, discipline, and correction of God (Jer. 3:22; Heb. 12:7–13).

Christian counselors minister with the expectation that the Spirit will provide miraculous power to produce healing and change. Jesus told his disciples that they would do even greater miracles than he had (John 14:12). Miracles are the supernatural energizing or operating of works of power. In fact, the Greek word translated as *miracles* in 1 Corinthians 12:10 is *dunamis*, meaning "the outward expression of wondrous or miraculous power." The power of God operating through the Spirit enabled Peter to raise Dorcas from the dead (Acts 9:40) and Paul to raise Eutychus (Acts 20:7–12). Not all miracles are spectacular events. The key characteristic is that they produce changes that lie beyond natural causes and explanations. They require the power of the Spirit.

The Spirit of the Knowledge of God and the Fear of God

While the previous two dimensions address the various expressions of spiritual gifts, this component has a different focus. "The Spirit of the knowledge of God and the fear of God" is not a subdivision of the various gifts of the Spirit; it is expressed in *the gift of the Spirit himself.*

The Spirit of the knowledge and fear of God prompts us to recognize our unregenerate condition and confess our sin. The Spirit leads us to a reverent fear of the awesome holiness of God and our absolute dependence on his mercy and grace (Eccl. 12:13–14). The Spirit manifests the gift of salvation through faith in Christ (Eph. 2:8, Heb. 6:4), and he enables us to relate to God as a child to the Father (Gal. 4:6–7).

This dimension expresses the role of God the Holy Spirit in our lives. We are to acknowledge the Spirit's presence in all our counseling activities, and we must never offend him. Jesus warned us of the eternal consequences of speaking against the Holy Spirit (Matt. 12:31–32). While the exact meaning of blasphemy against the Holy Spirit has been the subject of debate for centuries and a full discussion is beyond the scope of this book, Christ's admonition or word of caution emphasizes the fact that we dismiss the Holy Spirit at our own peril. Willful refusal to answer God's question, "Where are you?" has eternal consequences. We must not quench the Gift of the Holy Spirit (1 Thess. 5:16). We must not grieve the Spirit of God (Eph. 4:30). Isaiah tells us that the Messiah comes as redeeming Savior, but those who grieve his Spirit will experience his wrath (Isa. 63:9–10).

Rather than resisting the Spirit (Acts 7:51) and being stiff-necked, we should yield to his direction and Word and be his ambassadors, revealing God's presence.

The Spirit of the knowledge of God and the fear of God drives us to say, along with David:

> Create in me a clean heart, O God,
> And renew a steadfast spirit within me.
> Do not cast me away from Your presence
> And do not take Your Holy Spirit from me.
> Restore to me the joy of Your salvation
> And sustain me with a willing spirit.
> *Then* I will teach transgressors Your ways,
> And sinners will be converted to You (Ps. 51:10–13).

David was anointed with the mighty Spirit of God (1 Sam. 16:13), but Psalm 51 describes a man who had lost the joy of God's salvation. He had turned his eyes away from God. In fear and reverence, he asked God to create something new in him, a new heart and a renewed willingness to be obedient. David would express his new resolution in service to others, teaching even his enemies the ways of God and leading them to him.

The disturbing outcome of those people who disgrace Christ by expressing only a superficial commitment and not fully experiencing the heavenly gift of the Holy Spirit stands as a warning to the faithful counselor (Heb. 6:4–6). Christian counselors who are filled with the Spirit never take God for granted; they live in a holy fear of stepping outside his will. They are resolved to represent God in total obedience to his Spirit and to use their gifts, skills, and abilities to glorify the Lord.

An Example of the Spirit's Work

My friend Dr. Jim Headrick was teaching an interim-term graduate course a few years ago. These courses jam the sixteen weeks of course material covered in a regular semester into one or two weeks of classes. Both the teaching and the learning under these conditions are stressful. Students have difficulty concentrating. They sit from early morning until late in the afternoon every day, and physical endurance tends to take precedence over study and concentration on the course material. One day the class subject focused on belief and prayer. In the middle of talking about theory and principles, Jim sensed that God wanted him to confront his students with the practical nature of the subject and to test their faith.

Jim was faced with a choice. He could continue with the lecture and discussion, or he could step out in faith and follow the prompting of the Holy Spirit. He believed that God was acting in the situation and that he was not responding impulsively to some wild idea or personal agenda.

Jim began by challenging his students, "How many of you really believe God answers prayer?" All students agreed that they did. "Do you really believe?" he challenged them. One of the students had an obvious hearing problem, which made learning in a classroom setting difficult. The student lacked money to buy even reconditioned hearing aids, so Jim pressed his challenge.

"I am going to ask God to provide hearing aids for David this week," said Jim. "But I want you to pray only if you really believe."

The students sensed that the class had taken a new direction. The professor, under the prompting and direction of the Spirit, had led them onto the field of faith, where belief and prayer were no longer esoteric topics for theological discussion but active, living mediums for the work of the Spirit of God. You either believe, or you don't. If you believe, even with a modicum of faith, then mountains move (Mark 11:22–24).

During the morning break a student came up to Jim and asked if he could speak privately with him. "God has spoken to me, and I want to contribute an anonymous donation of one thousand dollars for David," he said. At lunchtime he went to his church, wrote them a check for

$1,000, and they cut a check for David on their stationery to assure anonymity. When classes resumed that afternoon, some students had gathered around David's chair. On the chair was a collection of money. When David returned to his seat, Jim asked him to count it. The sum was $200.

"How much will the hearing aids cost?" asked Jim. David told him that reconditioned hearing aids would cost $1,200. Jim handed him the check for $1,000. The response from the class was electric. Their emotions and senses were now attuned to God, and they were intent on offering praise to him.

The next day the student who gave the anonymous check asked to speak privately with Jim again. When he had arrived home the previous evening, the student told his wife what he had done. Although their budget would be strained, she affirmed his decision, assuring him that his actions were the will of God. Later they began opening the afternoon mail. In the mail was an envelope from a little company they had invested in years ago. The company had not done well, and they had long ago written off their money as a bad deal. In the envelope was a return on their investment—a check for $4,000. The student replaced the $1,000 he had taken out of his checking account and gave the remaining $3,000 anonymously to a ministry that another student in the class had requested specific prayer for its needs.

A few weeks later I was having lunch with Jim when David happened to enter the restaurant. He immediately came over to us and began to describe his experience with the audiologist. He had told the audiologist previously that he lacked the funds for hearing aids, even reconditioned ones. So when David came into his office with the money, the audiologist was naturally curious. David told the story of what had happened. The audiologist was so impressed he told David that he was going to contribute by giving David two brand-new hearing aids at an original cost of $4,400 for only $1,200 plus change.

In a letter of thanks to Jim, David tried to express his feeling over what had transpired in his life over that week. Notice what David mentions first, an indication of what he considered to be the most important event to occur during that period.

> Dr. Headrick:
>
> In the past two and a half years in seminary, this past week has been the most dynamic and awesome time of my life. I saw my daughter come to know Christ; I was given a monetary gift to purchase desperately needed new hearing aids; my wife has been hired to work with Down syndrome people; and my son was transferred at the spur of the moment to a new school which will work with his ADD.
>
> Dr. Headrick, you have been a role model to all of us this week, and this has changed the way I think of my family. God is doing some great things through you, and it is my prayer that God will keep you at the seminary to minister to other students.
>
> I thank God that I had this opportunity to experience him more through you.
>
> Thank you for a great week.
>
> In Christ's Love,
> David

What began as a normal and mundane lesson on belief and prayer became a transforming, supernatural experience of the power of God. It all started when a servant of God was willing to take seriously the Word of God, respond to the prompting of the Holy Spirit, and challenge those around him to pray and to step out in faith. Because of the faithful leadership of a seminary professor, many students were blessed, not just materially but also in their spirits. They will never forget what happened, and the effects of the event continue even today.

There are times when the Holy Spirit wants to teach us an important lesson during the ordinary activities of our lives. Counseling sessions, in particular, are situations where Christians need to be particularly attentive to God's direction in people's lives. We may have planned and prepared our work, but then the Spirit prompts us to take a new path. Paul, for example, was planning to go to Asia and Bithynia with the gospel. His motives were godly, but the Holy Spirit thwarted him in his mission, and he was given a vision of a man from Macedonia pleading for help. Paul was at a crossroads in his ministry, but his plans were always flexible and open to the prompting of the Spirit. He went to Macedonia (Acts 16:6–10).

Our responsibility as Christians, and as Christian counselors, is to be conscious of the Spirit working in a situation. Plan wisely but listen for the prompting voice of the Spirit directing you in the way that you should go.

Summary

1. The Holy Spirit empowers Christians in the ministry of counseling. Counselors need to seek the guidance and power of the Spirit in every counseling encounter.

2. Faithful Christian counselors give evidence of the fruit of the Spirit in their ministry. Love, joy, peace, patience, gentleness, goodness, faithfulness, meekness, and self-control are essential features of the mature Christian (Gal. 5:22–23), and they are more accurate measures of our identity in Christ than the possession of gifts.

3. The gifts of the Holy Spirit empower counselors to model the Master Counselor, Jesus Christ. They are dynamic and practical expressions of the one Spirit of Jehovah: the Spirit of wisdom and understanding, the Spirit of counsel and power, the Spirit of knowledge and of the fear of the Lord (Isa. 11:2). Counselors need to accept and use the gifts granted them by the Spirit. The gifts may manifest themselves in specific situations, and counselors need to be sensitive to the prompting of the Spirit and his empowering influence in the exercise of these gifts.

Where Do We Go from Here?

The Holy Spirit and his gifts provide counselors with the divine equipment for a counseling ministry. The next chapter will explore this area further by examining the character of a Christian counselor and the biblical traits and spiritual disciplines that support an effective and competent biblical counseling ministry.

Questions and Exercises for Reflection

1. Describe the role of the Holy Spirit in the ministry of counseling. How can the church and Christian counselors, in particular, increase awareness of the work of the Spirit in ministry?
2. The gifts and work of the Spirit were connected to the characteristics of the Messiah identified in Isaiah 11:2 and the ministry of Jesus. Find other examples in the Old Testament of the Holy Spirit that might have a particular application to counseling.
3. What are your spiritual gifts? Identify your gifts and explain how they relate, in particular, to a ministry of counseling.
4. Find a story from the Bible that illustrates the intervening power of the Holy Spirit. What principles can be drawn from the story that have an application in counseling?
5. How might the fruit of the Spirit be revealed in a counseling session? Describe the expressions of the fruit of the Spirit in terms that are relevant to the counseling process.

References

Sanders, J. Oswald. *The Holy Spirit of Promise: The Mission and Ministry of the Comforter.* London: Marshall, Morgan & Scott, 1940.

Endnotes

1 J. Oswald Sanders, *The Holy Spirit of Promise: The Mission and Ministry of the Comforter* (London: Marshall, Morgan & Scott, 1940), 12–13.

10

BIBLICAL TRAITS AND THE SPIRITUAL DISCIPLINES IN COUNSELING

The Biblical Traits in Counseling
The Spiritual Disciplines in Counseling
The Character of a Christian Counselor
Accessing God's Resources in Counseling

T he character of biblical Christian counselors is shaped by their relationship to God and by service to other people. The God-given qualities that make us unique are developed through biblical traits and spiritual disciplines. Counselors mature in their faith and in their counseling ministry as they nurture and develop the biblical traits identified in Scripture and the spiritual disciplines. Biblical traits and spiritual disciplines are tangible expressions of an active faith and competent counseling. Evidence of these traits and disciplines should be apparent throughout the counseling process.

The Biblical Traits in Counseling

A survey and Delphi study [1] by Kevin Forrester asked prominent biblical and Christian counselors in the United States to identify the biblical traits and spiritual disciplines they believed had particular relevance to counselors and a counseling ministry. His goal was to develop a reliable list of biblically based, spiritual disciplines and biblical traits that Christian counselors could employ in their counseling ministry. The counselors reached a consensus on fifty-six biblical traits with strong agreement on forty-nine, and thirty-six spiritual disciplines with strong agreement on twenty.[2]

While there is a great deal of overlap between these traits and disciplines, we will distinguish between them by defining *biblical traits* as "those characteristics of believers described in the Bible that are outward manifestations of our inward faith in God and our relationship to Him," and *spiritual disciplines* as "the ancient (classical) practices of the Christian church that are revealed in Scripture and are designed to strengthen and enrich the individual by the power and presence of God, so that the individual will be able to walk and work in God's grace to do what man cannot do by direct effort."[3] Biblical traits are oriented more toward outward service and for the benefit of others, while the spiritual disciplines tend to have an inner direction with the purpose of personal spiritual maturation. The spiritual disciplines are activities or exercises that are practiced and developed for spiritual growth in the life of a Christian counselor, though this distinction between outward service and inner spiritual development is not valid in all cases. Richard Foster, for example, identified twelve spiritual disciplines in the Christian life. He divided these twelve into three groups: the inward disciplines of meditation, prayer, fasting, and study; the outward disciplines of simplicity, solitude, submission, and service; and the corporate disciplines of confession, worship, guidance, and celebration.[4] These traits and disciplines are not limited to actions or behavior; they may also refer to attitudes, emotional affect, and cognitive disposition. An important function of these traits and disciplines is that, in their active practice, they will improve spiritual effectiveness in counseling.

The following two sections contain brief comments and observations on the traits and disciplines in Forrester's study. Some terms appear on both lists or are also expressions of the fruit of the Spirit or the gifts of the Spirit. The biblical references given for the traits and disciplines are not comprehensive, and Christian counselors would benefit from the further study of these concepts. Counselors can begin a self-assessment of their biblical traits and spiritual disciplines by completing the checklists in tables 1 and 2.

"Love, joy, peace, patience, kindness, goodness, faithfulness, gentleness, self-control" (1 Cor. 13; Gal. 5:22–23)

The first nine traits identified by the counselors in Forrester's survey are also the fruit of the Spirit. They provide a foundation in counseling for qualities of inward stability, a godly attitude, and a godly conduct toward others. They shape the temperament of counselors, as we are conformed to the image of Christ. The remaining traits are listed beginning with those that emphasize relationship to God and moving through to traits that address the self and relationship to others. Some traits clearly overlap in meaning with others; however, the order of listing and the groupings are suggestive, not definitive, and should not imply discrete categories of relationship to God, self, and our neighbor. The brief summary of each trait along with the biblical references provides an initial point of departure for meditation and further study.

Living by the Spirit (Gal. 5:16,25)

In Galatians 5, Paul contrasts slavery, the law, and acts of the sinful nature with freedom in Christ, faith, and living by the Spirit. Those people who are led by the Spirit have crucified their sinful nature of passions and desires and now produce the fruit of the Spirit. Counselors are living by the Spirit, as they place an absolute faith and trust in the work of the Spirit in their lives.

Longing for God (Pss. 10:17; 73:25–26)

Christians who long for God will find their hearts strengthened and their prayers answered (Ps. 10:17). "Whom have I in heaven but You? And besides You, I desire nothing on earth. My flesh and my heart may fail, but God is the strength of my heart and my portion forever" (Ps. 73:25–26). Counselors long for the teachings of God to guide them (Ps. 119:40,174–176), and they wait on God to provide for them (Isa. 26:6; 30:18).

Walking with the Lord (1 John 1:7)

People who walk with the Lord are in agreement with him. They operate in the will of God, and they are not soiled by unclean elements in the world (Rev. 3:2). God promised Solomon that if he would walk with him as his father David had, then he would establish the throne of his kingdom over Israel forever. Walking with the Lord means to have integrity of heart and uprightness, to be responsive to the prompting of the Spirit of God, and to obey the commands or Word of God (1 Kings 9:4–5; Isa. 38:3).

Using the Armor of God (Eph. 6:10–18)

Christians are new people, born of the Spirit; they clothe themselves with the Lord Jesus Christ (Rom. 13:14). In Ephesians 6, Paul describes the spiritual clothing in terms of armor: the belt of truth, the breastplate of righteousness, sandals of readiness grounded in the gospel of peace, the shield of faith, the helmet of salvation, and the sword of the Spirit. The armor prepares Christians for battle against the spiritual forces of evil. God provides for our defense against attacks, and he gives us the offensive weapons of His Word and prayer. Counselors need to be equipped with the armor of God.

Knowledge of God's Word (Josh. 1:8; Ps. 119)

We succeed and prosper when we keep the Word of God in our minds and hearts and allow it to guide us. As we meditate upon the Word, our knowledge of God increases. Nearly every verse of Psalm 119 (1–176) contains words of description about, praise for, and instruction in God's Word. (The possible exceptions are verses 122 and 132, and they both deal with God's protection and mercy toward us.) This psalm emphasizes the importance of knowing the Word of God and applying it in our lives. "I will study your teachings and follow your footsteps. I will take pleasure in your laws and remember your words" (Ps. 119:15–16 CEV). Counselors must be thoroughly familiar with the Word of God.

Work toward Biblical Goals (Matt. 6:31–34; Luke 16:17)

Rather than focus on our problems, we Christians should seek the kingdom of God first, and allow God to take care of our needs (Matt. 6:31–34; Phil. 3:14; Ps. 27:4). Counselors encourage others to trust God and to work toward goals that honor him. "If you trust the LORD, you will never miss out on anything good. Come, my children, listen as I teach you to respect the LORD. Do you want to live and enjoy a long life? Then don't say cruel things and don't tell lies. Do good instead of evil and try to live at peace. If you obey the LORD, he will watch over you and answer your prayers" (Ps. 34:10b–15 CEV).

Giving God the Glory (Num. 14:11–20; Phil. 1:11)

To give glory to God is to acknowledge our own inadequacy and to confess our sins (Josh. 7:19–21; Jer. 13:16). Christian counselors seek to help others in ways that bring glory and praise to God (Phil. 1:11). They recognize that God is in control and that every good thing that occurs in counseling ultimately derives from him (Prov. 19:21). They are not motivated to draw attention and praise to themselves but to direct others to healing and wholeness in God.

Purity of Heart (Matt. 5:8)

In contrast to the Old Testament rituals and ceremonies of purification and an external morality, Christians must nurture an inward purity. We have a great high priest who allows us to "draw near with a sincere heart in full assurance of faith, having our hearts sprinkled *clean* from an evil conscience and our bodies washed with pure water" (Heb. 10:22). The pure in heart have a transparent honesty and sincerity in their attitude and actions. Such counselors seek the best for others and counsel with a spirit and attitude of faith, hope, and love. They are motivated to find the will of God in every situation.

Knowing Self (Rom. 12:3)

Christians should have honest and sober self-appraisals and not allow pride and boastfulness to cause them to think too highly of themselves. Counselors need to know their personal strengths and weaknesses and embrace the gifts apportioned to them through the measure of their faith (Rom. 12:3; 2 Cor. 10:13).

Renewed Mind (Rom. 12:2)

Christians seek obedience to Christ. Through conversion and spiritual maturation, they are able to exchange conformity to the world with a new life and new motives and goals made possible only by the power of God. As they progress toward righteousness and obedience to Christ, Christians seek to be transformed by the renewal of their minds. More than simply a new way of thinking, a renewed mind is part of a spiritual transformation and a new life in Christ that is dependent on the renewing work of his Spirit. "Don't be like the people of this world, but let God change the way you think" (Rom. 12:2 CEV).

Thoughts Obedient to Christ (2 Cor. 10:5)

Christians are empowered with the Holy Spirit, who demolishes every thought and prideful attitude that opposes the knowledge of God. They voluntarily submit their minds and thoughts in obedience to Christ and allow his reasoning and understanding to be manifest in their hearts and lives.

Wisdom (Proverbs; Col. 3:16; Eph. 1:17)

Wisdom has been discussed previously in connection with the Messiah (chapter 6) and the gifts of the Spirit (chapter 9). The emphasis that Scripture places on this biblical trait suggests that Christian counselors should seek to grow in wisdom and actively solicit the blessing of divine wisdom. "But if any of you lacks wisdom, let him ask of God, who gives to all generously and without reproach, and it will be given to him" (James 1:5).

Discernment (Phil. 1:9–11)

Discernment is one of the gifts of the Spirit (1 Cor. 12:10). Paul prayed for the Philippians that their love would "abound more and more in knowledge and depth of insight," so that they would "be able to discern what is best" and be pure and blameless (Phil. 1:9–11 NIV). Spiritual discernment is the ability to have the correct understanding or to see the right thing to do in a situation from God's perspective.

Prayerful Attitude (1 Thess. 5:17)

A prayerful attitude acknowledges that God is our refuge and deliverer from troubles and expresses an unconditional faith, trust, and hope in him (Ps. 31). Such an attitude calls out to God for insight and searches diligently for understanding (Prov. 2:3–5). Brother Lawrence, the seventeenth-century Carmelite lay brother, said that "the time of business does not differ with me from the time of prayer."[5] In other words, communion with God can occur under any conditions and circumstances, including before, during, and after counseling. Biblical Christian counselors desire to be in continuous communication with God, and they repetitively petition him as a child seeking direction from a father (1 Thess. 5:17).

Thankfulness (Col. 3:12–17)

Christians express gratitude to God by the way they live their lives. All their words and actions are done in the name of Christ as a means of giving thanks to God the Father through the Lord Jesus. They express a heart of thankfulness to God in all their work and activities. Counselors express thankfulness to God in counseling situations for what he has done and what he will do in their lives.

Hope (1 Cor. 13:13)

Christians are born again into a living hope through the resurrection of Jesus Christ (1 Pet. 1:3). Hope, along with faith and love, is a fundamental element of Christian character. Christ is the object of a believer's hope (Eph. 1:18; 4:4; 1 Tim. 1:1; Col. 1:27), and this hope enables Christian counselors to offer healing and empowerment beyond anything secular counseling interventions are capable of producing. Hope is a necessary part of successful therapeutic counseling.

Humility (Phil. 2:3–5; Eph. 4:2; Col. 3:12; 1 Pet. 5:5)

An attitude of humility acknowledges our spiritual condition in relation to God. The Latin etymology of *humble* conveys the idea of "lowly" as in low ground. Within a counseling context, the term supports a "one-down" attitude, in which we recognize the insufficiency of our wisdom and knowledge in comparison to God and our inability to comprehend and understand completely the problems and issues our counselees face. Philippians 2:3–5 tells us that we should consider others ahead of ourselves and care for their interests. God gives his grace to those people who clothe themselves with humility toward others (1 Pet. 5:5).

Self-Giving (Phil. 2:5–11)

Christians follow the example of Christ, who gave himself completely, taking on the nature of a servant and a physical body to serve and to save others through the atoning sacrifice of his life on the cross.

Endurance (2 Tim. 3:10–11; 4:5)

Paul encouraged Timothy to endure hardship just as he had endured persecution and had depended on God to rescue him (2 Tim. 3:10–11; 4:5). *Endurance* means "having the ability to stay in the race until its completion; to withstand opposition, problems, difficulties, temptations and sin, by keeping our eyes on Jesus." Endurance increases the more our faith is tested (Heb. 12:1–2; James 1:3–4). Counseling requires endurance as you encounter difficult situations, destructive and dysfunctional attitudes and behaviors, and opposing temporal and spiritual forces.

Hunger and Thirst for Righteousness (Matt. 5:6)

The Bible enjoins Christians to strive for righteousness as they seek the establishment of God's will and way in every area of life. While the condition of right standing before God cannot be attained outside the righteousness of Christ and his sacrificial gift of salvation (Rom. 3:21–26; 5:18–21), all Christians are expected to live by faith and allow Christ to produce the fruit of righteousness in their lives (Phil. 1:11). Such righteousness will be expressed in exemplary moral conduct and the fruit of the Spirit (Gal. 5:22). Christian counselors hunger and thirst for righteousness as they model Christ and live their lives by faith through the grace of God. In the process, their personal conduct and counseling activities draw people toward the spiritual food and living water (John 4:13–14) that will provide eternal comfort and peace, regardless of current afflictions, problems, and circumstances.

Biblical Morality (James 1:22–25)

Biblical morality does more than lend lip service to rules, guidelines, and the Word of God. We must hide the Word of God in our heart (Ps. 119:11). Christian counselors need to develop an intrinsic sense of right and wrong that reflects the truth of God. "Obey God's message! Don't fool yourselves by just listening to it. If you hear the message and don't obey it, you are like people who stare at themselves in a mirror and forget what they look like as soon as they leave. But you must never stop looking at the perfect law that sets you free. God will bless you in everything you do, if you listen and obey, and don't just hear and forget" (James 1:22–25 CEV).

Not Practicing Worldliness (Rom. 12:2)

Christians must not be double minded and torn between God and the practices of the world (James 4:4–8). They must exercise faith, not doubt (James 1:5–8), and not conform to the patterns and expectation of the world. Paul listed numerous examples of worldly practices that believers must avoid (e.g., Gal. 5:19–21; Col. 3:5–10).

Integrity (1 Kings 9:4)

The Bible speaks of the "integrity of the heart" (e.g., Gen. 20:5–6; 1 Kings 9:4) or a thorough and complete honesty, trustworthiness, and an authenticity that breeds righteousness (Ps. 7:8). Christian counselors must ensure that integrity is a hallmark of their ministry to others.

Truthfulness (Eph. 4:25)

A truthful witness is one who does not deceive people (Prov. 14:5). The biblical trait of truthfulness is a state of habitual trustworthiness. We stand firm in truth (Eph. 6:14). A Christian counselor seeks to reveal the truth of God in Christ (John 14:6; Col. 1:5–6) and to separate truth from falsehood in life (Prov. 12:17,19).

Acceptance (Rom. 15:16)

Because Christians are in Christ and belong to him, God accepts them, and they serve him (Rom. 7:4). They express this acceptance through their obedience to Christ (1 John 2:3–6), and they model his acceptance and love toward others, including those who may be considered weak or inconsequential, such as children (Matt. 19:13–15) and even enemies (Matt. 5:43–48). Christian counselors express an attitude of acceptance toward people in need that invites them to seek peace and healing in the will of God.

Respect (John 4:1–15)

Christians honor God by showing respect or fear toward him and obeying his commands (Eccl. 12:13; Mal. 1:6). We respect whatever is honorable to God and to others (2 Cor. 8:21; Rom. 12:17). As counselors understand the love of God for his creation, they show respect toward all people, despite their spiritual condition or situation. The respect and value Christ conveyed to the woman at the well (John 4:1–15) provides counselors with a model to emulate.

Compassion (Col. 3:12)

Compassion is the genuine concern and consideration for the physical, mental, relational, and spiritual needs of others, and it is expressed in the desire to render aid and support. Jesus felt compassion for people because they were distressed and dispirited and they had no one to assist them. He challenged his followers to pray for helpers (Matt. 9:36–38). Compassion motivated the good Samaritan to bandage and pour oil and wine on the wounds of a man who was beaten and robbed and to carry him to safety (Luke 10:33–34). Colossians 3:12 tells us that we are to "put on a heart of compassion," that is, an inner yearning for mercy that drives us to show pity and to aid others.

Meekness (Matt. 5:5; 11:28–30)

Meekness is a character quality associated with gentleness and humility; it is a mild and friendly demeanor, not to be confused with weakness. God listens to the meek and lowly (Ps. 138:6). Meekness is a quality of those people who will inherit the earth. Condescension or meekness is a quality of God (Ps. 18:35) and a godly leader. The godly ruler champions the cause of truth and acts in meekness and righteousness (Ps. 45:4). Paul talks of the meekness and gentleness of Christ, and he describes his own attitude as meek or lowly when he is with the Corinthians (2 Cor. 10:1). The guidance and teaching of Jesus, which bring rest for souls, were done with a gentle and humble attitude (Matt. 11:28–30). We should imitate Christ in our counseling by developing a meek and gentle spirit.

Merciful (Matt. 5:7)

The Bible describes God as "merciful and gracious, slow to anger and abundant in lovingkindness and truth" (Ps. 86:15). A merciful spirit shows sympathy and tenderness toward others and engages in responsive and compassionate actions to meet needs, following the example of Christ. Through the incarnation, Christ became like us in every respect. He became a merciful or sympathetic and faithful high priest, in order to atone for the people's sins (Heb. 2:16–17). In like manner we demonstrate mercy and sympathy through our desire to help others, even our enemies, and to provide for their needs. These acts of mercy are characteristic of those people who will inherit the kingdom. In showing mercy we receive mercy from God (Matt. 24:34–36; Luke 6:35–36). The merciful man is good to his own soul (Prov. 11:17).

Empathy (Heb. 4:15)

Empathy is the ability to comprehend and understand the feelings and experience of other people, to look through their eyes and walk in their shoes for a time. It does not mean that we agree with their morality or condone their behavior. Christ is able to "sympathize with our weaknesses" because he "has been tempted in every way, just as we are—yet was without sin" (Heb. 4:15 NIV). This empathy enabled him to minister to people like Matthew the tax collector and the woman caught in adultery. His attitude and actions provide a model for us to follow in developing genuine empathy for people who need our help.

Forgiveness (Eph. 4:32)

We must be willing to forgive others for what they have done to us (Mark 11:25–26). At the heart of forgiveness is the recognition of the sacrifice and forgiveness God has extended to us through Christ (Eph. 4:32; Col. 3:13). Forgiveness is found in the Golden Rule that tells us to treat others in the same way we wish to be treated and to be kind and forgiving even to those people who are ungrateful and cruel to us (Luke 6:27–37). "So be careful what you do. Correct any followers of mine who sin, and forgive the ones who say they are sorry. Even if one of them mistreats you seven times in one day and says, 'I am sorry,' you should still forgive that person" (Luke 17:3–4 CEV). Christian counselors need to model a forgiving attitude to their counselees.

Ability to Relate Well to Others

Paul challenges us to "not lose heart in doing good" and to take the opportunity to "do good to all people, especially those who are in the household of the faith" (Gal. 6: 9–10). Our ability to relate well to others enables us to show benevolence to all people, both Christian and non-Christian. Paul used the model of being all things to all people (1 Cor. 9:22) as a means of developing relationships that enabled him to share the gospel. Effective Christian counselors are able to adjust to the location of people in terms of their language, culture, situation, and needs, enabling them to "do good" as they learn to relate well to others.

Approachable (1 Tim. 3:1–3)

Christian counselors should develop an approachable spirit or attitude that invites confidence and conveys a sincere desire to help others. Approachable people are friendly and hospitable toward others (Heb. 13:2; 1 Pet. 4:9). They serve and care for others (3 John 5–6).

Able to Teach (1 Tim. 2:24; 3:2; 2 Tim. 1:13–14)

Christian counselors should develop their teaching skills as part of their caregiving ministry. Teaching involves the ability to instruct, train, and coach people in knowledge, relationships, communication skills, and other aspects of problem solving.

Giving Comfort and Encouragement (2 Cor. 1:3–7; Ps. 10:17)

We are to encourage (from the Greek *parakaleo*) one another and support or build up one another (1 Thess. 5:11). Comfort and encouragement are functions of the Holy Spirit (Acts 9:31). The Spirit comforts us in our afflictions, empowering us to comfort and encourage others (2 Cor. 1:3–7). The grace of God comforts our hearts and encourages us to express good deeds and words (2 Thess. 2:16–17). Counselors offer comfort and encouragement to people in need.

Avoiding Quarrels (2 Tim. 2:23–26)

The Bible tells us that we must not quarrel with God (Isa. 45:9) or engage in controversial questions and disputes and wrangles about words that undermine a biblical witness and doctrine (1 Tim. 6:3–4; 2 Tim. 2:14; Titus 3:9). We must not let our emotions get the better of us and allow envy to lead to strife and quarreling. Instead, out of pure motives we must ask God to meet our needs (James 4:1–3). Counselors must not have a quarrelsome spirit; instead, they should nurture a spirit of love and reconciliation.

Peacemakers (Matt. 5:9; James 3:18)

Peace and peacemaking are virtues of God (Heb. 13:20; Rom. 16:20), and he is able to grant us peace in every circumstance or situation (2 Thess. 3:16). Christians are reconciled with Christ, and they have been given a ministry of reconciliation whereby others may come to know the peace of God that passes all understanding (2 Cor. 5:18–21; Phil. 4:7). As peacemakers, we reflect the likeness of God. One of the activities of counseling is to plant seeds of peace that produce righteous living (James 3:18).

Holding Others Accountable (Matt. 18:15–16)

We are expected to support others by helping them see their errors and faults and by seeking their restoration, but we must exercise caution that we don't overlook our own weaknesses or yield to temptation (Gal. 6:1; Matt. 7:4–5). Matthew 18 describes the steps we must take in the process of accountability, forgiveness, and reconciliation.

Confrontation (Matt. 18:15–17; 1 Thess. 5:12–14)

Christians have an obligation to warn and remind others of the consequences of their behavior and to be a godly influence through wise advice and biblical correction (Col. 1:28; 3:16). Biblical confrontation directs people toward virtuous living and the redemptive plan of God.

An Example to Those Served (1 Tim. 4:12)

Christian counselors and leaders are to be an example to others whom they seek to serve (1 Pet. 5:3), just as Christ set an example of humility and service for his disciples (John 13:12). Paul told Timothy to be an example in his speech, behavior, love, faith, and purity (1 Tim. 4:12).

Table 1. Biblical Traits in Counseling Checklist

Identify your biblical traits by placing a ☑ next to the ones you actively practice and an ☒ next to the ones where you think you need improvement. Write in any additional traits you believe are essential for you in counseling.					
Love (1 Cor. 13; Gal. 5:22–23)		Knowing self (Rom. 12:3; 2 Cor. 10:13)		Respect (John 4:1–15; Rom. 12:17)	
Joy (Gal. 5:22–23)		Renewed mind (Rom. 12:2)		Compassion (Col. 3:12)	
Peace (Gal. 5:22–23)		Thoughts obedient to Christ (2 Cor. 10:5)		Meekness (Matt. 5:5; 11:28–30)	
Patience (Gal. 5:22–23)		Wisdom (Prov.; Col. 3:16; Eph. 1:17)		Merciful (Matt. 5:7; Prov. 11:17)	
Kindness (Gal. 5:22–23)		Discernment (Phil. 1:9–11)		Empathy (Heb. 4:15)	
Goodness (Gal. 5:22–23)		Prayerful attitude (1 Thess. 5:17)		Forgiveness (Eph. 4:32)	
Faithfulness (Gal. 5:22–23)		Thankfulness (Col. 3:12–17)		Ability to relate well to others (Eph. 4:1–3)	
Gentleness (Gal. 5:22–23)		Hope (1 Cor. 13:13; 1 Pet. 1:3; Col. 1:27)		Approachable (1 Tim. 3:1–3)	
Self–control (Gal. 5:22–23)		Humility (Phil. 2:3–5; Eph. 4:2; Col. 3:12; 1 Pet. 5:5)		Able to teach (1 Tim. 2:24; 3:2; 2 Tim. 1:13–14)	
Living in the Spirit (Gal. 5:16, 25)		Self–giving (Phil. 2:5–11)		Giving comfort and encouragement (2 Cor.1:3–7; Ps. 10:17)	
A Longing for God (Pss. 10:17; 73:25–26)		Endurance (2 Tim. 3:10–11; 4:5)		Avoiding quarrels (2 Tim. 2:14,23–26)	
Walking with the Lord (1 John 1:7)		Hunger & thirst for righteousness (Matt. 5:6)		Peacemakers (Matt. 5:9; James 3:18)	
Using the armor of God (Eph. 6:10–18)		Biblical morality (Jas. 1:22–25; Ps. 119:11)		Holding others account-able (Matt. 18:15–16)	
Knowledge of God's Word (Josh. 1:8; Ps. 119)		Not practicing worldliness (Rom. 12:2; Jas. 4:4–8)		Confrontation (Matt. 18:15–17; Col. 1:28; 3:16; 1 Thess. 5:12–14)	
Work toward biblical goals (Matt. 6:31–34; Luke 16:17)		Integrity (1 Kings 9:4; Ps. 7:8)		An example to those served (1 Tim. 4:12; 1 Pet. 5:3)	

| Giving God the glory (Num. 14:11–20; Phil. 1:11) | Truthfulness (Eph. 4:25) | |
| Pure in heart (Matt. 5:8; Heb. 10:21) | Acceptance (Rom. 15:16; Matt. 19:13–15) | |

Additional Biblical Traits for Study

Some additional biblical traits suggested by Christian counselors as important in caregiving include the attitude of mourning (Matt. 5:4), being salt of the earth and light of the world (Matt. 5:13–14), being a good minister (1 Tim. 4:6), and taking the bitter and making it sweet (Exod. 15:22–25). (See table 1 above, "Biblical Traits in Counseling Checklist.")

The Spiritual Disciplines in Counseling

The spiritual disciplines are the habits we practice and develop in order to increase our spiritual devotion and growth in the Lord.[6] Some of these disciplines have a direct correlation with the quality of our biblical counseling. The following disciplines were identified in Forrester's survey of Christian counselors; however, the list should not be considered exhaustive. As with the list of biblical traits, the disciplines follow a general order of emphasis on relationship to God, self, and finally our neighbor. The brief descriptions and comments are designed to help you identify and practice the spiritual disciplines and to encourage you to study them and to search the Scriptures for additional insights and direction.

Prayer (Matt. 6:5–13; 1 Thess. 5:17–18)

Prayer may take the form of intercession for ourselves or for the needs of others, as we make our requests known to God (Eph. 6:18–19). Prayers can be contemplative, as we remain receptive to him and ponder the experience and wonder of God (Pss. 46:10; 24:1–6), or we can learn to pray in the Spirit. Praying in the Spirit is a type of verbal prayer spoken by the Holy Spirit who intercedes for us (Rom. 8:26) or a spiritual language uttered as we talk with God (1 Cor. 12:10). Christian counselors need to be persistent in their prayers (Luke 18:1–8; Eph.

6:18) and pray in faith for their counselees that they may experience restoration and spiritual wholeness (James 5:13–18).

Listening Prayer (Ps. 130:5–6; 1 Sam. 3:8–10)

Listening prayer concentrates on receiving communication from God without the topical focus of contemplative prayer. The soul waits for the Lord to speak. Our tendency is to want to speak to God and tell him our problems. The discipline of listening prayer opens our hearts and minds to the Word of God without any impediment, distraction, or predetermined agenda on our part.

Praise (Heb. 13:15)

We learn to offer our praise and thanksgiving to God as we tell of his wonders and worship him (Ps. 9:1–2). We are to offer up continually a sacrifice of praise and give thanks to his name (Heb. 13:15). The practice of praise allows us to draw attention to the Author of truth and energizes us in the counseling process. Through praise to God, we learn to rely on his power and not our own, we avoid self–aggrandizement, and we overcome discouragement and the burdens that weigh us down in the counseling encounter.

Scripture: Counselor Proactive (2 Tim. 3:14–17; Col. 3:16)

Counselors learn to use Scripture to teach, help, admonish, correct, and train others in godly living and good deeds. The Bible provides the authoritative guide for the Christian counselor, and it should permeate the counseling process. Under the power of the Holy Spirit, wise counselors know the Word, live in the Word, and reveal the Word. They avoid abusing Scripture through misinterpretation, fostering personal agendas, or legalistic requirements that undermine the path to healing and wholeness.

Obedience (Phil. 2:5–8; 1 John 5:3)

Mature Christians learn to submit their wills and rights to the Lord; they obey his commands and follow the servanthood model of Christ. Our obedience is directly related to our belief in the Son of God and the receiving of the Holy Spirit (John 3:36; Heb. 5:9; Acts 5:32). The discipline of obedience provides a model to others of living in the will of God, as the fruits of the Spirit are more clearly manifest in the believer's life.

Listening and Guidance (Eccl. 3:7; Matt. 13:9,13; 1 Cor. 2:10–12; James 1:22)

Christian counselors should develop and practice the discipline of listening. They need to learn the times to be silent (Eccl. 3:7) and to develop an ear of understanding that comprehends the motives of the heart and the underlying dimensions and issues in a situation. Failure to listen carefully to counselees will result in an inability to locate them correctly and will lead subsequently to poor counsel. As part of a listening regimen, counselors learn both to receive and to give guidance. The primary sources of guidance for Christian counselors are the Holy Spirit and the Word of God. As they learn to trust in the Lord and not in their own understanding, the Holy Spirit will guide them on the right path (Prov. 3:5–6). Mature counselors also observe and listen to the wisdom of God expressed in his creation (Matt. 6:25–30). In addition, listening to capable and experienced teachers and a desire to learn and to receive instruction lead to wisdom (Prov. 19:20).

Being an Example (1 Tim. 4:12,16; 1 Pet. 5:3)

Counselors should practice exemplary character and avoid any behavior that may cause others to doubt or stray (Titus 2:6–8). They need to develop a lifestyle, following the example of Christ, that serves as a model of faith, hope, and discipline (2 Thess. 3:7–9; 1 Pet. 2:21). People who come to counseling should expect to find a counselor whose life demonstrates the healthy and spiritually wholesome lifestyle that they desire.

Maintaining Purity (Rom. 12:1–2)

Christians learn to remain pure regardless of the hardships, afflictions, abuses, and difficulties they encounter (2 Cor. 6:4–6). Christians must maintain a soundness or purity in doctrine (Titus 2:7) and in their relationships with others (1 Tim. 4:12; 5:2). This discipline is essential in the counseling ministry, where counselors face temptations, personal stress, and emotional, mental, physical, and spiritual exhaustion.

Thought Life (Phil. 4:8)

Christian counselors seek to think like Christ and to keep their minds on "whatever is true, pure, right, holy, friendly, and proper. Don't ever stop thinking about what is truly worthwhile and worthy of praise" (Phil. 4:8 CEV). Counselors train their thoughts to focus on things that are godly, healthy, truthful, and worthwhile. They assist others to develop thinking that is not just rational but biblical and righteous.

Discernment (1 John 4:1,6; Heb. 5:14)

Counselors need to develop a discerning spirit, whereby they are able to distinguish godly truth from falsehood. Through constant training, mature Christian counselors learn to know right from wrong (Heb. 5:14).

Confession/Repentance (Ps. 51:1–3; Acts 20:21)

Confession of sin and repentance are essential practices in the Christian life (1 John 1:8–10). We must acknowledge our transgressions before God and ask for his forgiveness (Ps. 32:5–6a). We also confess our faults to one another and pray for one another so that we might be healed (James 5:16). Confession and repentance are often central issues in a counseling situation, and wise counselors possess mature knowledge and experience in this area in their personal lives and in their counseling ministry.

Accountability (James 5; Heb. 10; 13)

Christians practice accountability in their own lives and in support of their brethren. They look for ways to "spur one another on toward love and good deeds" and encourage one another (Heb. 10:24–25 NIV). They must show accountability in their love for the church, their relationships with their families and with strangers, their self-control and personal attitudes, service to others, leadership responsibilities and relationships, financial matters, and doctrinal issues (Heb. 13; James 5).

Growth (Phil. 3:12)

Healthy Christians learn and grow in the Christian life. Paul spoke of pressing on toward the goal "to win the prize for which God has called me heavenward in Christ Jesus" (Phil. 3:12–16 NIV). He made clear that he had not arrived in perfection, but his spiritual maturation had changed his perception. God makes things clearer as you grow in the faith. Counseling and the discipline of growth focus on development and maturation in godly relationships and in the Christian faith.

Wisdom (James 1:5)

Christian counselors should actively seek wisdom from God and try to grow in wisdom through every counseling encounter and learning opportunity. Asking the questions "What did I learn from this situation or experience?" and "What is God teaching me?" should be part of the evaluative process of every counseling encounter. Counselors grow in wisdom when they take what they have learned and they are able to modify and apply such information therapeutically in subsequent counseling contexts. (Review chapters 6 and 9 for a more extended discussion on the role of wisdom in counseling.)

Agape Love (1 Cor. 12:31–13:13)

John defines the essential nature of God as one of love. We understand this love through the sacrificial life of Christ, and we must follow his example by loving one another and surrendering our lives in service to others (1 John 3:11–20; 4:7–12). Love is expressed in kindness, patience, rejoicing in the truth, supportiveness, loyalty, hope, and trust. It is the antidote to envy, jealousy, boastfulness, pride, rudeness, offensiveness, resentment, keeping an account of the wrongdoing of others, selfishness, and evil desires. Love motivates counselors to seek truth and righteousness (1 Cor. 13). "Love bears up under anything *and* everything that comes, is ever ready to believe the best of every person, its hopes are fadeless under all circumstances, and it endures everything [without weakening]" (1 Cor. 13:7 AMP).

Compassion (Matt. 9:36; Heb. 13:16; James 1:27a)

The righteous leader learns to show compassion toward the poor and the needy and to help them in the same way Christ responded to the distressed and dispirited people and healed the sick (Ps. 72:12–13; Matt. 9:6; 14:14). We develop compassion as we confess and forsake our sins (Prov. 28:13). Our acknowledgment of our own inadequacies and needs directs us to show consideration and caring toward others. Compassion motivates Christian counselors to share the love of God. Counselors who are unable to demonstrate compassion toward others in need are like the priest and the Levite in the story of the good Samaritan who devalue people by studious detachment and a failure to render genuine assistance.

Forgiveness (Eph. 4:32)

Christians learn to be compassionate and kind toward others and seek ways to find and express forgiveness, in the same manner as Christ has forgiven them. The forgiveness that God extends to us makes possible our forgiveness of others (Ps. 103:1–5,10–12). Christian counselors should develop the discipline of learning to forgive that demonstrates a freedom in Christ without dismissing or ignoring biblical accountability (Matt. 6:12–15; 18:21–35; Mark 11:25; Luke 17:3–4; 1 John 1:9).

Service (Matt. 20:26–28; 1 Pet. 4:10)

We follow the example of Christ by using our gifts to serve others. We use our freedom in Christ as an opportunity to engage in loving acts of service, fulfilling the command to "love your neighbor as yourself" (Gal. 5:13–14). The discipline of service draws upon the time, skills, abilities, knowledge, emotions, will, and even material resources of the counselor as a sacrificial offering to God for use in healing others and the promotion of his kingdom.

Caring (Luke 10:34–35; 1 Tim. 3:5)

As members of the one body of Christ, Christians must care for one another to the extent that if one person suffers, all experience the suffering (1 Cor. 12:25–26). Caring expresses itself in the earnest desire and actions that lead to healing within the individual, family, or group at all levels (spiritual, physical, cognitive, affective, behavioral, social), in relationship to God, to self, and to others. Effective Christian counselors develop caring attitudes and actions.

Ministering to All Needs (Matt. 25:31–46)

Christ made clear that he expected believers to minister to all needs. We are to provide for the hungry, the thirsty, the stranger, the one needing clothes, the sick, and the imprisoned, as though they were Christ himself. We must see the image of God in all people, as ones created and loved by him. We do not abandon a person when we lack skill or competence in meeting a need. Instead, we find assistance for the person through referral or alternative support and counsel. When necessary and where possible, counselors seek to improve and extend their skills in ministering to needs.

Additional Spiritual Disciplines

Some additional spiritual disciplines identified by the counselors in Forrester's survey include fellowship one with another (2 Cor. 13:14), active Scripture reading by the client (Ps. 119:9–16; 2 Tim. 2:15), Scripture reading in general (2 Tim. 3:16–17; Ezra 7:10), solitude and silence (Pss. 46:10; 131:2), religious imagery, simplicity (Matt. 6:22–34; Col. 3:1–5), healing (Mic. 6:13; James 5:14–15), Bible study (Heb. 4:12–13), yielding and submission (John 12:24–25; 2 Cor. 12:9–10; Eph. 5:21; Matt. 5:38–42), journal keeping (Psalms), deliverance (Matt. 10:8), and witnessing (John 3:16; Rom. 8:31–32). (See table 2.)

Table 2. Spiritual Disciplines in Counseling Checklist

Place a ☑ next to the spiritual disciplines that you actively practice and an ☒ next to the ones where you need improvement. Write in any additional spiritual disciplines you believe are essential for you in counseling.	
Prayer (Matt. 6:5–13; Luke 18:1–8; 1 Thess. 5:17–18; James 5:13–18)	Confession/repentance (Ps. 51:1–3; Acts 20:21)
Listening prayer (Ps. 130:5–6; 1 Sam. 3:8–10)	Accountability (James 5; Heb. 10, 13)
Praise (Heb. 13:15; Ps. 9:1–2)	Growth (Phil. 3:12–16)

Scripture: counselor proactive (2 Tim. 3:14–17; Col. 3:16)	Wisdom (James 1:5)
Obedience (Phil. 2:5–8; 1 John 5:3)	Agape love (1 Cor. 12:31–13:13)
Listening and guidance (Prov. 3:5–6; Eccl. 3:7; Matt. 13:9, 13; 1 Cor. 2:10–12; James 1:22)	Compassion (Matt. 9:36; Heb. 13:16; James 1:27a)
Being an example (1 Tim. 4:12,16; 1 Pet. 5:3; Titus 2:6–8)	Forgiveness (Eph. 4:32)
Maintaining purity (Rom. 12:1–2)	Service (Matt. 20:26–28; 1 Pet. 4:10)
Thought life (Phil. 4:8)	Caring (Luke 10:34–35; 1 Tim. 3:5; 1 Cor. 12:25–26)
Discernment (1 John 4:1,6; Heb. 5:14)	Ministering to all needs (Matt. 25:31–46)

The Character of a Christian Counselor (Based on 1 Thess. 5:14–24)

A beneficial exercise for Christian counselors who wish to develop their spiritual acuity is to study Scripture through the eyes of a caregiver and ask themselves how particular passages apply to their ministry. In other words, they can glean counseling principles and procedures from the narratives and teachings in the Word of God. For example, if you read 1 Thessalonians 5:14–24 from the perspective of pastoral care and counseling, you will find fifteen biblical qualities of an effective biblical counselor.

A wise pastoral counselor:

- Warns those people who are failing to act correctly (v. 14).
- Encourages and supports and empowers those people who are reluctant to act or feel left out (v. 14).
- Helps or assists those people who are not capable or strong enough to act alone (v 14).
- Remains patient with everyone (v. 14), even as God is patient, wanting everyone to turn from their sin (2 Pet. 3:9,15).
- Intervenes to prevent retribution or repayment of evil for evil (v. 15).
- Expresses kindness and goodness toward others (v. 15).

- Continuously expresses joy and the fruit of the Spirit—an indication of the presence of God (v. 16; cf. Ps. 139).
- Repeatedly petitions God and maintains an attitude of prayer at all times—an awareness and an acknowledgment of the presence of God in every situation and a desire to communicate with him at all times (v. 17).
- Gives thanks to God that he is acting in all situations (v. 18).
- Does not ignore God or reject the guidance of his Spirit (v. 19). (The opposite of love is not hate but indifference. Do not quench or dismiss the Spirit of God.)
- Looks for the plans (prophecies) of God in all situations (v. 20).
- Thoroughly evaluates everything and retains that which is good (v. 21).
- Actively practices avoiding evil (v. 22).
- Has a personal goal of growing in godliness (v. 23).
- Recognizes that only God is capable of producing and accomplishing these things! (v. 24). (We must depend on God at all times and in every way.)

Accessing God's Resources in Counseling

God has provided us with the gift of his Spirit, the fruit of the Spirit, and spiritual gifts. Christians can also nurture and develop biblical traits and spiritual disciplines. God gives his children an abundance of healthy spiritual food to help them grow and mature, but some Christians appear to be on a spiritual starvation diet. They wander past the spiritual supermarket and ignore or fail to see God's provisions. Their spiritual muscles atrophy, and they develop spiritual anemia. These believers spend their lives in a state of spiritual weakness because they fail to respond to God's call to consume his spiritual resources.

Another group will enter the store, but they are afraid to take the food. They may nibble at some of the items on the lower shelves, but they avoid the abundance on the other aisles and on the higher shelves. They may fear what will happen to them if they eat too much or if they try something different. These Christians have some spiritual energy, but they lack the spiritual fortification that builds endurance, and they tend to falter under heavy loads and harsh conditions.

A third group yields to the guidance of the Spirit. They explore the many aisles and accept the gifts and the spiritual sustenance. They reach for the resources on the higher shelves; and their spiritual strength, faith, and hope grow as they consume the healthy food. These believers look for opportunities to exercise their spiritual muscles; they thrive in situations that strain the faith and test the resources of other believers.

The challenge for Christian counselors is to be a part of the third group. Too many counselors fail to access all the riches God provides. They look to their own strength, knowledge, and abilities and overlook the bountiful spiritual resources at their disposal. They need to embrace the power of his Spirit and minister to others out of an abundant life (John 10:10b).

Summary

1. A survey of biblical and Christian counselors identified nearly fifty biblical traits and twenty spiritual disciplines that enhance the effectiveness of a counseling ministry. These traits and disciplines were briefly described, and two checklists were included for counselor self-assessment.

2. A brief summary of the character of a biblical Christian counselor, based on 1 Thessalonians 5:14–24, was given as an example of applying biblical truth to a counseling ministry.

3. A final challenge was issued to Christian counselors to take advantage of the abundant spiritual resources God has made available to us. Counselors need to allow the Spirit to do his work through the ministry of counseling and nurture the fruit of the Spirit, the gifts of the Spirit, biblical traits, and spiritual disciplines.

Where Do We Go from Here?

The abundant spiritual resources supplied by God and the counseling guidelines found in the model of the Messiah and the ministry of Christ provide a foundation for a ministry of caregiving. The final chapter will examine the way we can evaluate counseling approaches and how we should relate to one another as we deal with disagreements over the nature and content of biblical Christian counseling.

Questions and Exercises for Reflection

1. What biblical traits and spiritual disciplines on the two lists would you add or delete? Give reasons for your additions and deletions.
2. What are the most important biblical traits and spiritual disciplines in counseling? Give reasons for your selection.
3. After you have completed the two checklists, develop a personal plan for improvement in the practice of biblical traits and spiritual disciplines.
4. Describe a situation in which you have applied your biblical traits and spiritual disciplines in a ministry of care to others.
5. What are some reasons people give for failing to use the spiritual resources that God provides for us? How would you develop these resources in a counseling ministry?

References

Brother Lawrence. *The Practice of the Presence of God*. Peabody, Mass.: Hendrickson, 2004.

Forrester, Kevin Scott. "Determining the Biblical Traits and Spiritual Disciplines Christian Counselors Employ in Practice: A Delphi Study." Ph.D. Dissertation. Fort Worth, Tex.: Southwestern Baptist Theological Seminary, 2002.

Foster, Richard. *Celebration of Discipline: The Path to Spiritual Growth*. London: Hodder & Stoughton, 1978.

Whitney, Donald S. *Spiritual Disciplines for the Christian Life*. Colorado Springs, Colo.: NavPress, 1991.

Endnotes

1 The Delphi method is an interactive form of research. It involves surveying acknowledged experts for their opinions in a field of study. Each expert is then given the opportunity to respond to the opinions of the other experts. Revised surveys are repeated until a consensus emerges.

2 Kevin Scott Forrester, "Determining the Biblical Traits and Spiritual Disciplines Christian Counselors Employ in Practice: A Delphi Study," Ph.D. Dissertation, Fort Worth, Tex.: Southwestern Baptist Theological Seminary, 2002, 151–57.

3 Ibid., 42–43.

4 Richard Foster, *Celebration of Discipline: The Path to Spiritual Growth* (London: Hodder & Stoughton, 1978).

5 Brother Lawrence, *The Practice of the Presence of God* (Peabody, Mass.: Hendrickson, 2004). At the time he said this, he was working in the monastery kitchen as a cook.

6 Donald S. Whitney, *Spiritual Disciplines for the Christian Life* (Colorado Springs, Colo.: NavPress, 1991), 17.

11

ESTABLISHING THE LOCATION
OF COUNSELORS

The Bible establishes our location in relationship to God and our neighbor. It reveals Christ and provides counselors with the authoritative guide to human nature and the spiritual resources available to Christians for the ministry of caregiving. The field of counseling is comprised of numerous theories, models, techniques, philosophies of care, and theological perspectives that vary widely in their agreement and differences with the biblical view. Biblical Christian counselors need to evaluate carefully the field and seek the wisdom of God in developing their counseling theory and skills. Strong opinions exist within the community of faith regarding the correct biblical approach to counseling, the selection and use of resources outside of Scripture, the appropriate context for counseling, the requirements for training, and the definition and nature of biblical counseling.

Counselors need to study these issues; however, they also need to remember the foundation of unity in Christ upon which all Christians rest (Eph. 2:13–22). The church is the body of Christ on earth, and we have a responsibility to care for one another and acknowledge the function that various parts of the body play (1 Cor. 12:14–26). Where we hold strong differences of opinion, we need to be reminded of our foundation and our function within the church. We need to express a biblical attitude in dealing with differences and disagreements, to be clear about the meaning of the words and concepts we use, to evaluate wisely books on counseling, and to be aware of the temptations and potential pitfalls associated with our own counseling positions.

"You're a counselor? So what do you think of . . . ?" The question is a common one. Upon learning that I am a counselor, the inquirer will want to know what I think of a particular therapist. "So what do you think of Freud?" some people will ask. Other individuals, who are more aware of the Christian counseling field, will want my opinion on a prominent Christian counselor or a model of therapy. These inquirers are not always interested in learning from me so much as they are attempting to determine my theological and biblical position. They are thinking, *Is he one of us, or is he one of those other people who must be challenged, corrected, or avoided?* They are trying to find my theological and philosophical position and, possibly, my spiritual condition. Their question is just a quick way of establishing my location.

We use a shorthand approach in everyday conversation to ascertain where people are coming from or their current location. What appears to be trivial or cliché conversation is actually a means by which we can discover the status of a relationship. The response to a simple "Hi, how are you?" will inform us about the condition of the person we are greeting. If the person says he is "fine," we must still decide about his state or location by taking his total response into account. What was his tone of voice? Did he make eye contact when he spoke? Was he being dismissive or did he smile? Did his actions tell me he was in a hurry and he didn't want to talk further, or did he appear to want to stop and engage in a serious discussion? Even in the simplest of conversations, it is not always easy to read people and establish their true position or condition. Actions and words occur in a context that requires interpretation derived from our knowledge and cultural proficiency. We have all had experiences where we misinterpreted a person's comment or someone has misunderstood us.

Research on conversations between married couples has revealed that the health of the relationship is correlated with the positive or negative interpretation a person has of his or her spouse's words and actions. In other words, couples who experience marital difficulties are more likely to have a negative response to a spouse's comments or actions, even when that spouse is trying to be helpful and positive. When we no longer trust people, we tend to question their motives, and we find it difficult to believe that they might have our best interests at heart or that they are being truthful. A similar principle applies in relationships between nations and even between and within Christian communities.

Jesus Christ: Our Criterion for Acknowledgment

While it might be helpful to determine a counselor's location in relationship to other Christian therapists and their theories, the Bible tells us that it is more important to identify our position in relationship to God. The vertical dimension should dictate our horizontal relationships. The Bible gives us a succinct question to ask when we evaluate any teaching. The more biblical question should not be, "What do you think of a particular therapist or theory?" but, "What do you think of Jesus Christ?"

This question is paramount according to 1 John 4:1–4. John tells us that we must test the spirits to see whether they are from God. We need to evaluate teachings, but what is the criterion for evaluation? What standard should we use to decide on the veracity of a person's words and writings? Should we use another person or theory as the standard?

The criterion for evaluation is acknowledgment of Jesus Christ. Is Jesus Christ accepted as the fully human and fully divine manifestation of God? The common ground for truth and relationship among all Christians is acceptance of Jesus as Savior and Lord (1 John 2:22–23; 4:15; 5:11–12; John 10:30; 14:6; Rom. 10:9–10). There is a corollary point to this truth. The unity we share in Christ demands that we show love and respect toward others (1 John 3:23; 4:7–12,21). Once again we are reminded of the importance of the Greatest Commandment.

When we use a standard other than the preeminence of Christ to evaluate people and determine relationships, we end up bickering and fighting like couples in an unhappy marriage. Some of Paul's most strident words were leveled at the church in Corinth. In the first chapter of 1 Corinthians, he reprimanded them for creating divisions within the church. Before dealing with issues that included gross sin and immorality and differences of opinion on marriage and food offered to idols, Paul addressed the problem of taking sides. Rather than displaying unity, the people were arguing and quarreling among themselves. How did they divide themselves? They separated into groups using horizontal criteria (1 Cor. 1:11–12). Some people identified themselves as Paul followers, others as the Apollos group and the Cephas group. A pious group claimed to be followers of Christ. You can almost hear the sanctimonious intonation of their voices as they claimed the higher ground in an air of superiority. Their claim had a spiritual resonance, but their actions and motives were still carnal and divisive. They were operating on the horizontal level, using the name of Christ as a tool of separation among the body.

Paul appealed to the Corinthians "in the name of our Lord Jesus Christ" to end their divisiveness. He expected them to be united in "mind and thought." Does this mean that they were to be in total agreement with one another and that they were never to have honest differences of opinion and interpretation? Paul accepted that there would be differences of opinion. He and Barnabas had quarreled in the past (Acts 15:36–41). What Paul understood, even in his disagreement with Barnabas, was that differences among Christians could be handled so long as there was absolute unity of mind in Christ Jesus (1 Cor. 1:10; Eph. 4:1–6).

When the vertical dimension was the dominant relationship uniting the brethren, disagreements among the Corinthians could occur without disagreeableness and division. When God was first, unity prevailed. Hence, while Paul could identify the divisions and open sins in the Corinthian church, he could, nevertheless, honestly greet them as people who were "sanctified" and "called to be holy" (1 Cor. 1:2). His words, actions, and motives were governed by the primacy of Christ in his life, and this relationship directed his entire being. He understood that dissension in the community of faith was harmful if it took precedence over a focus on Christ and seeking his mind and will. This principle applied not only to open sin that needed correcting but also to the attitudes that led to theological divisions.

It is possible to disagree without being divisive.

Differences of opinion are not the only important factor in our conversation; our physical demeanor and nonverbal expressions also convey acceptance or rejection. Both our actions and our attitudes toward others must reflect our relationship to God. "Anyone who does not do what is right is not a child of God; nor is anyone who does not love his brother" (1 John 3:10 NIV). Our attitudes and actions can convey humility and the love of God, or they can be dismissive and judgmental. Compassion, love, gentleness, humility, and respect are more likely to generate harmony and openness to the Spirit of God than contentiousness and insults (1 Pet. 3:8, 15–16).

The radical nature of the Christian attitude and behavior is expressed in the biblical requirement that we love our enemies. We are expected to pray for their happiness, treat them well, ask God to bless them, feed them if they are hungry and give them water if they are thirsty, be kind to them, and do them favors (Prov. 25:21–22; Matt. 5:44; Luke 6:27–28; 6:35). Sometimes in the heat of theological conflict, Christians are far more kind and forgiving toward their secular opponents and enemies and willing to give the benefit of the doubt than they are toward their fellow believers. Christian counselors must seek peace and harmony in all relationships, even those contacts that contain strong and sincere disagreements. Paul made clear that we are to be friendly and earn the respect of others, even those who mistreat and oppose us (Rom. 12:14–21). If Christian counselors are unable to handle disagreements among their brethren in a peaceful and harmonious manner, then what sort of model and witness are they presenting to their counselees and the world in general?

Trust and love are determined as much by the recipient as the giver. If people do not perceive themselves as being loved or trusted, it makes little difference if the giver remonstrates to the contrary. Counselors who claim a higher biblical ground in their approaches to counseling must still be careful to express their views with humility and in ways that communicate to others who hold differing opinions that they are genuinely respected and loved. In Romans 12:10, Paul emphasized the need for love in the church by combining Greek words for love (*phileo* and *storge*) to stress the importance of what he was saying—be devoted to one another in brotherly or familial love.

The Importance of "One Anothering"

We are called to serve and to love our neighbor (Gal. 5:13–14). The Bible stresses the importance of this relationship by using the phrase "one another" approximately 160 times, 125 of which occur in the New Testament. (In the New Testament the phrase is usually a translation of the Greek word *allelon*.) When the more neutral uses of "one another" are excluded (for example, "talked to one another"), we find that the term occurs over 80 percent of the time in the New Testament in a context of positive support and affirmation. Christians have a responsibility to develop, support, and maintain *koinonia* relationships with one another.

Christian counselors are to encourage and support one another (1 Thess. 4:18; 5:11; Heb. 3:13; 10:25), honor one another (Rom. 12:10), love one another (John 13:34; 1 Thess. 3:12; Heb. 13:1; 1 Pet. 1:22; 4:8; 1 John 3:11,23; 4:7; 2 John 5), seek peace and harmony with one another (Mark 9:50; Rom. 12:16; 12:18; 1 Cor. 1:10; 1 Thess. 5:13; 1 Pet. 3:8), teach and correct one another (Col. 3:16), greet one another and be hospitable (Rom. 16:16; 1 Cor. 16:20; 1 Pet. 4:9; 1 John 1:7), be humble and consider the needs of one another (1 Cor. 10:24; 12:25; Phil. 2:4; 1 Pet. 5:5; 1 John 3:16), serve and help one another (Gal. 5:13; 1 Pet. 4:10), be patient with one another (Eph. 4:2; Col. 3:13), speak truthfully to one another (Eph. 4:25), be kind and compassionate to one another

(Eph. 4:32; 1 Thess. 5:15), forgive one another (Eph. 4:32; Col. 3:13), and pray for one another (James 5:16) (see appendix).

Christian Integrity and Varied Approaches

One of the ways we achieve harmony in the Christian fellowship is to recognize and accept the biblical view of division rather than model the prejudices and discriminatory divisions we find in the world. Paul tells us that all believers have been baptized into Christ and have clothed themselves with Christ. "There is neither Jew nor Greek, there is neither slave nor free man, there is neither male nor female; for you are all one in Christ Jesus" (Gal. 3:26–28). The Bible divides people into two primary spiritual groups: those who are in Christ and those who are not in Christ. We are all either adopted children of God or spiritual orphans, claimed and abused by the father of lies. Yet Christians tend to expend a great deal of energy in the task of subdividing people.

Within the community of faith, important issues must be addressed related to how we are to associate with others and our duties as part of the body of Christ. In pastoral care and counseling there are significant differences of opinion on the biblical requirements and expectations in the field. These differences should not be overlooked, dismissed, or diluted into a spiritually weak soup of compromise; however, regardless of our views and affiliation, any division into Christian "camps" in counseling runs the risk of violating the biblical imperative to love one another and has the possibility of undermining our unity in Christ.

We must not compromise our beliefs or accept anything less than the complete inspiration of Scripture, but we need to establish a clear foundation and to use spiritual discernment. Our first imperative is to love God, and we express this love by keeping his commandments, loving one another, and following the example of Jesus (1 John 2:3–6, 10–11). Our disagreements can be healthy if there is common respect and agreement in Christ.

Understanding the Differences
Differing Functions

In some cases our differences are based on the different functions of the church. We may fail to distinguish the variety of expressions of care and ministry in the body of Christ, or we may assume that our particular area is the most important and show disdain toward the work of others. The Bible warns us against such critical and contemptuous attitudes (1 Cor. 3:1–9). We need to remember that there are different gifts but the same Spirit. There are different kinds of service, and there are different ways to accomplish things (1 Cor. 12:4–6). When we observe differences in counseling approaches, we need to ascertain the nature of the variations. Are they simply different expressions of the church body and the spiritual gifts or a reflection of variations in our personalities that affect our working styles, or is there a more fundamental divergence that could be harmful to the church?

Differing Definitions and Interpretations

In some cases misunderstandings and lack of agreement exist on the definition of terms and concepts in counseling. The meaning we give words influences our view of the world. Our interpretations may do more to reflect our counseling group affiliation or identity than to clarify any differences and issues of disagreement. The tendency to focus either on the truth or the falsehood of a concept often depends on how a person chooses to define or categorize the source of information. If we distrust the source, we are far more likely to suspect the quality and value of the teaching.

In some counseling circles, for example, you can mention the term *psychology* in connection with Christian counseling and theology, and it will barely raise an eyebrow, while in other circles it will be greeted with disdain and sometimes with passionate disapproval. Beyond the difficulty of clearly defining this word, we are confronted with the variety of emphases in the field. There is historical psychology, experimental psychology, social psychology, clinical psychology, neuropsychology, and even parapsychology, to mention a few. The same diversity appears in the field of sociology, in most other sciences, and even in theology. A similar range of responses will greet you when you mention the word *religion* among groups of secular counselors.

There are many different meanings for words like *psychology* and *religion*. Years ago I did a study on the word *religion* and discovered more than fifty different definitions for the term. Even the etymology of the word is unclear. It could be derived from the Latin *religere*, which means "to read again" and refers to rituals or repetitive behaviors designed to discover God's purposes. (Cicero favored this view.) It could come from the Latin *religare*, which means "to bind back again" or "to bind together," reflecting the idea of the gathering together of a group, or a fellowship of believers. Webster's dictionary says it is from the Latin word *religio*, meaning "fear of the gods" or "reverence." The definition you choose will reflect a particular interpretation or understanding of the nature of true religion. Imagine the debates on religion and the confusion that can occur between two people when they are unaware that they are arguing from two completely different perspectives and interpretations of the term.

The term *psychology* has changed in meaning since it first appeared in the sixteenth century.[1] The literal understanding of psychology as a study of the soul no longer applies in the field of secular science, where it now means the scientific study of human and animal behavior and mental processes. We can argue over which is the "true" or the "false" definition though I am not sure what benefit will be derived from such disputes. We may be better served by examining the origin of diverse definitions and studying the sources and motivations behind the descriptions and explanations of concepts that lead to such variations in the understanding and interpretation of counseling.

Some Christians may want to jettison words like *psychology, psychotherapy,* or even the word *counseling* from the vocabulary of their caregiving ministries, believing that these terms have accumulated too much secular baggage and are now more misleading and confusing than helpful.[2] Another possibility is to acknowledge the differences in definitions and clearly articulate our own position. One additional alternative is to adapt and even transform terms and concepts, giving them meanings and applications that reflect a biblical worldview.

Adopting, Adapting, and Transforming Terms

Approaches to counseling often adopt terms and concepts from other theories and models in the field. Some of these words are simply descriptive and generic. Attending skills, influencing skills, and guidelines for posture and communication are basic to effective human interaction. These people-helping skills find general agreement in definition and acceptance in most versions of counseling, regardless of any theoretical position. Other terms may be common to a number of counseling theories, but the meaning and content of these words may vary. The concepts of treatment planning and therapeutic interventions, for example, have a variety of descriptions, each reflecting a particular counseling approach. Christian counselors need to study these concepts carefully and have a clear understanding of how they are defined and applied in the different theories and approaches to counseling.

If we view the use of terms in Christian counseling that are common in secular models of counseling as "borrowing," then we are more likely to be skeptical and even critical of their biblical efficacy. Borrowing implies lack of ownership; something borrowed doesn't belong to us, and its structure and contents may be harmful to us. If, on the other hand, we consider such use as a legitimate enterprise practiced in all professions, where words are freely taken and modified to suit the design and purpose of a particular group, then such actions are less insidious. The primary responsibility then becomes clearly articulating what you mean when you use the term, with the understanding that other groups will have different definitions and interpretations.

Moral: *Clearly define your own terms in counseling and be slow to judge the terms of other Christian counselors.*

Some biblical Christian counseling approaches may choose to move beyond redefining and modifying of counseling terms to a more radical transformation of a word. Such changes are common in our language. We noted in chapter 4, for example, that change has occurred over the last few decades with the English words *gay* and *bad*. In Shakespeare's time the word *let* meant prevent; today it means allow. Rapid changes in technology have also given rise to new words. In counseling Christians have taken words, in some instances from the Greek and the Hebrew, and interpreted and applied them specifically to the counseling field.

The transformation of even common, everyday words is nothing new in Christian history. John and other biblical writers, in the power of the Holy Spirit, revolutionized the word *agape*. The etymology of *agapao* (verb) and *agape* (noun) is not clear. The verb appeared frequently in Homer and Greek literature, but the noun was of late Greek construction. The only reference to the noun outside of the Bible was its use as a title for goddess Isis. The verb carried a bland connotation of expressing fondness.[3] The fact that the term was associated with a pagan god seems to have been no problem for the biblical writers. The New Testament changed this rather innocuous word and transformed it into the divine loving presence of God—either in God expressing his love toward us or of Christians reflecting the Lord's presence through the love of others.[4]

Martin Luther did something similar in his use of *Beruf*, the German word for "work." He took a word that referred to everyday work and labor and infused it with a divine imperative. Prior to Luther, the word had no spiritual connotation at all, but Luther transformed its meaning. His interpretation meant that any labor could now be part of God's calling, not just the work of the professional priesthood. His new use of the word had profound implications for the concept of a divine calling and the doctrine of the priesthood of the believer. Calling, as it related to the work of the Lord, no longer applied solely to the function of an exclusive group of clergy separated from the laity of the church; now it applied to all Christians as part of a priesthood of all believers. Any honorable work could become a spiritual activity to glorify God.

Becoming Multilingual in Counseling

Christian counselors need to be proficient in the language of counseling. They need to be skilled in learning the language of the people they are seeking to help; they need training in the biblical truths of caregiving, and they will benefit from learning the language of research that helps reveal the truths of God in his creation. In addition, they will need to learn the formal languages and concepts of counseling and psychotherapy existing in their culture if they wish to understand and communicate with other practitioners. Knowledge of these languages, particularly the formal and secular ones, does not imply agreement with the contents or underlying worldviews.

Beginning counselors must decide the degree to which they will need to be conversant in the multiple counseling worldviews. The *lingua franca* of psychotherapy in the United States is defined in the *Diagnostic and Statistical Manual of Mental Disorders* (DSM).[5] The DSM identifies, categorizes, and defines psychological disorders; and it provides a means of determining the presence and intensity of such problems. This book represents a particular philosophy of caregiving that has been roundly criticized in both Christian and secular fields, yet it is in such common use that it is difficult to ignore. Systems and family therapists and social workers, in particular, have offered some of the more articulate arguments against its individualistic and pathologizing portrayal of human nature.[6] Being aware of the DSM language does not mean that you agree entirely with the descriptions, categories, and diagnostic criteria. It may mean that you *are equipped to* converse with others who use that language. If you wish to communicate with family therapists, however, then you will need to learn the language of systems theory.

Evaluating Counseling Literature

One of the activities I occasionally do with my students is to display a number of books on counseling. After briefly describing the contents of each book, I ask the students to list the books in order of preference for use in their counseling ministry. Invariably, students will rate the books based either on the amount of Scripture references contained in a book or their knowledge of a particular author. Their inclination is to see a high positive correlation between a correct biblical view of counseling and the number of Scripture references.

One of the books I display is comprised of a list of topics related to counseling and pastoral care. Under each topic is a series of Bible verses. Students usually rate this text highly until they discover that the publisher is from outside the mainstream of Christian theology. Another book contains a reasoned exposé of psychiatry along with documented evidence of abuses in the field. All the examples in the book, as far as I know, are accurate, but it is always changed to a lower rating when the publisher is identified as a well-known cult group. We tend to rate the quality of a work not just by its content but also by the affiliation of the author. The students are struggling with the problem of assessment. What criteria do we use to determine the value of a book in counseling?

When the Bible is placed on the list, it is always rated the highest, as you would expect among seminary students. Things get more complicated when I place different translations of the Bible or my Greek and Hebrew versions on the list. Now differences may arise based upon a student's knowledge of translations and the original languages. The consensus among students, however, is that the Bible is in a separate class from all other books.

Biblical Christian counselors recognize that all literature can be divided into two distinct divisions: the Word of God and all other books. The Bible is the revealed Word of a single, supreme Author, produced over the course of centuries through individual writers under the inspiration of the Holy Spirit, and it is absolute truth uncontaminated by error. All human works contain admixtures of truth and error, including the book you are now reading—an admission that may surprise some of you and confirm the suspicions of others! All counseling books, with the exception of Scripture, contain various degrees of error and truth since they all reflect and incorporate elements of the self and finite knowledge and human wisdom.

Once students grasp this differentiation, they have a new way to read and evaluate books other than the Bible. Biblical Christian counselors will still use resources in addition to Scripture, but they will read these books with the assumption that they are imperfect. Even those of us who would choose to use only the Bible in counseling also read other books on counseling and even write books in the field. Obviously, the purpose of most of these works is to explain aspects of biblical counseling and how Christians should practice it. The authors also expect their books to be read and accepted as truthful and even authoritative in the field, but an examination of the references and footnotes in many of these books will reveal that they have drawn information not only from Scripture but also from both Christian and non-Christian sources.

Criteria for Evaluation

There is a tendency to want to further divide books into "acceptable" and "unacceptable" in Christian counseling rather than view them all on a continuum of truth and error in various categories and entirely separate from the inerrant Scripture. The Roman Catholic Church historically has provided a seal of approval or "Divine Imprimatur" upon works they deem acceptable to the faith, and church officials have used banning along with the threat of excommunication to control the contents and publication of books among their flock. Their criteria for evaluation usually have been a mixture of tradition, cultural context, and biblical interpretation. The purpose behind this practice has been to separate truth from error and to protect readers from the dangers inherent in falsehood.

How should evangelical Christians evaluate the quality of counseling books? The obvious answer is that all information should be appraised by the standard, principles, and truth of Scripture. We use what is perfect to judge and evaluate the imperfect. All information from alternative sources is considered to be of lesser authority and requiring conformity to the correct interpretation of Scripture. Disagreements usually center on the quantity and quality or value of alternative sources, and determining the correct interpretation of Scripture. These issues suggest that biblical Christian counselors should have training in biblical languages and hermeneutics as well as skills in research and statistical analysis.

Some considerations for evaluating a counseling book, in addition to determining the source and standard of authority, include the author's background and area of expertise, the intended audience and the language used, the categories and subjects covered by the book, the understanding and use of Scripture, and identification of its purpose and intended use.

What are the background and training of the author? In chapter 3 we examined the connection between personal experiences and subsequent theories of counseling. Knowing something about the biography, historical context, social and cultural influences, education, and spiritual development of the author can assist in understanding the contents and perspective of a book. This connection also applies to Christian authors and may help explain differences of opinion in the Christian counseling field.

Who are the intended readers, and what language is used in the book? The sophistication or simplicity of a book must be evaluated in terms of the intended audience. Books may be written for novices or for specialists, for counselees or for the public at large. They may be intended for a general readership and use a popular writing style with an uncomplicated terminology. Such books lack sophisticated reasoning and technical information. Other books are intended for basic and advanced theorists and practitioners in counseling; and they contain varying levels of highly technical language, research, and thought.

Some counseling books use the language of science; others may use the language of theology. A book written in highly technical scientific or theological language may require that readers understand not only the terminology but also the author's particular definitions and frame of reference.[7] Some readers may be more comfortable with a particular writing style; however, they need to recognize that other people may favor alternate styles. A book they rate poorly may find acceptance and be considered an important resource for others simply on the basis of communication preferences and knowledge differences.

What are the variations in quality in the categories and subjects covered by the book? Part of the evaluation process is recognizing that books may offer important contributions in some areas yet may be weak in others. Astute readers understand that important observations in one part of a book do not require acceptance of all information and views in the remainder of the work as holding equal value. Conversely, the discovery of falsehoods should not automatically lead to the dismissal of all other information in a book. The same observation holds true for entire fields such as research and science.

Although books outside the Word of God are flawed and ideas generated by humans have weaknesses, this fact does not mean that all these books and ideas are to be rejected. Such an attitude would have prevented any progress in medicine, technology, and all the physical and social sciences.

As one who has taken graduate-level courses in advanced statistical analysis and taught courses in research and statistics, I can attest that even this field is not a precise science that provides absolute proof. Nor does it claim to be. Some books are rich in research and provide extensive statistical data and biblical study on issues in counseling, while others give only anecdotal evidence and illustrations. Various research designs and both quantitative and qualitative methods are used to study the effectiveness of counseling. All of these approaches have strengths and weaknesses. One of the first things I learned in research was that every quantitative and qualitative study has flaws and limitations. There are no exceptions. The effect of this discovery was not to breed discouragement but to shift the focus to determine whether the weaknesses must necessarily invalidate the hypotheses and conclusions. Mistakes and flaws can also contribute to our knowledge. As we learn more in the field, we adjust to and incorporate the new information and improve our understanding.[8] Similar progress has occurred in biblical Christian counseling where God has rewarded our study with greater insights into caregiving and ministry development.

How is Scripture used in the book? Some books exegete Bible verses to glean counseling principles; others may use biblical references for illustration, analogy, or support of a viewpoint. Readers must evaluate both the appropriateness and the accuracy of the use of Scripture in a book.

A book that I use occasionally in counseling contains an extensive listing of Scriptures arranged alphabetically by issues and problems. (This is not the same book that I use in my evaluation of counseling books activity in class.) While the book is helpful, it also has limitations. Scripture verses that I consider relevant are overlooked under some topics. In addition, the selection and arrangement of verses in this form separates them from their context in Scripture and could lead to misinterpretation. Consequently, even a book that is comprised entirely of Bible verses can be both useful and misleading.

What is the purpose of the book, and how will it be used? Readers need to understand the intention of the author and the subject the book proposes to cover. Some books are introductions to counseling; these cover a wide range of issues. The breadth of their subject matter means that they are unable to provide much depth on an issue. Other books focus on a limited number of issues and seek to give extensive information. Some books provoke; others promote. Some books are designed to raise questions and to stimulate thinking and speculation; other books are written to provide answers and solidify support for a position. It is unfair to judge a book as inadequate simply because it fails to meet an expectation that lies beyond the scope and intention of the author.

Readers need to decide how helpful or functional the book will be in their particular context. Beyond evaluating the purpose of a book, counselors must identify the need they are trying to fill by reading the book. Does the book provide answers to their dilemma or focus of interest? Does it give counselors the information they seek?

If you were stranded on a deserted island, a book on how to build a boat might be more useful to you than one on landscaping or even one on the theory of flotation devices. Yet, depending on your situation, a book on how to find water or catch a fish might be more necessary than one on boat building. Your location and condition determine your needs. If you are studying cross-cultural counseling, a book that gives you insights into the characteristics and customs among various cultural groups may be a valuable asset, despite its lack of a biblical orientation. Books of little value in one situation might serve a useful purpose in another.

One of the most widely read books among Christians in the Soviet Union in the 1960s was published by the Communists. It attacked the Christian faith and sought to expose errors in the Bible. Since the book included direct quotations from Scripture, Christians could read and study biblical truths with impunity, while either disregarding or learning to respond to the Communist challenges. They extracted the precious from the worthless in a book that attacked their Christian faith. Sometimes we have to use creatively what we have available to us.

In a course I took on the philosophy of religion in seminary, the class studied a book that challenged Christianity to the point that the author actually questioned the historical existence of Jesus. On the surface the book would appear to have little value for Christians. It was filled with arguments against some basic tenets of the faith. Yet my professor used the book effectively to help his students identify and eloquently defend these philosophical attacks on the faith.

Learning to Look for Truth

I have a secondhand textbook on a subject in Christian counseling in my library. The previous owner, whom I do not know, had marked the book with personal comments. The notes are revealing for what they tell me about the person. Some observations support the author of the book, but many challenge his views. Occasionally a comment implies that the author is not only wrong but also unbiblical. When I read these comments, my reaction to many of them was, "This reader is misunderstanding," or, "This reader is failing to see that her comment and the author's position can both be true." The comments told me that the reader was relatively young in the field of Christian counseling. To her credit, she was thinking about and interacting with the material she was reading, and I found myself agreeing with a few of her reactions. But I also picked up on her tendency to challenge and reject some of the author's views rather than question them with a desire to pursue the truth.

As a reader, you have a choice. You can question and evaluate ideas with an attitude that says, "Let me think about this matter, study it a little more, and see if there is any truth in it," or you can dismiss an author's ideas and views with a mind that is already made up and assumes a rejection of the material.

One additional point is significant. I have met the author of this textbook, and I am aware of his desire to honor God in his ministry. This relationship leads me to be more predisposed to giving him the benefit of the doubt and to having a more positive interpretation of his work. This attitude, as we shall see, does carry with it the danger of overlooking incorrect or misleading information.

We need to acknowledge our tendency to be more lenient and flexible with authors with whom we agree and more critical of those who fail to support our counseling position. We are apt to evaluate books according to our knowledge of the author's affiliation. Is he one of *us*, or is he one of *them*? If he is one of ours, then we will tend to read his work with an eye for truth and be less critical of any apparent errors in the work. If he is not associated with our position, then we will be more likely to examine the book critically and miss some possible truths or insights. We would like to think that authors who share our beliefs are without fault in their writings or at least that any shortcomings are minor. In contrast, we want to find mistakes, weaknesses, and falsehoods in the works of those with whom we disagree.

Try the following exercise: Read a counseling book written by someone closely aligned with your position as though it were written by an author who disagreed with your views. Keep the author's opposition uppermost in your mind until you find yourself critically evaluating the contents of the book. What did you discover? You probably found yourself questioning some of the information and claims in the book.

Now reverse the exercise and read a book that lies outside the zone of acceptance in your approach to counseling. Imagine that the most articulate proponent of your position wrote the book. You will find this exercise extremely difficult. It is hard to imagine someone we support is presenting views that are aberrant to the point of being unbiblical.

We would prefer to think that the person has lost his mind, is playing devil's advocate, or that there has been a mistake in authorship. If you are able to complete this exercise, you will probably find yourself trying to make some of the information fit into your biblical frame of reference by searching for, reinterpreting, and extracting bits of truth.

Moral: *Use the same critical discernment to evaluate all books that you read on counseling, both the ones you are likely to disagree with and, in particular, the ones written by an author whom you are inclined to support.*

Developing and Embracing Counseling Approaches and Models

What are the characteristics of authentic biblical Christian counseling? Such counseling seeks to be biblical as opposed to nonbiblical, perfect rather than imperfect, right rather than wrong, and true rather than false. I have yet to meet a genuine Christian counselor who wants to be nonbiblical, imperfect, wrong, or misinformed.

- Biblical versus nonbiblical: Christian counselors acknowledge the authority of Scripture and allow the Word to direct them under the power of the Holy Spirit. The Bible provides the standard for evaluation of all Christian counseling practices.
- Perfect versus imperfect: Christian counselors accept that they are in a process of growing in wisdom and knowledge; they seek to develop and improve in their counseling skills and ministry with the goal of perfection in Christ.
- Right versus wrong: Christian counselors seek to express a biblical morality and identify the correct and godly way to proceed in counseling. Christian counseling addresses the correct, just, and godly thing to do, rather than simply the most convenient or utilitarian.
- True versus false: Christian counselors look for evidence of truth and seek to correct falsehood.

If we can affirm that these are common goals among biblical Christian counselors and accept that Christians are genuine in their desire to manifest these objectives in their counseling practices, then we have a foundation for agreement upon which we can build collegial communication in addition to our unity in Christ. Differences appear among biblical Christian counselors regarding how we define these goals and how they are to be achieved. The most common area of contention is how Christian counselors should deal with information and ideas that arise from sources outside of Scripture.

The Danger of the Ditches

In our attempts to develop counseling models and approaches or to decide which counseling groups and associations are worthy biblically of our support, we face disparate concerns based on the path we choose. Each position has attendant hazards. As we align ourselves with a particular group or perspective, we tend to look critically at others who fail to share our views. In looking for the specks in others' eyes, we may overlook the logs in our own eyes (Matt. 7:3–5; Luke 6:41–42). We must be careful not to judge others while failing to recognize and understand the weaknesses in our own position (Rom. 2:1).

Our knowledge of counseling and the strength of our theological position do not prevent our straying off track and falling into ditches that render us less effective as biblical Christian counselors. The issue of the roles of Scripture and scientific research in counseling serve to illustrate some of these dangers and temptations.

Inflexible Phariseeism and Syncretistic Samaritanism

If we are inclined to accept the Bible as our only resource in counseling, then we are unlikely to be tripped by misleading scientific studies and psychotherapies. We face the danger of falling into the ditch of rigidity and legalism. While we are less likely to accept any falsehoods from the world, our position can lead to a false sense of security and even a smugness that gives rise to a critical spirit. We are tempted to focus on the letter of Scripture and miss the Spirit of the Word; our attitudes and actions may imply that the Sabbath is not made for man, but man for the Sabbath (Mark 2:27). Rather than consider each situation on its own merits, we may condemn every Christian who draws observations from other fields or who associates with and appears to defend adulterers and other sinners. We can become inflexible Pharisees.

If we are inclined to use counseling research and information from the sciences along with or under the authority of Scripture, then we are less likely to be rigid and legalistic in our relationships with other counselors who take different approaches. But we may fall into an uncritical acceptance of anything presented as scientific truth in counseling. We are tempted to mix Scripture and counseling models and ideas without a clear standard of authority and truth. We can become spiritual and syncretistic Samaritans, worshipping at the wrong place and in the wrong way (John 4:21–24).

Isolationism and Naïve Inclusiveness

Our fear of spiritual contamination and our desire to remain pure in the Word of God may leave us so isolated that we avoid fellowship with other Christian counselors who have a suspect theology. We favor exclusivity over the dangers accompanying inclusiveness and relaxed membership requirements. One effect of this isolation is that we only read and consult with those counselors who share our particular worldview. This shield of protection against harmful ideas can lead us to a position where we are no longer able to communicate effectively with other counselors or some people in need because we do not think it is necessary to learn their language of care. In our desire to remain pure and faithful to the Word of God, we may find ourselves in the ironic position of trying to protect God from contamination, with an underlying implication that, in the battle between good and evil, God is the weaker party.

If we believe that it is important to study and learn from the various theories and models and the research in counseling, we face the danger of falling into a ditch of naïve inclusiveness. We favor a more open policy and a broader field upon which to discover truth, leaving it to God to separate the wheat from the tares (Matt. 13:28–30). We may fear being perceived as judgmental or narrow-minded, and so we readily learn and even embrace the latest trends and ideas in counseling in order to communicate effectively with others. We may desire acceptance in and respect from representative groups in mainstream counseling; consequently, we may try to hide or disguise our Christian identity. In the process we may fail to articulate clearly our biblical position and standard of authority. In an attempt to avoid opposing or condemning any position in counseling and to promote a "harmless as doves" demeanor, we may overlook our biblical responsibility to be "wise as serpents" (Matt. 10:16 KJV).

Demonization and Trivialization

As we try to honor and remain faithful to the Word of God, we are tempted to cast aspersions upon individuals or groups in the Christian community who claim a different biblical interpretation of counseling. Our focus becomes one of exposing errors, but in the process we may overlook important truths. We become adept at identifying flaws and faults, but we may also become blinded to possible lessons that God might be teaching us. As we move further to an extreme position, we may unilaterally declare any counseling done by those people who are not like us as work of the devil. We demonize them as worse than secular counselors because they are trying to "serve two masters" (Matt. 6:24; Luke 16:13), and we treat them as spiritual pariahs who are no longer our Christian brethren.[9]

As we find our counseling approaches challenged, we are tempted to ignore or reject people whom we perceive as our opponents. We may dislike disputes; consequently, we are likely to dismiss comments that we interpret (correctly or incorrectly) as personal attacks, unsophisticated arguments, crude reasoning, or misrepresentations of an issue. We are tempted to turn a deaf ear to the critical assessments and label them as trivial or unworthy of consideration. We treat them like fleas on a dog's back: irritating, occasionally scratched but better ignored. In the process we risk developing an attitude of false superiority and intellectual smugness as our search for "truth" leads us to overlook possible errors or treat flaws in our position as inconsequential and unimportant. We are tempted to trivialize the comments of our critics; and in the process we may miss valuable insights, cautions, and correctives.

Eisegesis and Intellectualism

The more we attempt to support our personal counseling theories and theological position from Scripture, the more we are vulnerable to the danger of eisegesis. Eisegesis is the act of reading things into Scripture that are not present in the text itself. We incorporate our beliefs, theories, and preferences into our interpretation of a Bible verse or passage. Consequently, we distort the intended meaning as we conscript Scripture in the promotion of our personal interests and agendas. We unintentionally try to create God in our own image.

The more we attempt to support our counseling theories and theological positions from the field of science and through human reasoning, the more we are vulnerable to humanistic intellectualism and rationalism. Insights we gain from scientific inquiry may lead us to place too high a value on human wisdom. We may be tempted to spend most of our time and energy pursuing scientific truth to the neglect of biblical research and study. Our broad-mindedness may become a narrow-minded pursuit of the rational and the elevation of self as we eschew biblical authority and revelation.

Words and Deeds, Claims and Practices

Perhaps we should be more interested in the actual practice of counseling than in what counselors describe as their counseling theory or approach. I am aware of some Christian and biblical counselors whose writings and words make me uncomfortable theologically; nevertheless, I would recommend them as counselors because I know that, regardless of what they write and say about counseling, in an actual counseling situation they are keenly intent on discovering the will of God for the person in need; they have a genuine love for people; they are sensitive to every opportunity to reveal the healing power of Christ; and they affirm the authority of Scripture.

On the other hand, I am sure that there are counselors who claim an approach to counseling that is biblically unimpeachable, but in their practice these counselors are insensitive and unable to communicate the healing message. Jesus said, "You will know [recognize] them by their fruits" (Matt. 7:20). Is the counselor "in Christ"? Is he the good person who "brings good things out of the good stored up in his heart" (Luke 6:45)? Despite his words and ambiguity in print, does he actively pursue the will of God in his actual ministry to others (Matt. 21:28–32)? While it is important to be clear in what we say and write, Christ is interested, in particular, in our heart and our motives.

Jesus had some unexpected comments in this area. When his disciples discovered a person using the authority of Jesus to cast out demons, they tried to stop him because he was unwilling to follow along with them. But Jesus told them not to hinder the man because "he who is not against you is for you" (Luke 9:49–50). Jesus seems to be accepting a broad principle that affirms any healing that does not reject God and accepts the authority of Christ even if it falls outside of official guidelines and patronage. Paul also acknowledged that the motives of some people may not have been pure; but if they proclaimed Christ, then he was satisfied and could rejoice (Phil. 1:15–18). The path to salvation is narrow, certain, and nonnegotiable (John 14:6), but the freedom that comes with life in Christ has broad options and possibilities for ministry. In Christ, "everything is permissible," though not everything is beneficial or constructive. Our guide and goal should be to glorify God and to please our neighbor (1 Cor. 10:23–33 NIV).

Summary

1. Just as Christian counselors seek to discover the location of people in need, they also try to determine the position of others in their field. The temptation is to separate counselors by standards other than Scripture and the person and nature of Christ. We find unity in Christ, who is our criterion for evaluation.

2. All Christians have a responsibility to maintain the bond of love and unity in Christ and to express love and support toward all people. Loving our neighbor even includes our critics, theological opponents, and enemies.

3. The horizontal way of the world is to divide people into various groups, whether by nationality, race, gender, and culture or by

philosophical, scientific, or even theological difference. The biblical way divides people into only two groups: those who are in Christ and all others who need to be (Gal. 3:26–28; Eph. 2:19–22).

4. We have different functions in the body of Christ. In biblical Christian counseling some people are called to minister to the church body, and some people are called in a missionary service to counsel people in the world; some counselors are called to minister to particular groups and issues, while others are not equipped or gifted in these areas and have a calling to other types of counseling. Each area and calling requires particular gifts and skills, but wise counselors distinguish between different functions and unbiblical alternatives.

5. We need a clear understanding of terminology in counseling. Words and definitions vary in the field, and differences of opinion exist among Christian counselors concerning the meaning, value, and application of concepts in counseling. Some counselors choose to avoid confusion by rejecting words associated with nonbiblical approaches; other counselors seek to adapt and transform terms to fit a biblical worldview. Regardless of our approach, we need to be accurate in our understanding of how others define a term, and we need to be clear in our own definitions.

6. The more counselors learn about the different languages in counseling, the better equipped they will be to communicate with others in the field. Communication in these languages does not mean agreeing with the content or underlying worldview. Like Paul, we need to keep our foundation solid, as we use varied methods to locate and join with those people who need God's healing word (1 Cor. 9:19–23).

7. Counselors should examine the presuppositions and standard of authority in counseling literature. Other considerations include understanding the purpose of the book, biographical information and influences, the intended audience, the language used, the scope of the book, the role of Scripture, and the functional need for the book.

8. In our efforts to develop biblical approaches to counseling, we face possible hazards. These potential concerns include the dangers of inflexible Phariseeism and syncretistic Samaritanism, isolationism and naïve inclusiveness, demonization and trivialization, and eisegesis and intellectualism. In our efforts to reveal and defend biblical truth, we may fail to love our brethren. Alternatively, we may focus on our service to others to the extent that we disregard God.

9. We must strive for consistency in our words and actions. We need to recognize this potential failing in our own ministry and be prepared to acknowledge the contributions and application of wise counseling in others with whom we might disagree, particularly in their published counseling positions.

While we do need to evaluate critically and separate truth from error (1 John 4:1; Prov. 14:15; 1 Thess. 5:21), exposing error and revealing truth are not necessarily the same thing. We should not assume that pointing out the faults and weaknesses in a position or view will automatically lead to the discovery and acceptance of truth. Part of our ministry should be the encouragement to become colaborers with others in the search for godly truth and wisdom in counseling.

Finally, we need to be careful of our language and our attitude toward others in the field of counseling. Comments that draw accusations of meanness, ignorance, misrepresentation of position, and allegations of exegetical ineptitude and unholy alliances may rally troops to our side, but they are unlikely to promote a spirit of "one anothering" in the pursuit of Christlikeness and loving our neighbor. Developing theological shibboleths to guard and determine entrance into our inner counseling circles may have the unintentional effect of weakening rather than simply purifying the church. Christian counselors have a choice. They can limit their service to viewing their own position in counseling as biblical, accurate, effective, and worthy of replication and describing differing views in Christian counseling as unbiblical, inaccurate, and ultimately ineffective, or they can look for ways and opportunities to support and encourage all Christian counselors to be worthy representatives of Christ in their caregiving ministry.

Questions and Exercises for Reflection

1. When you discuss counseling issues, are you primarily listening for error or for truth? You may say that you are listening for both, but invariably you will find yourself focusing on one over the other. Describe your listening predisposition or tendency in such conversations and the conditions that might determine your preference. What do these choices and inclinations reveal about you?

2. When you meet other counselors, what are you most interested in discovering about them? What information do you tend to seek about their counseling position and their relationship to Christ?

3. How would you apply 1 Corinthians 9:19–23 to counseling and to how we should relate to other people and views in the field?

4. Which dangers identified in the chapter (inflexible Phariseeism and syncretistic Samaritanism, isolationism and naïve inclusiveness, demonization and trivialization, and eisegesis and intellectualism) are you more likely to face in your own approach to counseling? Give reasons for your selections and develop a plan to deal with the dangers.

5. Identify and describe some things that have been most beneficial to you in this book. What are some weaknesses or limitations in the book? What areas were difficult for you to understand or need further explanation?

References

Bobgan, Martin and Deirdre. *Competent to Minister: The Biblical Care of Souls*. Santa Barbara, Calif.: EastGate Publishers, 1996.

Duncan, Barry L., and Scott D. Miller. *The Heroic Client: Doing Client-Directed, Outcome-Informed Therapy*. San Francisco: Jossey-Bass, 2000.

Günther, W., and H. G. Link. "Love." In Colin Brown, gen. ed., *The New International Dictionary of New Testament Theology*, vol. 2. Grand Rapids, Mich.: Zondervan, 1976: 538–47.

Hunt, Morton. *The Story of Psychology*. New York: Doubleday, 1993.

Jones, Ian F. "Research in Christian Counseling: Proving and Promoting Our Valued Cause." In *Competent Christian Counseling. Vol. 1: Foundations & Practice of Compassionate Soul Care*. Ed. Timothy Clinton and George Ohlschlager. Colorado Springs, Colo.: WaterBrook Press, 2002.

Kirk, Stuart A., and Herb Kutchins. *The Selling of DSM: The Rhetoric of Science in Psychiatry*. Hawthorne, N.Y.: Aldine de Gruyter, 1992.

Kutchins, Herb, and Stuart A. Kirk. *Making Us Crazy. DSM: The Psychiatric Bible and the Creation of Mental Disorders*. New York: Free Press, 1997.

Endnotes

1 Marulic, a Serbo-Croatian, used the word *psychologia* in a manuscript in 1520, and in 1590 Rudolf Goeckel (Latin name: Goclenius) published a book entitled *Psychologia Hoc Est. de Hominis Perfectione (Psychology This Is. On the Improvement of Man)*. See Morton Hunt, *The Story of Psychology* (New York: Doubleday, 1993), 59. Study on the nature of the soul, of course, was being done long before the sixteenth century.

2 See, for example, Martin and Deirdre Bobgan, *Competent to Minister: The Biblical Care of Souls* (Santa Barbara, Calif.: EastGate Publishers, 1996).

3 Isis was the wife of Osiris and a national deity in Egypt. She became a leading goddess throughout the Hellenistic Mediterranean world. An Isis mystery cult developed in Greece that included initiation rites and dramas that celebrated the death and resurrection of Osiris. See Thomas Allan Brady, "Isis," in M. Cary, et al. eds, *The Oxford Classical Dictionary* (Oxford: The Clarendon Press, 1949), 459–60.

4 W. Günther & H. G. Link, "Love," in Colin Brown, gen. ed., *The New International Dictionary of New Testament Theology,* vol. 2 (Grand Rapids, Mich.: Zondervan, 1976), 539.

5 American Psychiatric Association, *Diagnostic and Statistical Manual of Mental Disorders,* 4th ed. (Washington, D.C.: American Psychiatric Association, 2000).

6 See, for example, Barry L. Duncan and Scott D. Miller, *The Heroic Client: Doing Client-Directed, Outcome-Informed Therapy* (San Francisco: Jossey-Bass, 2000), 46–54; Stuart A. Kirk and Herb Kutchins, *The Selling of DSM: The Rhetoric of Science in Psychiatry* (Hawthorne, N.Y.: Aldine de Gruyter, 1992); and Herb Kutchins and Stuart A. Kirk, *Making Us Crazy. DSM: The Psychiatric Bible and the Creation of Mental Disorders* (New York: Free Press, 1997).

7 One of the problems readers have in evaluating books is distinguishing between theoretical or philosophical "science" and demonstrable or empirical science. A similar problem also exists in theology.

8 Ian F. Jones, "Research in Christian Counseling: Proving and Promoting Our Valued Cause," in *Competent Christian Counseling. volume 1: Foundations & Practice of Compassionate Soul Care,* ed. Timothy Clinton and George Ohlschlager (Colorado Springs, Colo.: WaterBrook Press, 2002), 641–57.

9 Among the expressions of our sinful nature listed in Galatians 5:19–20 that undermine our new life in the Holy Spirit, Paul included factionalism or sects (Greek: *hairesis*). The New Living Translation (1996) paraphrases the term as "the feeling that everyone is wrong except those in your own little group" (Gal. 5:20 NLT).

CONCLUSION

WHERE DO YOU GO FROM HERE?

H uman history exists between the question and the call, between Genesis and Revelation. We live between the first words spoken by God after the fall: "Where are you?" (Gen. 3:9) and his final words to us in the biblical revelation: "The Spirit and the bride say, 'Come.' And let the one who hears say, 'Come.' And let the one who is thirsty come; let the one who wishes take the water of life without cost" (Rev. 22:17). The Alpha and the Omega, the One who is the beginning and the end (Rev. 21:6) comes to us with a question and a call. The question is one of location, and the call gives us the promise of life. Throughout this book we have addressed the importance of location and finding direction in relationship to God, self, and neighbor. The call of God reminds us that the ultimate answers to life and the path of salvation are found in Christ, the Giver of living water.

Biblically based counselors need a clear understanding of the question and a commitment to the call of God upon their lives. Such counselors:

- Accept the supreme authority of Scripture and the biblical view of human nature and the human condition.
- Begin with the question, "Where are you?" as they seek to locate people in need in their relationship to God, self, and others.
- Are God-centered and counselee serving as they emulate and apply the Greatest Commandment.

- Follow the model of Jesus the Messiah, our Master Counselor of heaven on earth in the components of wisdom and understanding, planning and power, and the knowledge and fear of the Lord.
- Clearly communicate truth as they assist people to "extract the precious from the worthless" by looking for the hand of God in every situation.
- Rely upon the Holy Spirit, our current Counselor of heaven on earth, for guidance and the expression of spiritual gifts.
- Develop and use biblical traits and spiritual disciplines in their ministry.
- Seek every opportunity to learn and incorporate information and tools of application into the counseling process that allow therapeutic biblical connection and communication with people in need (1 Cor. 9:19–23).
- Encourage love and support among their counseling peers, are knowledgeable about the counseling field, careful and fair in their evaluation of counseling approaches and publications, continuing to learn, and humble in the assessment of their own position.

Christian counselors are representatives of God in the counseling encounter. In addition to locating people who are in pain and guiding them toward healing, Christian counselors have a responsibility to imitate and demonstrate Christ in their lives as a model for people in need.

For some Christians, counseling will be a primary focus of their ministry. They need to be conversant in the field and continue to learn and grow in their skills and knowledge. They need discernment in reaching decisions on licensure, training, continuing education, and appraisement of all the information available to them. For others, counseling will be a peripheral interest or minor part of their ministry. God will call upon them occasionally to bring a word of counsel to a hurting individual. Regardless of the degree of involvement in counseling, developing godly relationships and finding our identity in Christ are essential to the pilgrimage of all Christians.

So what do you think of Jesus Christ?

Appendix

"One Anothering" Relationships

Old Testament

Most references to "one another" in the Old Testament refer to forms of communication, such as speaking to one another (e.g., Gen. 11:3; 37:19; 42:1,21,28; Exod. 10:23; 16:15; Num. 14:4; Judg. 6:29; 10:18; 1 Sam. 10:11; 2 Kings 7:3,6,9; Jer. 22:8; 23:27; 49:29; Ezek. 24:23; 33:30; Mal. 3:16). The phrase is also used in reference to observing one another (e.g., Gen. 43:33; Exod. 25:20; Isa. 13:8), and examples and warnings about lying to or harming one another (e.g., Lev. 19:11; 25:14,46; 2 Kings 3:23; 2 Chron. 20:23; Ps. 12:2; Isa. 3:5; Zech. 7:10; 8:10).

New Testament

The New Testament also uses the phrase in reference to communication (e.g., Mark 4:41; 8:16; 9:10,34; 12:7; 14:4; 16:3; Luke 2:15; 4:36; 6:11; 7:32; 8:25; 12:1; 20:14; 24:14,17,32; John 4:33; 7:35; 11:56; 12:19; 16:17,19; 19:24; Acts 2:12; 4:15; 21:5, 26:31; 28:4), observing one another (e.g., John 13:22), and conflict situations, and harmful or unholy relationships (e.g., Matt. 24:10; Mark 15:31; John 5:44; 6:43,52; Acts 7:26; 15:39; 19:38; 28:25; Rom. 1:24,27; 2:15; 14:13; 1 Cor. 4:6; 7:5; Gal.

5:15,17,26; Col. 3:9; Titus 3:3; James 4:11; 5:9; Rev. 6:4; 11:10). The phrase most often translates the Greek term *allelon*.

When the neutral references, such as those related to communication, are excluded, we find that over 80 percent of the references to "one another" in the New Testament occur in a context of affirmation and support of others. Most of these references are found in the epistles to the churches, and they form a clear mandate that we must "love our neighbors as ourselves" and seek unity in Christ in the church fellowship.

Encourage, Support, Edify One Another

Romans 1:12	Be mutually encouraged by each other's faith.
Romans 14:19	To mutual edification (building up one another).
Ephesians 5:19	Speak to one another with psalms, hymns, and spiritual songs.
1 Thessalonians 4:18	Encourage one another.
1 Thessalonians 5:11	Encourage one another.
1 Thessalonians 5:11	Build up one another.
Hebrews 3:13	Encourage one another daily.
Hebrews 10:24	Spur on one another.
Hebrews 10:25	Encourage one another.

Belong or Be Devoted to, and Honor One Another

Romans 12:15	Belong to one another.
Romans 12:10	Be devoted to one another.
Romans 12:10	Honor one another.

Love One Another

John 13:34	A new commandment . . . that you love one another.
John 13:35	If you have love for one another.
John 15:12	That you love one another.
John 15:17	That you love one another.
Romans 13:8	Except the continuing debt to love one another.

1 Thessalonians 3:12	May the Lord make your love increase and overflow for each other.
1 Thessalonians 4:9	Love one another.
2 Thessalonians 1:3	The love . . . for each other is increasing.
Hebrews 13:1	Love one another.
1 Peter 1:22	Love one another.
1 Peter 4:8	Fervent in your love for one another.
1 John 3:11	Love one another.
1 John 3:23	Love one another.
1 John 4:7	Love one another.
1 John 4:11	We also ought to love one another.
1 John 4:12	But if we love one another.
2 John 5	Love one another.

Seek Agreement, Peace, Harmony, and Accept One Another

Mark 9:50	Be at peace with one another.
Romans 12:16	Live in harmony with one another.
Romans 12:18	Live at peace with one another.
Romans 15:5	A spirit of unity among yourselves.
Romans 15:7	Accept one another.
1 Corinthians 1:10	Agree with one another.
1 Thessalonians 5:13	Live in peace with one another.
1 Peter 3:8	Live in harmony with one another.

Teach and Correct One Another

Romans 15:14	Competent to instruct one another.
Colossians 3:16	Teach one another.
Colossians 3:16	Admonish one another.

Greet One Another, Meet Together, and Be Hospitable

Romans 16:16	Greet one another with a holy kiss.
1 Corinthians 16:20	Greet one another with a holy kiss.
2 Corinthians 13:12	Greet one another with a holy kiss.
Hebrews 10:25	Meet with one another.
1 Peter 4:9	Offer hospitality to one another.

1 Peter 5:14	Greet one another with a kiss of love.
1 John 1:7	Have fellowship with one another.

Consider the Needs of One Another (Ahead of Your Own) and Be Humble

John 13:14	Ought to wash one another's feet.
1 Corinthians 10:24	Look out for one another.
1 Corinthians 11:33	Wait for each other.
1 Corinthians 12:25	Have equal concern for one another.
Ephesians 5:21	Submit to one another.
Philippians 2:4	Look to the interests of one another.
Philippians 2:3	In humility consider others better than yourselves.
1 Peter 5:5	Clothe yourselves with humility toward one another.
1 John 3:16	Lay down your lives for one another.

Serve and Help One Another

Galatians 5:13	Serve one another.
Galatians 6:2	Carry one another's burdens.
1 Peter 4:10	Employ (your gift) in serving one another.

Persevere with One Another

Ephesians 4:2	Bear with one another.
Colossians 3:13	Bear with one another.

Confess and Speak Honestly to One Another

Ephesians 4:25	Speak truthfully with one another.
James 5:16	Confess your sins to one another.

Be Kind and Compassionate to One Another

Ephesians 4:32	Be kind to one another.
Ephesians 4:32	Be compassionate to one another.
1 Thessalonians 5:15	Be kind to one another.

Forgive One Another

Ephesians 4:32   Forgive one another.

Colossians 3:13   Forgive one another.

Pray for One Another

James 5:16   Pray for one another.

GENERAL INDEX

Abraham, 21, 22
Adam, 20, 21, 31–33, 42,
    85, 142
  new, 17, 18, 21, 141
  old, 141
adultery, 1, 75, 101,
    126, 189
advice, 52, 80, 97, 107,
    108, 128, 132,
    150,159, 167, 191
advocate, 157, 158, 159
agape, 68, 197, 215
Alpha and Omega, 117
armor of God, 182
Augustine, 8, 12, 71, 74

Bacon, Francis, 5
Beck, J. T., 64
Behaviorism, 12
behavioral, 25, 26, 125
behaviorist, 26
Bereans, 10
blasphemy, 171
Breuer, Josef, 49
bronze, 115–116

Calvin, John, 8, 13
Calvinism, 7
Chambers, Oswald, 114,
    135
Charcot, Jean, 49
comfort, 158, 169, 170,
    186, 190
comforter, 158, 159
commandments, 74, 75, 77
  Greatest Command-
    ment, 55, 69, 73,
    74, 75–79, 84,
    86–87, 137, 205,
    235
  Ten Commandments,
    73–75, 76, 77
common grace, 8, 45
communication, 10, 59,
    61–62, 126, 128,
    185, 190, 194
  and gender, 129–130

and use of Scripture,
    133–136
  biblical principles,
    131–133
community, 19, 20, 42, 211
counseling
  associations and orga-
    nizations, 3
  definition, biblical
    Christian, 59
  licensed, 4
  process, 34–36, 59ff.,
    179
  secular, 25ff., 68, 111,
    185
  skills, 1, 43, 99, 127,
    224
  theories, 25, 27, 45, 47,
    48, 52, 55, 205,
    214, 228
Creator, 5, 7, 8, 15–18, 19,
    20, 21, 29, 32, 33,
    39, 43, 47, 54, 65,
    117
crisis, 28, 80, 83, 86, 144
  crisis counseling, 28,
    31, 79, 88
  crisis intervention, 145
cure of souls, 1, 62, 70

David, 113, 126–127, 172,
    181
deception, 21–23, 34, 169
Delitzsch, Franz, 64, 71
*Diagnostic and Statistical
    Manual* (DSM), 216
discipleship, 33, 60, 111

ego, 50, 64, 65, 71, 125
eisegesis, 228, 232
Elijah, 144–146, 147, 170
Elisha, 144, 146–147
Eusebius, 147
evangelism, 33, 60, 166

fear, 21, 22, 33, 80, 97, 144,
    146, 147, 148, 168,
    171, 172, 188

of God, 115, 117–120,
    159, 171, 172
  of the Lord, 95, 96, 117,
    118, 119, 166,
    172, 236
  true and false fear,
    118–119
Fletcher, Scott, 64–65
forgiveness, 24, 66, 133,
    149, 189, 196, 198
Forrester, Kevin, 2, 179–
    181, 193, 199
Freud, Sigmund, 26, 44–51
fruit, 16, 17, 95, 172, 166,
    186
fruit of the Spirit, 163–164,
    180, 181, 186, 195,
    201, 202

Galileo, 5
gift of the Spirit, 160, 161,
    170, 171
gifts of the Spirit, 161,
    164–166, 171, 180,
    184, 202
grace, 5, 93, 98, 144, 165
  common, 8, 45
  of God, 5, 13, 89, 190

Headrick, Jim, 2, 173, 175
health, mental, 26
health, relationship, 46
hermeneutics, 45, 135, 218
human nature, 7, 8, 15, 25,
    26, 27, 96, 104, 120,
    205, 216
humble, 9, 43, 68, 97, 185,
    188, 210, 236, 240
humility, 67, 119, 185, 188,
    191, 209, 210, 240

iatrogenic effects, 63
identity, 19, 20, 67, 141
  in Christ, 67, 141, 236
image, 17, 19, 20, 21, 33,
    181
  of God, 17, 19, 20, 26,
    33, 199

243

SCRIPTURE INDEX

CPSIA information can be obtained
at www.ICGtesting.com
Printed in the USA
LVHW091054031020
667439LV00003B/4